A Child
Called "It"

and

The Lost Boy

One Child's Courage
to Survive

A Child
Called "It"

and

The Lost Boy

One Child's Courage
to Survive

Dave Pelzer

Health Communications, Inc.
Deerfield Beach, Florida

Permission to reprint *I Never Knew* was given by Cindy Adams.

ISBN 0-7394-0061-4

Publisher: Health Communications, Inc.
       3201 S.W. 15th Street
       Deerfield Beach, Florida 33442-8190

Cover design by Ileana M. Wainwright

A Child
Called "It"

This book is dedicated to my son Stephen,
who, by the grace of God, has taught me
the gift of love and joy through
the eyes of a child.

This book is also dedicated to
the teachers and staff members of
Thomas Edison Elementary School to include:

Steven E. Ziegler
Athena Konstan
Peter Hansen
Joyce Woodworth
Janice Woods
Betty Howell
and the School Nurse

To all of you, for your courage and for
putting your careers on the line
that fateful day, March 5, 1973.
You saved my life.

Contents

Contents

*A*cknowledgments

After years of intensive labor, sacrifice, frustration, compromises and deception, this book is finally *published* and available in bookstores everywhere. I wish to take a moment and pay homage to those who truly believed in this crusade.

To Jack Canfield, co-author of the phenomenal bestseller *Chicken Soup for the Soul*, for his extreme kindness and opening a big door. Jack is indeed a rare entity who, without reservation, assists more individuals in a single day than many of us can help in a lifetime. Bless you Sir.

To Nancy Mitchell and Kim Wiele at the Canfield Group for their enormous enthusiasm and guidance. Thank you ladies.

To Peter Vegso at Health Communications, Inc., as well as Christine Belleris, Matthew Diener, Kim Weiss and the entire friendly staff at HCI for their honesty, professionalism and everyday courtesy that make publishing a pleasure. Kudos galore to Irene Xanthos and Lori Golden for their tenacious drive and for picking up the slack. And a gargantuan thank you to the Art Department for all your hard work and dedication.

A special thank you to Marsha Donohoe, editor extraordinaire, for her hours of reediting and eradicating "the Wahoo" out of the *tome* (that's *book* for those of you who reside in Yuba/Sutter Counties in Northern CA), so to provide the reader with a clear, precise sense of this story through the eyes of a child. For Marsha, it was a matter of ". . . Farmer's Trust."

To Patti Breitman, of Breitman Publishing Projects, for her initial work and for giving it a good run for the money.

To Cindy Adams for her unwavering faith when I needed it the most.

A special thank you to Ric & Don at the Rio Villa Resort, my then home away from home, for providing the perfect sanctuary during the process of this project.

And lastly, to Phyllis Colleen. I wish you happiness. I wish you peace. May God bless you.

*A*uthor's Notes

Some of the names in this book have been changed in order to maintain the dignity and privacy of others.

This book, the first part of the trilogy, depicts language that was developed from a child's viewpoint. The tone and vocabulary reflect the age and wisdom of the child at that particular time.

This book is based on the child's life from ages 4 to 12.

The second part of the trilogy, *The Lost Boy*, is based on his life from ages 12 to 18.

CHAPTER

1

The Rescue

*M*arch 5, 1973, Daly City, California—*I'm late. I've got to finish the dishes on time, otherwise no breakfast; and since I didn't have dinner last night, I have to make sure I get something to eat. Mother's running around yelling at my brothers. I can hear her stomping down the hallway towards the kitchen. I dip my hands back into the scalding rinse water. It's too late. She catches me with my hands out of the water.*

SMACK! Mother hits me in the face, and I topple to the floor. I know better than to stand there and take the hit. I learned the hard way that she takes that as an act of defiance, which means more hits, or worst of all, no food. I regain my posture and dodge her looks, as she screams into my ears.

I act timid, nodding to her threats. "Please," *I say to myself,* "just let me eat. Hit me again, but I have to have food." *Another blow pushes my head against the tile counter top. I let the tears of mock defeat stream down my face as she storms out of the kitchen, seemingly satisfied with herself. After I count her steps, making sure she's gone, I breathe a sigh of relief. The act worked. Mother can beat me all she wants, but I haven't let her take away my will to somehow survive.*

I finish the dishes, then my other chores. For my reward I receive breakfast—leftovers from one of my brother's cereal bowls. Today it's Lucky Charms. There are only a few bits of cereal left in a half of a bowl of milk, but as quickly as I can, I swallow it before Mother changes her mind. She has done that before. Mother enjoys using food as her weapon.

She knows better than to throw leftovers in the garbage can. She knows I'll dig it out later. Mother knows most of my tricks.

Minutes later I'm in the old family station wagon. Because I'm so late with my chores, I have to be driven to school. Usually I run to school, arriving just as class begins, with no time to steal any food from other kids' lunch boxes.

Mother drops my oldest brother off, but keeps me for a lecture about her plans for me tomorrow. She is going to take me to her brother's house. She says Uncle Dan will "take care of me." She makes it a threat. I give her a frightened look as if I am truly afraid. But I know that even though my uncle is a hard-nosed man, he surely won't treat me like Mother does.

Before the station wagon comes to a complete stop, I dash out of the car. Mother yells for me to return. I have forgotten my crumpled lunch bag, which has always had the same menu for the last three years—two peanut butter sandwiches and a few carrot sticks. Before I bolt out of the car again, she says, "Tell 'em . . . Tell 'em you ran into the door." Then in a voice she rarely uses with me, she states, "Have a nice day." I look into her swollen red eyes. She still has a hangover from last night's stupor. Her once beautiful, shiny hair is now frazzled clumps. As usual, she wears no makeup. She is overweight, and she knows it. In all, this has become Mother's typical look.

Because I am so late, I have to report to the administrative office. The gray-haired secretary greets me with a smile. Moments later, the school nurse comes out and leads me into her office, where we go through the normal routine. First, she examines my face and arms. "What's that above your eye?" she asks.

I nod sheepishly, "Oh, I ran into the hall door . . . by accident."

Again she smiles and takes a clipboard from the top of a cabinet. She flips through a page or two, then bends down to show me. "Here," she points to the paper. "You said that last Monday. Remember?"

I quickly change my story, "I was playing baseball and got hit by the bat. It was an accident." Accident. I am always supposed to say that. But the nurse knows better. She scolds me so I'll tell the truth. I always break down in the end and confess, even though I feel I should protect my mother.

The nurse tells me that I'll be fine and asks me to take off my clothes. We have been doing this since last year, so I immediately obey. My long-sleeve shirt has more holes than Swiss cheese. It's the same shirt I've worn for about two years. Mother has me wear it every day as her way to humiliate me. My pants are just as bad, and my shoes have holes in the toes. I can wiggle my big toe out of one of them. While I stand clothed only in my underwear, the nurse records my various marks and bruises on the clipboard. She counts the slash-like marks on my face, looking for any she might have missed in the past. She is very thorough. Next, the nurse opens my mouth to look at my teeth that are chipped from having been slammed against the kitchen tile counter top. She jots a few more notes on the paper. As she continues to look me over, she stops at the old scar on my stomach. "And that," she says as she takes a deep swallow, "is where she stabbed you?"

"Yes, ma'am," I reply. *"Oh no!"* I tell myself, "I've done something wrong . . . again." *The nurse must have seen the concern in my eyes. She puts the clipboard down and hugs me.* "God," I tell myself. "She is so warm." *I don't want to let go. I want to stay in her arms forever. I hold my eyes tightly shut, and for a few moments nothing else exists. She pats my head. I flinch from the swollen bruise Mother gave me this morning. The nurse then breaks the embrace and leaves the room. I rush to put my clothes back on. She doesn't know it, but I do everything as fast as possible.*

The nurse returns in a few minutes with Mr. Hansen the principal, and two of my teachers, Miss Woods and Mr. Ziegler. Mr. Hansen knows me very well. I've been in his office more than any other kid in school. He looks at the paper, as the nurse reports her findings. He lifts my chin. I'm afraid to look into his eyes, which is mostly a habit from trying to deal with my mother. But it's also because I don't want to tell him anything. Once, about a year ago, he called Mother to ask about my bruises. At that time, he had no idea what was really going on. He just knew I was a troubled kid who was stealing food. When I came to school the next day, he saw the results of Mother's beatings. He never called her again.

Mr. Hansen barks he's had enough of this. I almost leap out of my skin with fear. "He's going to call Mother again!" *my brain screams. I break down and cry. My body shakes like jello and I mumble like a baby, begging Mr. Hansen not to phone Mother.* "Please!" *I whine,* "Not today! Don't you understand, it's Friday?"

Mr. Hansen assures me he's not going to call Mother, and sends me off to class. Since it's too late for homeroom class, I sprint directly to Mrs. Woodworth's English class. Today's a spelling test on all the states and their capitals. I'm not prepared. Usually I'm a very good student, but for the past few months I gave up on everything in my life, including escaping my misery through my schoolwork.

Upon entering the room, all the students plug their noses and hiss at me. The substitute teacher, a younger woman, waves her hands in front of her face. She's not used to my smell. At arm's length she hands my test to me, but before I can take my seat in the back of the class by an open window, I'm summoned back to the principal's office. The entire room lets out a howl at me—the reject of the fifth grade.

I run to the administration office, and I'm there in a flash. My throat is raw and still burns from yesterday's "game" Mother played against me. The secretary leads me into the teachers' lounge. After she opens the door, it takes a moment for my eyes to adjust. In front of me, sitting around a table, are my homeroom teacher Mr. Ziegler, my math teacher Miss Moss, the school nurse, Mr. Hansen and a police officer. My feet become frozen. I don't know whether to run away or wait for the roof to cave in. Mr. Hansen waves me in, as the secretary closes the door behind me. I take a seat at the head of the table, explaining I didn't steal anything . . . today. Smiles break everyone's depressed frowns. I have no idea that they are about to risk their jobs to save me.

The police officer explains why Mr. Hansen called him. I can feel myself shrink into the chair. The officer asks that I tell him about Mother. I shake my head no. Too many people already know the secret, and I know she'll find out. A soft voice calms me. I think it's Miss Moss. She tells me it's all right. I take a deep breath, wring my hands and reluctantly tell them about Mother and me. Then the nurse has me stand up and show the policeman the scar on my chest. Without hesitation, I tell them it was an accident; which it was—Mother never meant to stab me. I cry as I spill my guts, telling them Mother punishes me because I am bad. I wish they would leave me alone. I feel so slimy inside. I know after all these years there is nothing anyone can do.

A few minutes later, I am excused to sit in the outer office. As I close the door, all the adults look at me and shake their heads in an approving way. I fidget in my chair, watching the secretary type papers. It seems forever before Mr. Hansen calls me back into the room. Miss Woods and Mr. Ziegler leave the lounge. They seem happy, but at the same time worried. Miss Woods kneels down and wraps me in her arms. I don't think I will ever forget the smell of the perfume in her hair. She lets go, turning away so I won't see her cry. Now I am really worried. Mr. Hansen gives me a lunch tray from the cafeteria. "My God! Is it lunch time already?" I ask myself.

I gobble down the food so fast I can hardly taste it. I finish the tray in record time. Soon the principal returns with a box of cookies, warning me not to eat so fast. I have no idea what's going on. One of my guesses is that my father, who is separated from my mother, has come to get me. But I know it's a fantasy. The policeman asks for my address and telephone number. "That's it!" I tell myself. "It's back to hell! I'm going to get it from her again!"

The officer writes down more notes as Mr. Hansen and the school nurse look on. Soon he closes his note pad and tells Mr. Hansen that he has enough information. I look up at the principal. His face is covered with sweat. I can feel my stomach start to coil. I want to go to the bathroom and throw up.

Mr. Hansen opens the door, and I can see all the teachers on their lunch break staring at me. I'm so ashamed. "They know," *I tell myself.* "They know the truth about my mother; the real truth." *It is so important for them to know that I'm not a bad boy. I want so much to be liked, to be loved. I turn down the hall. Mr. Ziegler is holding Miss Woods. She is crying. I can hear her sniffle. She gives me another hug and quickly turns away. Mr. Ziegler shakes my hand.* "Be a good boy," *he says.*

"Yes, sir. I'll try," is all I can say.

The school nurse stands in silence beside Mr. Hansen. They all tell me goodbye. Now I know I am going to jail. "Good," *I tell myself.* "At least she won't be able to beat me if I'm in jail."

The police officer and I walk outside, past the cafeteria. I can see some of the kids from my class playing dodge ball. A few of them stop playing. They yell, "David's busted! David's busted!" *The policeman touches my shoulder, telling me everything is okay. As he drives me up the street, away from Thomas Edison Elementary School, I see some kids who seem to be fazed by my departure. Before I left, Mr. Ziegler told me he would tell the other kids the truth—the real truth. I would give anything to have been there in class when they found out I'm not so bad.*

In a few minutes, we arrive at the Daly City Police Station. I sort of expect Mother to be there. I don't want to get out of the car. The officer opens the door and gently takes me by the elbow, into a big office. No other person is in the room. The policeman sits in a chair, in the corner, where he types several sheets of paper. I watch the officer closely as I slowly eat my cookies. I savor them as long as I can. I don't know when I will be eating again.

It's past 1:00 P.M. when the policeman finishes his paperwork. He asks for my telephone number again.

"Why?" *I whine.*

"I have to call her, David," *he says gently.*

"No!" I command. "Send me back to school. Don't you get it? She mustn't find out I told!"

He calms me down with another cookie, as he slowly dials 7-5-6-2-4-6-0. I watch the black dial turn as I get up and walk towards him, straining my whole body while trying to hear the phone ringing on the other end. Mother answers. Her voice scares me. The policeman waves me away, and takes a deep breath before saying, "Mrs. Pelzer, this is Officer Smith from the Daly City Police Department. Your son David will not be coming home today. He will be in the custody of the San Mateo Juvenile Department. If you have any questions, you can call them." He hangs up the phone and smiles. "Now that wasn't so hard, was it?" he asks me. But the look on his face tells me he is assuring himself, more than he is me.

A few miles later, we are on highway 280, heading towards the outskirts of Daly City. I look to my right and see a sign that reads, "THE MOST BEAUTIFUL HIGHWAY IN THE WORLD." The officer smiles with relief, as we leave the city limits. "David Pelzer," he says, "you're free."

"What?" I ask, clutching my only source of food. "I don't understand. Aren't you taking me to some kind of jail?"

Again he smiles, and gently squeezes my shoulder. "No, David. You have nothing to worry about, honest. Your mother is never going to hurt you again."

I lean back against the seat. A reflection from the sun hits my eyes. I turn away from the rays as a single tear runs down my cheek.

"I'm free?"

CHAPTER
2

Good Times

*I*n the years before I was abused, my family was the "Brady Bunch" of the 1960s. My two brothers and I were blessed with the perfect parents. Our every whim was fulfilled with love and care.

We lived in a modest two-bedroom house, in what was considered a "good" neighborhood in Daly City. I can remember looking out of our living room bay window on a clear day, to gaze at the bright orange towers of the Golden Gate Bridge and the beautiful skyline of San Francisco.

My father, Stephen Joseph, supported his family as a fireman, working in the heart of San Francisco. He stood about five feet ten inches tall, and he weighed about 190 pounds. He had broad shoulders and forearms that would make any muscle man proud. His thick black eyebrows matched his hair. I felt special when he winked at me and called me "Tiger."

My mother, Catherine Roerva, was a woman of average size and appearance. I never could remember the color of her hair or eyes, but Mom was a woman who glowed with love for her children. Her greatest asset was her determination. Mom always had ideas, and she always took command of all family matters. Once, when I was four or five years old, Mom said she was sick, and I remember feeling that she did not seem to be herself at all. It was a day when Father was working at the fire station. After serving dinner, Mom rushed from the table and began painting the steps that led to the garage. She coughed as she frantically brushed the red paint onto every step. The paint had not fully dried, when Mom began tacking rubber mats to the steps. The red paint was all over the mats and Mom. When she finished, Mom went into the house and collapsed on the couch. I remember asking her why she had put the mats down before the paint dried. She smiled and said, "I just wanted to surprise your dad."

When it came to housekeeping, Mom was an absolute clean fiend. After feeding my two brothers, Ronald and Stan, and me breakfast, she would dust, disinfect, scour and vacuum everything. No room in our house was left untouched. As we grew older, Mom made sure we did our part by keeping our rooms neat. Outside, she would meticulously tend a small flower garden, which was the envy of the neighborhood. With Mom, everything she touched turned to gold. She didn't believe in doing anything halfway. Mom often told us that we must always do the best we could, in whatever we did.

Mom was truly a gifted cook. Of all the things she did for her family, I think creating new and exotic meals was her favorite. This was especially true on those days when Father was home. Mom would spend the better part of the day preparing one of her fantastic meals. On some days when Father was working, Mom would take us on exciting sight-seeing tours around the city. One day, she took us to Chinatown in San Francisco. As we drove around the area, Mom told us about the culture and history of the Chinese people. When we returned, Mom started her record player, and our home was filled with beautiful sounds from the Orient. She then decorated the dining room with Chinese lanterns. That evening, she dressed in a kimono and served what seemed to us as a very exotic but delicious meal. At the end of dinner, Mom gave us fortune cookies and read the captions for us. I felt that the cookie's message would lead me to my destiny. Some years later, when I was old enough to read, I found one of my old fortunes. It said, "Love and honor thy mother, for she is the fruit that gives thou life."

Back then our house was full of pets—cats, dogs, aquariums filled with exotic fish and a gopher tortoise named "Thor." I remember the tortoise best because Mom let me pick a name for it. I felt proud because my brothers had been chosen to name the other pets and it was now my turn. I named the reptile after my favorite cartoon character.

The five- and ten-gallon aquariums seemed to be everywhere. There were at least two in the living room, and one filled with guppies in our bedroom. Mom creatively decorated the heated tanks with colored gravel and colored foil backs; anything she thought would make the tanks more realistic. We would often sit by the tanks while Mom told us about the different species of fish.

The most dramatic of Mom's lessons, came one Sunday afternoon. One of our cats was behaving in an odd way. Mom had us all sit down by the cat while she explained the process of birth. After all the kittens had slipped safely out of the mother cat, Mom explained in great detail the wonder of life. No matter what the family was doing, she somehow came up with a constructive lesson; though we were not usually aware that we were being taught.

For our family—during those good years—the holidays started with Halloween. One October night, when the huge harvest moon was in full view, Mom hurried the three of us out of our house, to gaze at the "Great Pumpkin" in the sky. When we returned to our bedroom, she told us to peek under our pillows where we found Matchbox race cars. My two brothers and I squealed with delight as Mom's face was flushed with pride.

The day after Thanksgiving, Mom would disappear to the basement, then bring up enormous boxes filled with Christmas decorations. While standing on a ladder, she tacked strings of ornaments to the ceiling beams. When she was finished, every room in our house had a seasonal touch. In the dining room Mom arranged different sizes of red candles on the counter of her prized oak hutch. Snowflake patterns graced every window in the living room and dining room. Christmas lights were draped around our bedroom windows. Every night I fell asleep while staring at the soft, colorful glow of the Christmas lights that blinked on and off.

Our Christmas tree was never even an inch under eight feet, and it took the whole family hours to decorate it. Each year one of us was honored by being allowed to place the angel at the top of the tree, while Father held us up in his strong arms. After the tree was decorated and dinner was finished, we would pile into the station wagon and cruise the neighborhood, admiring the decorations on other homes. Mom always rambled on about her ideas of bigger and better things for the next Christmas, even though my brothers and I knew our house was always the best. When we returned home, Mom sat us down by the fireplace to drink egg nog. While she told us stories, Bing Crosby sang "White Christmas" on the stereo. I was so excited during those holiday seasons that I couldn't sleep. Sometimes Mom would cradle me, while I fell asleep listening to the crackle of the fire.

As Christmas Day came nearer, my brothers and I became more and more excited. The pile of gifts at the base of the tree grew day by day. By the time Christmas finally arrived, there were dozens of gifts for each of us.

On Christmas Eve, after a special dinner and caroling, we were allowed to open one gift. Afterwards, we were sent to bed. I always strained my ears as I laid in bed, waiting for the sound of Santa's sleigh bells. But I always fell asleep before I heard his reindeer land on the roof.

Before dawn, Mom would creep into our room and wake us, whispering, "Santa came!" One year she gave each of us a yellow, plastic, Tonka hard hat and had us march into the living room. It took us forever to rip the colorful paper from the boxes, to discover our new Christmas toys. Afterwards, Mom had us run to the backyard in our new robes, to look back in through the window at our huge Christmas tree. That year, standing in the yard, I remember seeing Mom cry. I asked her why she was sad. Mom told me she was crying because she was so happy to have a real family.

Because Father's job often required him to work 24-hour shifts, Mother often took us on day trips to places like the nearby Golden Gate Park in San Francisco. As we slowly drove through the park, Mom explained how the areas were different and how she envied the beautiful flowers. We always visited the park's Steinhart Aquarium last. My brothers and I would blaze up the stairs and charge through the heavy doors. We were thrilled as we leaned over the brass, seahorse-shaped fence, looking far below at the small waterfall and pond that were home to the alligators and large turtles. As a child, this was my favorite place in the entire park. I once became frightened, as I thought about slipping through the barrier and falling into the pond. Without speaking a word, Mom must have felt my fear. She looked down at me and held my hand ever so softly.

Spring meant picnics. Mom would prepare a feast of fried chicken, salads, sandwiches and lots of desserts the night before. Early the next day, our family sped off to Junipero Serra Park. Once there, my brothers and I would run wild on the grass and pump higher and higher on the park's swings. Sometimes we would venture off on a new trail. Mom always had to pry us away from our fun, when it came time for lunch. We wolfed down our food, hardly tasting it, before my brothers and I blitzed off for parts unknown, in search of high adventure. Our parents seemed happy to lie next to each other on a blanket, sip red wine and watch us play.

It was always a thrill when the family went on summer vacation. Mom was always the mastermind behind these trips. She planned every detail, and swelled with pride as the activities came together. Usually we traveled to Portola or Memorial Park, and camped out in our giant, green tent for a week or so. But whenever Father drove us north across the Golden Gate Bridge, I knew we were going to my favorite place in the world—the Russian River.

The most memorable trip to the river for me, happened the year I was in kindergarten. On the last day of school, Mom asked that I be excused a half-hour early. As Father honked the horn, I rocketed up the small hill from the school, to the waiting car. I was excited because I knew where we were going. During the drive, I became fascinated at the seemingly endless fields of grapes. When we drove into the quiet town of Guerneville, I rolled my window down to smell the sweet air from the redwood trees.

Each day was a new adventure. My brothers and I either spent the day climbing an old, burnt tree stump with our special whomper-stomper boots or swimming in the river at Johnson's Beach. Johnson's Beach was a whole day's event. We would leave our cabin by nine and return after three. Mom taught each of us to swim in a small, trenched hole in the river. That summer Mom taught me how to swim on my back. She seemed so proud when I was finally able to do it.

Everyday seemed sprinkled with magic. One day after dinner, Mom and Dad took the three of us to watch the sunset. All of us held hands, as we crept past Mr. Parker's cabin to get to the river. The green river water was as smooth as glass. The bluejays scolded the other birds, and a warm breeze blew through my hair. Without a word, we stood watching the fireball-like sun as it sank behind the tall trees, leaving bright blue and orange streaks in the sky. From above, I felt someone hug my shoulders. I thought it was my father. I turned and became flushed with pride to find Mom holding me tightly. I could feel her heart beat. I never felt as safe and as warm as that moment in time, at the Russian River.

CHAPTER

3

Bad Boy

*M*y relationship with Mom drastically changed from discipline to punishment that grew out of control. It became so bad at times, I had no strength to crawl away—even if it meant saving my life.

As a small child, I probably had a voice that carried farther than others. I also had the unfortunate luck of getting caught at mischief, even though my brothers and I were often committing the same "crime." In the beginning, I was put in a corner of our bedroom. By this time, I had become afraid of Mom. Very afraid. I never asked her to let me come out. I would sit and wait for one of my brothers to come into our bedroom, and have him ask if David could come out now and play.

About this time, Mom's behavior began to change radically. At times while Father was away at work, she would spend the entire day lying on the couch, dressed only in her bathrobe, watching television. Mom got up only to go to the bathroom, get another drink or heat leftover food. When she yelled at us, her voice changed from the nurturing mother to the wicked witch. Soon, the sound of Mother's voice began to send tremors down my spine. Even when she barked at one of my brothers, I'd run to hide in our room, hoping she would soon return to the couch, her drink and her TV show. After a while, I could determine what kind of day I was going to have by the way she dressed. I would breathe a sigh of relief whenever I saw Mom come out of her room in a nice dress with her face made up. On these days she always came out with a smile.

When Mother decided that the "corner treatment" was no longer effective, I graduated to the "mirror treatment." In the beginning, it was a no-notice form of punishment. Mother would simply grab me and smash my face against the mirror, smearing my tear-streaked face on the slick, reflective glass. Then she would order me to say over and over again, "I'm a bad boy! I'm a bad boy! I'm a bad boy!" I was then forced to stand, staring into the mirror. I would stand there with my hands locked to my sides, weaving back and forth, dreading the moment when the second set of television commercials aired. I knew Mother would soon be stomping down the hall to see if my face was still against the mirror, and to tell me what a sickening child I was. Whenever my brothers came into the room while I was at the mirror, they would look at me, shrug their shoulders and continue to play—as if I were not there. At first I was jealous, but soon I learned that they were only trying to save their own skins.

While Father was at work, Mother would often yell and scream while forcing my brothers and me to search the entire house for something she had lost. The quest usually started in the morning and lasted for hours. After a while, I was usually sent to search in the garage which was under part of the house—like a basement. Even there, I trembled upon hearing Mother scream at one of my brothers.

The searches continued for months, and finally, I was the only one singled out to look for her things. Once, I forgot what I was looking for. When I timidly asked her what it was that I was to find, Mother smacked me in the face. She was lying on the couch at the time, and she didn't even stop watching her television show. Blood gushed from my nose and I began to cry. Mother snatched a napkin from her table, tore a piece and rammed it up my nose. "You know damn well what you're looking for!" she screamed. "Now go find it!" I scurried back down to the basement, making sure I made enough noise to convince Mother I was feverishly obeying her command. As Mother's "find the thing" became more common, I began to fantasize that I had found her missing item. I imagined myself marching upstairs with my prize and Mom greeting me with hugs and kisses. My fantasy included the family living happily ever after. But, I never found any of Mother's lost things, and she never let me forget that I was an incompetent loser.

As a small child, I realized Mom was as different as night and day when Father was home from work. When Mom fixed her hair and put on nice clothes, she seemed more relaxed. I loved it when Dad was home. It meant no beatings, mirror treatments or long searches for her missing things. Father became my protector. Whenever he went to the garage to work on a project, I followed him. If he sat in his favorite chair to read the newspaper, I parked myself at his feet. In the evenings, after the dinner dishes were cleared from the table, Father would wash them, and I would dry. I knew that as long as I stayed by his side, no harm would come to me.

One day before he left for work, I received a dreadful shock. After he said goodbye to Ron and Stan, he knelt down, held my shoulders tightly and told me to be a "good boy." Mother stood behind him with her arms folded across her chest, and a grim smile on her face. I looked into my father's eyes and knew right then that I was a "bad boy." An ice-cold chill rushed through my body. I wanted to hold on to him and never let go, but before I could give Father a hug, he stood up, turned and walked out the door, without saying another word.

For a short time after Father's warning, things seemed to calm down between Mother and me. When Dad was home, my brothers and I played in our room or outside, until about 3:00 P.M. Mother would then turn on the television so we could watch cartoons. For my parents, 3:00 P.M. meant "Happy Hour." Father would cover the kitchen counter top with bottles of alcohol and tall fancy glasses. He cut up lemons and limes, placing them in small bowls beside a small jar of cherries. They often drank from mid-afternoon, until my brothers and I climbed into bed. I remember watching them dance around the kitchen to music from the radio. They held each other close, and they looked so happy. I thought I could bury the bad times. I was wrong. The bad times were only beginning.

A month or two later, on a Sunday, while Father was at work, my brothers and I were playing in our room when we heard Mother rush down the hall, yelling at us. Ron and Stan ran for cover in the living room. I instantly sat down in my chair. With both arms stretched out and raised, Mother came at me. As she came closer and closer, I backed my chair towards the wall. Soon, my head touched the wall. Mother's eyes were glazed and red, and her breath smelled of booze. I closed my eyes as the oncoming blows began to rock me from side to side. I tried to protect my face with my hands, but Mother would only knock them away. Her punches seemed to last forever. Finally, I snaked my left arm up to cover my face. As Mother grabbed my arm, she lost her balance and staggered back a step. As she jerked violently to regain her stability, I heard something pop, and felt an intense pain in my shoulder and arm. The startled look on Mother's face told me that she had heard the sound, too, but she released her grip on my arm, and turned and walked away as if nothing had happened. I cradled my arm as it began to throb with pain. Before I could actually inspect my arm, Mother summoned me to dinner.

I plopped down at a TV tray to try to eat. As I reached for a glass of milk, my left arm did not respond. My fingers twitched upon command, but my arm tingled and had become lifeless. I looked at Mother, trying to plead with my eyes. She ignored me. I knew something was very wrong, but I was too afraid to utter a word. I simply sat there, staring at my tray of food. Mother finally excused me and sent me to bed early, telling me to sleep in the top bunk. This was unusual because I had always slept on the bottom. Sometime near morning I finally fell asleep, with my left arm carefully cradled in the other.

I hadn't slept long when Mother awakened me, explaining that I had rolled out of the top bunk during the night. She seemed to be deeply concerned about my condition, as she drove me to the hospital. When she told the doctor about my fall from the top bunk bed, I could tell by the look he gave me that he knew my injury was no accident. Again, I was too afraid to speak up. At home, Mother made up an even more dramatic story for Father. In the new version, Mother included her efforts to catch me before I hit the floor. As I sat in Mother's lap, listening to her lie to Father, I knew my mom was sick. But my fear kept the accident our secret. I knew if I ever told anyone, the next "accident" would be worse.

School was a haven for me. I was thrilled to be away from Mother. At recess I was a wild man. I blitzed through the bark-covered playground, looking for new, adventurous things to do. I made friends easily and felt so happy to be at school. One day in late spring, when I returned home from school, Mother threw me into her bedroom. She then yelled at me, stating I was to be held back from the first grade because I was a bad boy. I did not understand. I knew I had more "happy face" papers than anybody in the class. I obeyed my teacher and I felt she liked me. But Mother continued to roar that I had shamed the family and would be severely punished. She decided that I was banned from watching television, forever. I was to go without dinner and accomplish whatever chores Mother could dream up. After another thrashing, I was sent to the garage to stand until Mother called me to go to bed.

That summer, without warning, I was dropped off at my Aunt

Josie's house on the way to the campsite. No one told me about this and I could not understand why. I felt like an outcast as the station wagon drove away, leaving me behind. I felt so sad and hollow. I tried to run away from my aunt's house. I wanted to find my family, and for some strange reason, I wanted to be with Mother. I didn't get far, and my aunt later informed my mother of my attempt. The next time Father worked the 24-hour shift, I paid for my sin. Mother smacked, punched and kicked me until I crumpled to the floor. I tried to tell Mother that I had run away because I wanted to be with her and the family. I tried to tell her that I had missed her, but Mother refused to let me speak. I tried once more and Mother dashed to the bathroom, snatched a bar of soap and crammed it down my throat. After that, I was no longer allowed to speak unless I was instructed to do so.

Returning to the first grade was really a joy. I knew the basic lessons and was instantly dubbed the class genius. Since I was held back, Stan and I were in the same grade. During recess, I would go over to Stan's first-grade class to play. At school we were the best of friends; however, at home, we both knew I was not to be acknowledged.

One day I rushed home to show off a school paper. Mother threw me into her bedroom, yelling about a letter she had received from the North Pole. She claimed the letter said that I was a "bad boy" and Santa would not bring me any gifts for Christmas. Mother raged on and on, saying that I had embarrassed the family *again*. I stood in a daze, as Mother badgered me relentlessly. I felt I was living in a nightmare that Mother had created, and I prayed she would somehow wake up. Before Christmas that year, there were only a couple of gifts for me under the tree, and those came from relatives outside the immediate family. On Christmas morning, Stan dared to ask Mother why Santa had brought me only two paint-by-number pictures. She lectured him stating, "Santa only brings toys to *good* boys and girls." I stole a glance from Stan. There was sorrow in his eyes, and I could tell that he understood Mother's freakish games. Since I was still under punishment, on Christmas Day I had to change into my work clothes and perform my chores. While I was cleaning the bathroom, I overheard an argument between Mother and Father. She was angry with him for "going behind her back" to buy me the paintings. Mother told Father that *she* was in charge of disciplining "the boy" and that he had undermined her authority by buying the gifts. The longer Father argued his case, the angrier she became. I could tell he had lost, and that I was becoming more and more isolated.

A few months later, Mother became a den mother for the Cub Scouts. Whenever the other kids came to our home, she treated them like kings. Some of the other kids told me how they wished their mothers would be like mine. I never responded, but I wondered to myself what they would think if they knew the real truth. Mother only kept the den mother job for a few months. When she gave it up I was so relieved because it meant I could go to other kids' homes for the Wednesday meetings.

One Wednesday, I came home from school to change into my blue and gold Cub Scout uniform. Mother and I were the only ones in the house, and I could tell by the look on her face that she was after blood. After smashing my face against the bedroom mirror, she snatched my arm and dragged me to the car. During the drive to my den mother's house, Mother told me what she was going to do with me when we got home. I scooted to the far side of the front seat of the car, but it didn't work. She reached across the seat and seized my chin, lifting my head towards hers. Mother's eyes were bloodshot and her voice sounded as if she were possessed. When we arrived at the den mother's house, I ran to the door crying. I whined to her that I had been a bad boy and could not attend the meeting. The den mother smiled politely, saying that she would like me to come to the next meeting. That was the last time I saw her.

Once home, Mother ordered me to strip off my clothes and stand by the kitchen stove. I shook from a combination of fear and embarrassment. She then revealed my hideous crime. Mother told me that she had often driven to school to watch my brothers and me play during our lunch period recess. Mother claimed that she had seen me that very day playing on the grass, which was absolutely forbidden by her rules. I quickly answered that I never played on the grass. I knew Mother had somehow made a mistake. My reward for observing Mother's rules and telling the truth was a hard punch in the face.

Mother then reached over and turned on the gas burners to the kitchen stove. Mother told me that she had read an article about a mother who had her son lie on top of a hot stove. I instantly became terrified. My brain became numb, and my legs wobbled. I wanted to disappear. I closed my eyes, wishing her away. My brain locked up when I felt Mother's hand clamp my arm as if it were in a vice grip.

"You've made my life a living hell!" she sneered. "Now it's time I showed *you* what hell is like!" Gripping my arm, Mother held it in the orange-blue flame. My skin seemed to explode from the heat. I could smell the scorched hairs from my burnt arm. As hard as I fought, I could not force Mother to let go of my arm. Finally I fell to the floor, on my hands and knees, and tried to blow cool air on my arm. "It's too bad your drunken father's not here to save you," she hissed. Mother then ordered me to climb up onto the stove and lie on the flames so she could watch me burn. I refused, crying and pleading. I felt so scared I stomped my feet in protest. But Mother continued to force me on top of the stove. I watched the flames, praying the gas might run out.

Suddenly I began to realize the longer I could keep myself off the top of the stove, the better my chances were for staying alive. I knew my brother Ron would soon be coming home from his scout meeting, and I knew Mother never acted this bizzare when anyone else was in the house. In order to survive, I had to buy time. I stole a glance at the kitchen clock behind me. The second hand seemed to creep ever so slowly. To keep Mother off balance, I began to ask whining questions. This infuriated her even more, and Mother began to rain blows around my head and chest. The more Mother slugged me, the more I began to realize I won! Anything was better than burning on the stove.

Finally, I heard the front door fly open. It was Ron. My heart surged with relief. The blood from Mother's face drained. She knew she had lost. For a moment in time, Mother froze. I seized that instant to grab my clothes and race to the garage, where I quickly dressed. I stood against the wall and began to whimper until I realized that *I* had beaten her. *I* had bought a few precious minutes. *I* used my head to survive. For the first time, *I* had won!

Standing alone in that damp, dark garage, I knew, for the first time, that I could survive. I decided that I would use any tactic I could think of to defeat Mother or to delay her from her grizzly obsession. I knew if *I* wanted to live, *I* would have to think ahead. I could no longer cry like a helpless baby. In order to survive, *I* could never give in to her. That day I vowed to myself that I would never, ever again give that bitch the satisfaction of hearing me beg her to stop beating me.

In the coldness of the garage, my entire body trembled from both the cold anger and intense fear. I used my tongue to lick the burn and soothe my throbbing arm. I wanted to scream, but I refused to give

Mother the pleasure of hearing me cry. *I* stood tall. I could hear Mother talking to Ron upstairs, telling him how proud she was of him, and how she didn't have to worry about Ron becoming like David—a bad boy.

The Fight
for Food

*T*he summer after the burn incident, school became my only hope of escape. Except for the short duration of a fishing trip, things with Mother were touch and go, or smash and dash—she would smash me, and I would dash to the solitude of the basement/garage. The month of September brought school and bliss. I had new clothes and a shiny, new lunch pail. Because Mother had me wear the same clothes week after week, by October my clothes had become weathered, torn and smelly. She hardly bothered to cover my bruises on my face and arms. When asked, I had my ready-made excuses Mother brainwashed into me.

By then, Mother would "forget" to feed me any dinner. Breakfast wasn't much better. On a good day, I was allowed leftover cereal portions from my brothers, but only if I performed all of my chores before going to school.

At night I was so hungry, my stomach growled as if I were an angry bear. At night I lay awake concentrating on food. *"Maybe tomorrow I'll get dinner,"* I said to myself. Hours later, I would drift off to sleep, fantasizing about food. I mainly dreamt of colossal hamburgers with all the fixings. In my dreams I seized my prize and brought it to my lips. I visualized every inch of the hamburger. The meat dripped with grease, and thick slices of cheese bubbled on top. Condiments oozed between the lettuce and tomato. As I brought the hamburger closer to my face, I opened my mouth to devour my prize, but nothing happened. I'd try again and again, but no matter how hard I struggled, I could not taste a morsel of my fantasy. Moments later I would wake up, with my stomach more hollow than before. I could not satisfy my hunger; not even in my dreams.

Soon after I had begun to dream about food, I started stealing food at school. My stomach coiled with a combination of fear and anticipation. Anticipation because I knew that within seconds, I would have something to put in my stomach. Fear because I also knew that at any time, I could get caught stealing. I always stole food before school began, while my classmates were playing outside the building. I would sneak to the wall, right outside my homeroom, drop my lunch pail by another pail and kneel down so nobody could see me hunting through their lunches. The first few times were easy, but after several days, some students began to discover Twinkies and other desserts missing from their lunches. Within a short time, my classmates began to hate me. The teacher told the principal, who in turn informed Mother. The fight for food became a cycle. The principal's report to Mother led to more beatings and less food for me at the house.

On weekends, to punish me for my thefts, Mother refused to feed me. By Sunday night, my mouth would water as I began to plot new, fool-proof ways to steal food without getting caught. One of my plots was to steal from other first-grade rooms, where I wasn't known as well. On Monday mornings I would dash from Mother's car to a new first-grade classroom to pick through lunch boxes. I got away with it for a short time, but it didn't take long for the principal to trace the thefts back to me.

At the house, the dual punishment of hunger and violent attacks continued. By this time, for all practical purposes, I was no longer a member of the family. I existed, but there was little or no recognition. Mother had even stopped using my name; referring to me only as The Boy. I was not allowed to eat meals with the family, play with my brothers, or watch television. I was grounded to the house. I was not allowed to look at or speak to anybody. When I returned to the house from school, I immediately accomplished the various chores Mother assigned me. When the chores were finished, I went directly to the basement, where I stood until summoned to clean off the dinner table and wash the dishes. It was made very clear that getting caught sitting or lying down in the basement would bring dire consequences. I had become Mother's slave.

Father was my only hope, and he did all he could to sneak me scraps of food. He tried to get Mother drunk, thinking the liquor might leave her in a better mood. He tried to get Mother to change her mind about feeding me. He even attempted to make deals, promising her the world. But all his attempts were useless. Mother was as solid as a rock. If anything, her drunkenness made it worse. Mother became more like a monster.

I knew Father's efforts to help me led to stress between him and Mother. Soon, midnight arguments began to occur. From bed I could hear the tempo build to an ear-shattering climax. By then they were both drunk, and I could hear Mother scream every vulgar phrase imaginable. It didn't matter what issue started the fight, I would soon be the object of their battle. I knew Father was trying to help, but in bed I still shivered with fear. I knew he would lose, making things worse for me the next day. When they first began to fight, Mother would storm off in the car with the tires screeching. She usually returned home in less than an hour. The next day, they would both act as if nothing had happened. I was grateful when Father found an excuse to come down to the basement and sneak me a piece of bread. He always promised me he would keep trying.

As the arguments between Mother and Father became more frequent, he began to change. Often after an argument, he would pack an overnight bag and set off in the middle of the night for work. After he left, Mother would yank me out of bed and drag me to the kitchen. While I stood shivering in my pajamas, she'd smack me from one side of the kitchen to the other. One of my resistance techniques was to lie on the floor acting as though I didn't have the strength to stand. That tactic didn't last long. Mother would yank me up by the ears and yell into my face with her bourbon breath, for minutes at a time. On these nights, her message was always the same: I was the reason she and Father were having problems. Often I became so tired, my legs would shake. My only escape was to stare at the floor and hope that Mother would soon run out of steam.

By the time I was in the second grade, Mother was pregnant with her fourth child. My teacher, Miss Moss, began to take a special interest in me. She began by questioning me about my attentiveness. I lied, saying I had stayed up late watching television. My lies were not convincing, and she continued to pry not only about why I was sleepy, but also about the condition of my clothes and the bruises on my body. Mother always coached me on what to say about my appearance, so I simply passed Mother's story to the teacher.

Months crept by and Miss Moss became more persistent. One day, she finally reported her concerns to the school principal. He knew me well as the food thief, so he called Mother. When I returned to the house that day, it was as if somebody had dropped an atomic bomb. Mother was more violent than ever. She was furious that some "Hippie" teacher had turned her in for child abuse. Mother said that she would meet with the principal the next day to justify all the false accusations. By the end of the session, my nose bled twice and I was missing a tooth.

When I returned from school the next afternoon, Mother smiled as if she had won a million-dollar sweepstakes. She told me how she had dressed up to see the principal, with her infant son Russell in her arms. Mother told me how she had explained to the principal how David had an overactive imagination. Mother told him how David had often struck and scratched himself to get attention, since the recent birth of his new brother, Russell. I could imagine her turning on her snake-like charm as she cuddled Russell for the benefit of the principal. At the end of their talk, Mother said that she was more than happy to cooperate with the school. She said they could call her any time there was a problem with David. Mother said the staff at school had been instructed to pay no attention to my wild stories of child beating or not being fed. Standing there in the kitchen that day, listening to her boast, gave me a feeling of total emptiness. As Mother told me about the meeting, I could sense her heightened confidence, and her new confidence made me fear for my life. I wished I could dissolve and be gone forever. I wished I would never have to face another human being again.

That summer, the family vacationed at the Russian River. Although I got along better with Mother, the magical feeling had disappeared. The hayrides, the weenie roasts and storytelling were things of the past. We spent more and more time in the cabin. Even the day trips to Johnson's Beach were rare.

Father tried to make the vacation more fun by taking the three of us to play on the new super slide. Russell, who was still a toddler, stayed in the cabin with Mother. One day, when Ron, Stan and I were playing at a neighbor's cabin, Mother came out onto the porch and yelled for us to come in immediately. Once in the cabin, I was scolded for making too much noise. For my punishment, I was not allowed to go with Father and my brothers to the super slide. I sat on a chair in a corner, shivering, hoping that something would happen so the three of them wouldn't leave. I knew Mother had something hideous on her mind. As soon as they left, she brought out one of Russell's soiled diapers.

She smeared the diaper on my face. I tried to sit perfectly still. I knew if I moved, it would only be worse. I didn't look up. I couldn't see Mother standing over me, but I could hear her heavy breathing.

After what seemed like an hour, Mother knelt down beside me and in a soft voice said, "Eat it."

I looked straight ahead, avoiding her eyes. *"No way!"* I said to myself. Like so many times before, avoiding her was the wrong thing to do. Mother smacked me from side to side. I clung to the chair, fearing if I fell off she would jump on me.

"I said 'eat it!' " she sneered.

Switching tactics, I began to cry. *"Slow her down,"* I thought to myself. I began to count to myself, trying to concentrate. Time was my only ally. Mother answered my crying with more blows to my face, stopping only when she heard Russell crying.

Even with my face covered with defecation, I was pleased. I thought I might win. I tried to wipe the crap away, flicking it onto the wooden floor. I could hear Mother singing softly to Russell, and I imagined him cradled in her arms. I prayed he wouldn't fall asleep. A few minutes later my luck ran out.

Still smiling, Mother returned to her conquest. She grabbed me by the back of the neck and led me to the kitchen. There, spread out on the counter top, was another full diaper. The smell turned my stomach. "Now, you are going to eat it!" she said. Mother had the same look in her eyes that she had the day she wanted me to lie on top of the gas stove back at the house. Without moving my head, I moved my eyes, searching for the daisy-colored clock that I knew was on the wall. A few seconds later, I realized the clock was behind me. Without the clock, I felt helpless. I knew I needed to lock my concentration on something, in order to keep any kind of control of the situation. Before I could find the clock, Mother's hands seized my neck. Again she repeated, "Eat it!" I held my breath. The smell was overpowering. I tried to focus on the top corner of the diaper. Seconds seemed like hours. Mother must have known my plan. She slammed my face into the diaper and rubbed it from side to side.

I anticipated her move. As I felt my head being forced down, I closed my eyes tightly and clamped my mouth shut. My nose struck first. A warm sensation oozed from my nostrils. I tried to stop the blood from escaping by breathing in. I snorted bits of defecation back up my nose with the blood. I threw my hands on the counter top and tried to pry myself out of her grip. I twisted from side to side with all my strength, but she was too powerful. Suddenly Mother let go. "They're back! They're back!" she gasped. Mother snatched a wash cloth from the sink and threw it at me. "Clean the shit off your face," she bellowed as she wiped the brown stains from the counter top. I wiped my face the best I could, but not before blowing bits of defecation from my nose. Moments later, Mother stuffed a piece of napkin up my bloody nose and ordered me to sit in the corner. I sat there for the rest of the evening, still smelling traces of the diaper through my nose.

The family never returned to the Russian River again.

In September, I returned to school with last year's clothes and my old, rusted, green lunch pail. I was a walking disgrace. Mother packed the same lunch for me every day: two peanut butter sandwiches and a few limp carrot sticks. Since I was no longer a member of the family, I was not allowed to ride to school in the family station wagon. Mother had me run to school. She knew I would not arrive in time to steal any food from my classmates.

At school I was a total outcast. No other kid would have anything to do with me. During the lunch recesses, I stuffed the sandwiches down my throat as I listened to my former friends make up songs about me. "David the Food Thief" and "Pelzer-Smellzer" were two of the playground favorites. I had no one to talk to or play with. I felt all alone.

At the house, while standing for hours in the garage, I passed the time by imagining new ways to feed myself. Father occasionally tried to sneak scraps of food to me, but with little success. I came to believe if I were to survive, *I* would have to rely on myself. I had exhausted all possibilities at school. All the students now hid their lunch pails, or locked them in the coat closet of the classroom. The teachers and principal knew me and carefully watched me. I had little to no chance of stealing anymore food at school.

Finally, I devised a plan that might work. Students were not allowed to leave the playground during lunch recess, so nobody would expect me to leave. My idea was to sneak away from the playground and run to the local grocery store, and steal cookies, bread, chips or whatever I could. In my mind, I planned every step of my scheme. When I ran to school the next morning, I counted every step so I could calculate my pace and later apply it to my trip to the store. After a few weeks, I had all the information I needed. The only thing left was finding the courage to attempt the plan. I knew it would take longer to go from the school to the store because it was up a hill, so I allowed 15 minutes.

Coming back downhill would be easier, so I allowed 10 minutes. This meant I had only 10 minutes at the store.

Each day when I ran to and from school, I tried to run faster, pounding each step as if I were a marathon runner. As the days passed and my plan became more solid, my hunger for food was replaced with daydreaming. I fantasized whenever performing my chores at the house. On my hands and knees while scrubbing the bathroom tile, I imagined I was the prince in the story *The Prince and the Pauper*. As the Prince, I knew I could end the charade of acting like a servant any time I wanted. In the basement, I stood perfectly still with my eyes closed, dreaming I was a comic-book hero. But my daydream was always interrupted by hunger pangs, and my thoughts soon returned to my plan of stealing food.

Even when I was sure my plan was foolproof, I was too afraid to put it into action. During the lunch recess at school, I strolled around the playground making excuses to myself for my lack of guts to run to the store. I told myself I would get caught or that my timing calculations were not accurate. All through the argument with myself, my stomach growled, calling me a "chicken." Finally, after several days without dinner and only the small leftover portions for breakfast, I decided to do it. A few moments after the lunch bell rang, I blitzed up the street, away from the school, with my heart pounding and my lungs bursting for air. I made it to the store in half the time I allowed myself. Walking up and down the aisles of the store, I felt as if everybody was staring at me. I felt as though all the customers were talking about the smelly, ragged child. It was then that I knew my plan was doomed because I had not taken into account how I might look to other people. The more I worried about my appearance, the more my stomach became seized with fear. I froze in the aisle, not knowing what to do. I slowly began to count the seconds away. I began to think about all the times I had been starving. Suddenly without thinking, I grabbed the first thing I saw on the shelf, ran out of the store and raced back to school. Clutched tightly in my hand was my prize—a box of graham crackers.

As I came near the school I hid my possession under my shirt, on the side that didn't have any holes, as I walked through the school-yard. Inside, I ditched the food in the garbage can of the boys' rest-room. Later that afternoon, after making an excuse to the teacher, I returned to the restroom to devour my prize. I could feel my mouth begin to water, but my heart sank as I looked into an empty trash can. All my careful plans and all the pain of convincing myself that I would eat, were wasted. The custodian had emptied the trash can before I could slip away to the restroom.

That day my plan failed, but on other attempts I was lucky. Once, I managed to hide my treasure in my desk in homeroom, only to find on the next day that I had been transferred to the school across the street. Except for losing the stolen food, I welcomed the transfer. Now, I felt I had a new license to steal. Not only was I able to snitch food from my classmates again, but I also sprinted to the grocery store about once a week. Sometimes at the grocery store, if I felt things weren't just right, I didn't steal anything. As always, I finally got caught. The manager called Mother. At the house, I was thrashed relentlessly. Mother knew why I stole food and so did Dad, but she still refused to feed me. The more I craved food, the more I tried to come up with a better plan to steal it.

After dinner, it was Mother's habit to scrape the leftovers from the dinner plates into a small garbage can. Then she would summon me up from the basement, where I had been standing while the family ate. It was my function to wash the dishes. Standing there with my hands in the scalding water, I could smell the scraps from dinner in the small garbage can. At first my idea was nauseating, but the more I thought about it, the better it seemed. It was my only hope for food. I finished the dishes as fast as I could and emptied the garbage in the garage. My mouth watered at the sight of the food, and I gingerly picked the good pieces out while scraping bits of paper or cigarette butts away, and gobbled the food as fast as I could.

As usual, my new plan came to an abrupt halt when Mother caught me in the act. For a few weeks I quit the garbage routine, but I finally had to return to it, in order to silence my growling stomach. Once, I ate some leftover pork. Hours later I was bent over in extreme pain. I had diarrhea for a week. While I was sick, Mother informed me she had purposefully left the meat in the refrigerator for two weeks, to spoil before she threw it away. She knew I couldn't resist stealing it. As time progressed, Mother had me bring the garbage can to her so she could inspect it while she lay on the couch. She never knew that I wrapped food between paper towels and hid them in the bottom of the can. I knew she wouldn't want to get her fingers dirty, digging in the bottom of the trash can, so my scheme worked for awhile.

Mother sensed I was getting food some way, so she began sprinkling ammonia in the trash can. After that, I gave up on the garbage at the house and focused my sights on finding some other way to get food at school. After getting caught stealing from other kids' lunches, my next idea was to rip off frozen lunches from the school cafeteria.

I timed my restroom break so that the teacher excused me from the classroom just after the delivery truck dropped off its supply of frozen lunches. I crept into the cafeteria and snatched a few frozen trays, then I scurried to the restroom. Alone in the restroom, I swallowed the frozen hot dogs and tater tots in huge chunks so fast I almost choked myself in the process. After filling my stomach I returned to the classroom, feeling so proud that *I* had fed myself.

As I ran to the house from school that afternoon, all I could think about was stealing food from the cafeteria the next day. Minutes later, Mother changed my mind. She dragged me into the bathroom and slugged me in the stomach so hard that I bent over. Pulling me around to face the toilet, she ordered me to shove my finger down my throat. I resisted. I tried my old trick of counting to myself, as I stared into the porcelain toilet bowl, "One . . . two . . . ." I never made it to three. Mother rammed her finger into my mouth, as if she wanted to pull my stomach up through my throat. I squirmed in every direction in an effort to fight her. She finally let me go, but only when I agreed that I would vomit for her.

I knew what was going to happen next. I closed my eyes as chunks of red meat spilled into the toilet. Mother just stood behind me, with her hands on her hips and said, "I thought so. Your father's going to hear about this!" I tensed myself for the volley of blows that I knew was coming, but nothing happened. After a few seconds, I spun around to discover that Mother had left the bathroom. I knew the episode wasn't over. Moments later she returned with a small bowl, ordered me to scoop the partially-digested food out of the toilet and put it in the bowl. Since Father was away shopping at the time, Mother was gathering evidence for his return.

Later that night, after I finished all of my evening chores, Mother had me stand by the kitchen table while she and Father talked in the bedroom. In front of me was the bowl of hot dogs that I had vomited. I couldn't look at it, so I closed my eyes and tried to imagine myself far away from the house. A short time later, Mother and Father stormed into the kitchen. "Look at this, Steve," Mother barked, thrusting her finger in the direction of the bowl. "So you think The Boy is through stealing food, do you?"

By the look on Father's face, I could tell he was getting more and more tired of the constant "What The Boy has done now" routine.

Staring at me, he shook his head in disapproval and stammered, "Well, Roerva, if you would just let The Boy have *something* to eat." A heated battle of words broke out in front of me and, as always, Mother won. "EAT? You want The Boy to eat, Stephen? Well, The Boy is going to EAT! He can eat this!" Mother yelled at the top of her lungs, shoving the bowl towards me and stomping off to the bedroom.

The kitchen became so quiet I could hear Father's strained breathing. He gently placed his hand on my shoulder and said, "Wait here, Tiger. I'll see what I can do." He returned a few minutes later, after trying to talk Mother out of her demand. By the saddened look on his face, I knew immediately who won.

I sat on a chair and picked the clumps of hot dogs out of the bowl with my hand. Globs of thick saliva slipped through my fingers, as I dropped it in my mouth. As I tried to swallow, I began to whimper. I turned to Father, who stood looking through me with a drink in his hand. He nodded for me to continue. I couldn't believe he just stood there as I ate the revolting contents of the bowl. At that moment, I knew we were slipping further and further apart.

I tried to swallow without tasting, until I felt a hand clamp on the back of my neck. "Chew it!" Mother snarled, "Eat it! Eat it all!" she said, pointing to the saliva. I sat deeper in my chair. A river of tears rolled down my cheeks. After I had chewed the mess in the bowl, I tilted my head back and forced what remained, down my throat. I closed my eyes and screamed to myself to keep it from coming back up into my mouth. I didn't open my eyes until I was sure my stomach wasn't going to reject my cafeteria meal. When I did open them, I stared at Father who turned away to avoid my pain. At that moment I hated Mother to no end, but I hated Father even more. The man who had helped me in the past, just stood like a statue while his son ate something even a dog wouldn't touch.

After I finished the bowl of regurgitated hot dogs, Mother returned in her robe and threw a wad of newspapers at me. She informed me the papers were my blankets, and the floor under the table was now my bed. Again I shot a glance at Father, but he acted as though I was not even in the room. Forcing myself not to cry in front of them, I crawled, completely dressed, under the table, and covered myself with the newspapers, like a rat in a cage.

For months I slept under the breakfast table next to a box of kitty litter, but I soon learned to use the newspapers to my advantage. With the papers wrapped around me, my body heat kept me warm. Finally,

Mother told me that I was no longer privileged enough to sleep up-stairs, so I was banished downstairs to the garage. My bed was now an old army cot. To stay warm, I tried to keep my head close to the gas heater. But after a few cold nights, I found it best to keep my hands clamped under my arms and my feet curled towards my buttocks. Sometimes at night I would wake up and try to imagine I was a real person, sleeping under a warm electric blanket, knowing I was safe and that somebody loved me. My imagination worked for awhile, but the cold nights always brought me back to my reality. I knew no one could help me. Not my teachers, my so-called brothers or even Father. I was on my own, and every night I prayed to God that I could be strong both in body and soul. In the darkness of the garage, I laid on the wooden cot and shivered until I fell into a restless sleep.

Once, during my midnight fantasies, I came up with the idea of betting for food on my way to school. Even though the after-school "vomit inspection" was carried out every day when I returned to the house from school, I thought that any food I ate in the morning would be digested by the afternoon. As I began my run to school, I made sure I ran extra fast so I would have more time for my hunt for food. I then altered my course—stopping and knocking on doors. I would ask the lady who answered if she happened to find a lunch box near her house. For the most part, my plan worked. I could tell by looking at these ladies that they felt sorry for me. Thinking ahead, I used a fake name so nobody would know who I really was. For weeks my plan worked, until one day when I came to the house of a lady who knew Mother. My time-tested story, "I lost my lunch. Could you make me one?" fell apart. Even before I left her house, I knew she would call Mother.

That day at school I prayed for the world to end. As I fidgeted in the classroom, I knew Mother was lying on the couch, watching televi-sion and getting more drunk by the hour, while thinking of something hideous to do to me when I arrived at *her* house after school. Running to the house from school that afternoon, my feet felt as though they were encased in blocks of cement. With every step I prayed that Mother's friend had not called her, or had somehow mistaken me for another kid. Above me the skies were blue, and I could feel the sun's rays warm my back. As I approached Mother's house, I looked up towards the sun, wondering if I would ever see it again. I carefully cracked the front door open before slipping inside, and tiptoed down the stairs to the garage. I expected Mother to fly down the stairs and beat me on the cement floor any second. She didn't come. After changing into my work clothes, I crept upstairs to the kitchen and began washing Mother's lunch dishes. Not knowing where she might be, my ears became radar antennae, seeking out her exact location. As I washed the dishes, my back became tense with fear. My hands shook, and I couldn't concentrate on my chores. Finally, I heard Mother come out of her bedroom and walk down the hall towards the kitchen. For a fleeting moment I looked out the window. I could hear the laughter and screams of the children playing. For a moment I closed my eyes and imagined I was one of them. I felt warm inside. I smiled.

My heart skipped a beat when I felt Mother breathing down my neck. Startled, I dropped a dish, but before it could hit the floor I snatched it out of the air. "You're a quick little shit, aren't you?" she sneered. "You can run fast and find time to beg for food. Well . . . we'll just see how fast you really are." Expecting Mother to bash me, I tensed my body, waiting for her to strike. When it didn't happen, I thought she would leave and return to her TV show, but that didn't happen either. Mother remained inches behind me, watching my every move. I could see her reflection in the kitchen window. Mother saw it too, and smiled back. I nearly peed my pants.

When I finished the dishes, I began cleaning the bathroom. Mother sat on the toilet as I scoured the bathtub. While I was on my hands and knees scrubbing the tile floor, she calmly and quietly stood behind me. I expected her to come around and kick me in the face, but she didn't. As I continued my chores, my anxiety grew. I knew Mother was going to beat me, but I didn't know how, when or where. It seemed to take forever for me to finish the bathroom. By the time I did, my legs and arms were shaking with anticipation. I could not concentrate on anything but her. Whenever I found the courage to look up at Mother, she smiled and said, "Faster young man. You'll have to move much faster than that."

By dinner time, I was exhausted with fear. I almost fell asleep as I waited for Mother to summon me to clear the table and wash the evening dishes. Standing alone downstairs in the garage, my insides became unglued. I so badly wanted to run upstairs and go to the bathroom, but I knew without Mother's permission to move, I was a prisoner. *"Maybe that is what she has planned for me,"* I told myself. *"Maybe she wants me to drink my own pee."* At first the thought was too crude to imagine, but I knew *I* had to be prepared to deal with anything Mother might throw at me. The more I tried to focus on my options of what she might do to me, the more my inner strength drained away. Then an idea flashed in my brain: I knew why Mother had followed every step I took. She wanted to maintain a constant pressure on me, by leaving me unsure of when or where she would strike. Before I could think of a way to defeat her, Mother bellowed me upstairs. In the kitchen she told me that only the speed of light would save me, so I had better wash the dishes in record time. "Of course," she sneered, "there's no need to tell you that you're going without dinner tonight, but not to worry, I have a cure for your hunger."

After finishing the evening chores, Mother ordered me to wait downstairs. I stood with my back against the hard wall, wondering what plans she had for me. I had no idea. I broke out in a cold sweat that seemed to seep through to my bones. I became so tired I fell asleep while standing. When I felt my head roll forward, I snapped it upright, waking myself. No matter how hard I tried to stay awake, I couldn't control my head that bobbed up and down like a piece of cork in water. While in my trance-like state, I could feel the strain lift my soul away from my body, as if I too were floating. I felt as light as a feather until my head rolled forward again, jolting me awake. I knew better than to fall into a deep slumber. To get caught could be deadly, so I escaped by staring through the molded garage window, listening to the sounds of the cars driving by and watching the red flashes of planes flying overhead. From the bottom of my heart I wished that I could fly away.

Hours later after Ron and Stan went to bed, Mother ordered me to return upstairs. I dreaded every step. I knew the time had come. She had drained me emotionally and physically. I didn't know what she had planned. I simply wished Mother would beat me and get it over with.

As I opened the door, a calmness filled my soul. The house was dark except for a single light in the kitchen. I could see Mother sitting by the breakfast table. I stood completely still. She smiled, and I could tell by her slumped shoulders that the booze had her in a deep-six. In a strange way, I knew she wasn't going to beat me. My thoughts became cloudy, but my trance broke when Mother got up and strolled over to the kitchen sink. She knelt down, opened the sink cabinet and removed a bottle of ammonia. I didn't understand. She got a tablespoon and poured some ammonia into it. My brain was too rattled to think. As much as I wanted to, I could not get my numbed brain into gear.

With the spoon in her hand, Mother began to creep towards me. As some of the ammonia sloshed from the spoon, spilling onto the floor, I backed away from Mother until my head struck the counter top by the stove. I almost laughed inside. *"That's all? That's it? All she's going to do is have me swallow some of this?"* I said to myself.

I wasn't afraid. I was too tired. All I could think was, *"Come on, let's go. Let's get it over with."* As Mother bent down, she again told me that only speed would save me. I tried to understand her puzzle, but my mind was too cloudy.

Without hesitation I opened my mouth, and Mother rammed the cold spoon deep into my throat. Again I told myself this was all too easy, but a moment later I couldn't breathe. My throat seized. I stood wobbling in front of Mother, feeling as if my eyes were going to pop out of my skull. I fell on the floor, on my hands and knees. *"Bubble!"* my brain screamed. I pounded the kitchen floor with all my strength, trying to swallow, and trying to concentrate on the bubble of air stuck in my esophagus. Instantly I became terrified. Tears of panic streamed down my cheeks. After a few seconds, I could feel the force of my pounding fists weaken. My fingernails scraped the floor. My eyes became fixed on the floor. The colors seemed to run together. I began to feel myself drift away. I knew I was going to die.

I came to my senses, and felt Mother slapping me on the back. The force of her blows made me burp, and I was able to breathe again. As I forced huge gulps of air back into my lungs, Mother returned to her glass of booze. She took a long drink, gazed down at me and blew a mist of air in my direction. "Now, that wasn't so hard, was it?" Mother said, finishing her glass before dismissing me downstairs to my cot.

The next evening was a repeat performance, but this time in front of Father. She boasted to him, "This will teach The Boy to quit stealing food!" I knew she was only doing it for her sick, perverted pleasure. Father stood lifeless as Mother fed me another dose of ammonia. But this time, I fought back. She had to pry my mouth open, and by thrashing my head from side to side, *I* was able to make her spill most of the cleaner onto the floor. But not enough. Again I clenched my fingers together, beating the floor. I looked up at Father, trying to call out to him. My thoughts were clear, but no sound escaped from my mouth. He simply stood above me, showing no emotion, as I pounded my hands by his feet. As if she were kneeling to pet one of her dogs,

Mother again slapped me on the back a few times before I blacked out.

The next morning while cleaning the bathroom, I looked in the mirror to inspect my burning tongue. Layers of flesh were scraped away, while remaining parts were red and raw. I stood, staring into the sink, feeling how lucky I was to be alive.

Although Mother never made me swallow ammonia again, she did make me drink spoonfuls of Clorox a few times. But Mother's favorite game seemed to be dishwashing soap. From the bottle she would squeeze the cheap, pink liquid down my throat and command that I stand in the garage. My mouth became so dry, I sneaked away to the garage faucet and filled my stomach full of water. Soon I discovered my dreadful mistake, and diarrhea took hold. I cried out to Mother upstairs, begging her to let me use the toilet upstairs. She refused. I stood downstairs, afraid to move, as clumps of the watery matter fell through my underwear and down my pant legs, onto the floor.

I felt so degraded; I cried like a baby. I had no self-respect of any kind. I needed to go to the bathroom again, but I was too afraid to move. Finally, as my insides twisted and turned, I gathered the last of my dignity. I waddled to the garage sink, grabbed a five-gallon bucket and squatted to relieve myself. I closed my eyes trying to think of a way to clean myself and my clothes when suddenly, the garage door opened behind me. I turned my head to see Father, looking on dispassionately, as his son "mooned" him and as the brown seepage spilled into the bucket. I felt lower than a dog.

Mother didn't always win. Once, during a week when I was not allowed to attend school, she squeezed the soap into my mouth and told me to clean the kitchen. She didn't know it, but I refused to swallow the soap. As the minutes passed, my mouth became filled with a combination of soap and saliva. *I* would not allow myself to swallow. When I finished the kitchen chores, I raced downstairs to empty the trash. I smiled from ear to ear, as I closed the door behind me and spit out the mouthful of pink soap. At the trash cans by the garage door, I reached into one of the cans and plucked out a used paper towel, and wiped out the inside of my mouth ensuring that I removed every drop of soap. After I finished, I felt as though I had won the Olympic Marathon. I was so proud for beating Mother at her own game.

Even though Mother caught me in most of my attempts to feed myself, she couldn't catch me *all* the time. After months of being confined for hours at a time in the garage, my courage took over and I stole bits of frozen food from the garage freezer. I was fully aware that I could pay for my crime at any time, so I ate every morsel as if it were my last meal.

In the darkness of the garage I closed my eyes, dreaming I was a king dressed in the finest robes, eating the best food mankind had to offer. As I held a piece of frozen pumpkin pie crust or a bit of a taco shell, *I* was the king, and like a king on his throne, I gazed down on my food and smiled.

CHAPTER 5

The Accident

*T*he summer of 1971 set the tone for the remainder of the time that I lived with Mother.

I had not yet reached my 11th birthday, but for the most part, I knew what forms of punishment to expect. To exceed one of Mother's time limits on any of my multiple chores, meant no food. If I looked at her or one of her sons without her permission, I received a slap in the face. If I was caught stealing food, I knew Mother would either repeat an old form of punishment or dream up something new and hideous. Most of the time Mother seemed to know exactly what she was doing, and I could anticipate what she might do next. However, I always kept my guard up and tensed my entire body if I thought she might come my way.

As June turned to early July, my morale dwindled. Food was little more than a fantasy. I rarely received even leftover breakfast, no matter how hard I worked, and I was *never* fed lunch. As for dinner, I averaged about one evening meal every three days.

One particular July day began like any other mundane day, in my now slave-like existence. I had not eaten in three days. Because school was out for the summer, my options for finding food vanished. As always during dinner, I sat at the bottom of the stairs with my buttocks on top of my hands, listening to the sounds of "the family" eating. Mother now demanded that I sit on my hands with my head thrust backward, in a "prisoner of war" position. I let my head fall forward, half dreaming that I was one of them—a member of "the family." I must have fallen asleep because I was suddenly awakened by Mother's snarling voice, "Get up here! Move your ass!" she yelled.

At the first syllable of her order I snapped my head level, stood up and sprinted up the stairs. I prayed that tonight I would get something, anything, to soothe my hunger.

I had begun clearing the dishes from the dining room table at a feverish pace, when Mother called me into the kitchen. I bowed my head as she began to babble her time limits to me. "You have 20 minutes! One minute, one second more, and you go hungry again! Is that understood?"

"Yes, ma'am."

"Look at me when I'm talking to you!" she snapped.

Obeying her command, I slowly raised my head. As my head came up, I saw Russell rocking back and forth on Mother's left leg. The harsh tone of Mother's voice didn't seem to bother him. He simply stared at me through a set of cold eyes. Even though Russell was only four or five years old at the time, he had become Mother's "Little Nazi," watching my every move, making sure I didn't steal any food. Sometimes he would make up tales for Mother so he could watch me receive punishment. It really wasn't Russell's fault. I knew Mother had brainwashed him, but I had begun to turn cold towards him and hate him just the same.

"Do you hear me?" Mother yelled. "Look at me when I'm talking to you!" As I looked at her, Mother snatched a carving knife from the counter top and screamed, "If you don't finish on time, I'm going to kill you!"

Her words had no effect on me. She had said the same thing over and over again for almost a week now. Even Russell wasn't fazed by her threat. He kept rocking on Mother's leg as if he were riding a stick pony. She apparently wasn't pleased with her renewed tactic because she continued to badger on and on as the clock ticked away, eating up my time limit. I wished she would just shut up and let me work. I was desperate to meet her time limits. I wanted so much to have something to eat. I dreaded going to sleep another night.

Something looked wrong. Very wrong! I strained to focus my eyes on Mother. She had begun to wave the knife in her right hand. Again, I was not overly frightened. She had done this before too. *"Eyes,"* I told myself. *"Look at her eyes."* I did, and they seemed normal for her—half-glazed over. But my instincts told me there was something wrong. I didn't think she was going to hit me, but my body began to tense anyway. As I became more tense, I saw what was wrong. Partly because of Russell's rocking motion, and partly because of the motion of her arm and hand with the knife, Mother's whole body began to weave back and forth. For a moment I thought she was going to fall.

She tried to regain her balance, snapping at Russell to let go of her leg, while she continued to scream at me. By then, her upper body looked like a rocking chair that was out of control. Forgetting about her useless threats, I imagined that the old drunk was going to fall flat on her face. I focused all of my attention on Mother's face. Out of the corner of my eye I saw a blurred object fly from her hand. A sharp pain erupted from just above my stomach. I tried to remain standing, but my legs gave out, and my world turned black.

As I regained consciousness, I felt a warm sensation flowing from my chest. It took me a few seconds to realize where I was. I sat propped up on the toilet. I turned towards Russell who began chanting, "David's going to die. The Boy's going to die." I moved my eyes towards my stomach. On her knees, Mother was hastily applying a thick wad of gauze to a place on my stomach where dark red blood pumped out. I tried to say something. I knew it was an accident. I wanted Mother to know that I forgave her, but I felt too faint to speak. My head slumped forward again and again, as I tried to hold it up. I lost track of time as I returned to darkness.

When I woke up, Mother was still on her knees wrapping a cloth around my lower chest. She knew exactly what she was doing. Many times when we were younger, Mother told Ron, Stan and me how she had intended to become a nurse, until she met Father. Whenever she was confronted with an accident around the home, she was in complete control. I never doubted her nursing abilities for a second. I simply waited for her to load me in the car and take me to the hospital. I felt sure that she would. It was just a matter of time. I felt a curious sense of relief. I knew in my heart it was over. This whole charade of living like a slave had come to an end. Even Mother could not lie about this one. I felt the accident had set me free.

It took Mother nearly half an hour to dress my wound. There was no remorse in her eyes. I thought that, at the very least, she would try to comfort me with her soothing voice. Looking at me with no emotion, Mother stood up, washed her hands and told me I now had 30 minutes to finish the dishes. I shook my head, trying to understand what she had said. After a few seconds, Mother's message sunk in.

Just as in the arm incident a few years ago, Mother was not going to acknowledge what had happened.

I had no time for self-pity. The clock was running. I stood up, wobbled for a few seconds, then made my way to the kitchen. With every step, pain ripped through my ribs and blood seeped through my ragged T-shirt. By the time I reached the kitchen sink, I leaned over and panted like an old dog.

From the kitchen I could hear Father in the living room, flipping through his newspaper. I took a painfully deep breath, hoping that I could shove off and make my way to Dad. But I breathed too hard, and fell to the floor. After that I realized I had to take short, choppy breaths. I made my way into the living room. Sitting on the far end of the couch was my hero. I knew he would take care of Mother and drive me to the hospital. I stood before Father, waiting for him to turn his page and see me. When he did, I stuttered, "Father . . . Mo . . . Mo . . . Mother stabbed me."

He didn't even raise an eyebrow. "Why?" he asked.

"She told me if I didn't do the dishes on time, she . . . she'd kill me."

Time stood still. From behind the paper I could hear Father's labored breathing. He cleared his throat before saying, "Well . . . you ah . . . you better go back in there and do the dishes." My head leaned forward as if to catch his words. I couldn't believe what I had just heard. Father must have sensed my confusion when I saw him snap his paper and heard him raise his voice saying, "Jesus H. Christ! Does Mother know that you're here talking to me? You better go back in there and do the dishes. Damn it boy, we don't need to do anything that might make her more upset! I don't need to go through that tonight. . . ." Father stopped for a second, took a deep breath and lowered his voice, whispering, "I tell you what: you go back in there and do the dishes. I won't even tell her that you told, okay? This will be *our* little secret. Just go back in the kitchen and do the dishes. Go on now, before she catches the both of us. Go!"

I stood before Father in total shock. He didn't even look at me. Somehow I felt if he could at least turn a corner flap of the paper and search into my eyes, he would know; he would feel my pain, how desperate I was for his help. But, as always, I knew that Mother controlled him like she controlled everything that happened in her house. I think Father and I both knew the code of "the family"—if we don't acknowledge a problem, it simply does not exist. As I stood before

Father, not knowing what to do next, I looked down and saw droplets of blood staining the family's carpet. I had felt in my heart that he would scoop me up in his arms and take me away. I even imagined him ripping off his shirt to expose his true identity, before flying through the air like Superman.

I turned away. All my respect for Father was gone. The savior I had imagined for so long was a phony. I felt more angry at him than I did at Mother. I wished that somehow I could fly away, but the throbbing pain brought me back to reality.

I washed the dishes as fast as my body would let me. I quickly learned that moving my forearm resulted in a sharp pain above my stomach. If I sidestepped from the wash basin to the rinse basin, another pain raced through my body. I could feel what little strength I had, draining away. As Mother's time limit passed, so did my chances of getting fed.

I wanted to just lie down and quit, but the promise I made years ago kept me going. I wanted to show The Bitch that she could beat me only if I died, and I was determined not to give in, even to death. As I washed the dishes, I learned that by standing on my toes and leaning my upper body towards the counter top, I could relieve some of the pressure on my lower chest. Instead of sidestepping every few seconds, I washed a few dishes at a time, then moved over and rinsed them all together. After drying the dishes, I dreaded the task of putting them away. The cupboards were above my head, and I knew reaching for them would cause great pain. Holding a small plate, I stretched my legs as far as I could and tried to raise my arms above my head to put the dish away. I almost made it, but the pain was too great. I crumbled to the floor.

By now, my shirt was saturated with blood. As I tried to regain my footing, I felt Father's strong hands helping me. I brushed him away. "Give me the dishes," he said. "I'll put them away. You better go downstairs and change that shirt." I didn't say a word as I turned away. I looked at the clock. It had taken me nearly an hour and a half to complete my chore. My right hand clamped tightly onto the railing, as I slowly made my way downstairs. I could actually see the blood seep from my T-shirt with every step I took.

Mother met me at the bottom of the stairs. As she tore the shirt from my body, I could see Mother was doing it as gently as she could, however, she gave me no other comfort. I could see it was just a matter of business to her. In the past, I had seen her treat animals with more compassion than she did me.

I was so weak that I accidentally fell against her as she dressed me in an old, oversized T-shirt. I expected Mother to hit me, but she allowed me to rest against her for a few seconds. Then Mother set me at the bottom of the stairs and left. A few minutes later, Mother returned with a glass of water. I gulped it down as fast as I could swallow. When I finished, Mother told me that she couldn't feed me right away. She said she would feed me in a few hours when I felt better. Again, her voice was monotone—completely without emotion.

Stealing a glance, I could see the California twilight being overtaken by darkness. Mother told me I could play outside with the boys, on the driveway in front of the garage door. My head was not clear. It took me a few seconds to understand what she had said. "Go on, David. Go," she persisted. With Mother's help, I limped out of the garage to the driveway. My brothers casually looked me over, but they were much more interested in lighting their Fourth-of-July sparklers.

As the minutes passed, Mother became more compassionate towards me. She held me by the shoulders as we watched my brothers make figure eights with their sparklers. "Would you like one?" Mother asked. I nodded yes. She held my hand as she knelt down to light the sparkler. For a moment, I imagined the scent of the perfume Mother wore years ago. But she had not used perfume or made up her face for a long time.

As I played with my brothers, I couldn't help but think about Mother and the change in the way she was treating me. *"Is she trying to make up with me?"* I wondered. *"Are my days living in the basement finally over? Am I back in the family fold?"* For a few minutes I didn't care. My brothers seemed to accept my presence, and I felt a feeling of friendship and warmth with them that I thought had been buried forever.

Within a few seconds my sparkler fizzled out. I turned towards the retreating sun. It had been forever since I had watched a sunset. I closed my eyes, trying to soak up as much heat as I could. For a few fleeting moments my pain, my hunger and my miserable way of life disappeared. I felt so warm, so alive. I opened my eyes, hoping to capture the moment for the rest of eternity.

Before she went to bed, Mother gave me more water and fed me some small bites of food. I felt like a disabled animal being nursed back to health, but I didn't care.

Downstairs in the garage I laid on my old army cot. I tried not to think of the pain, but it was impossible to ignore as it crept throughout my body. Finally exhaustion took over and I drifted off to sleep. During the night I had several nightmares. I startled myself, waking up in a cold sweat. Behind me I heard a sound that scared me. It was Mother. She bent down and applied a cold wash cloth to my forehead. She told me that I had been running a fever during the night. I was too tired and weak to respond. All I could think about was the pain. Later, Mother returned to my brothers' downstairs bedroom, which was closer to the garage. I felt safe knowing she was nearby to watch over me.

Soon I drifted back into darkness, and with the fitful sleep came a dreadful dream of sheets of red, hot rain. In the dream I seemed to drench in it. I tried wiping the blood off my body only to find it quickly covered again. When I awoke the next morning, I stared at my hands which were crusted with dried blood. The shirt covering my chest was entirely red. I could feel the dried blood on parts of my face. I heard the bedroom door behind me open, and I turned to see Mother walking towards me. I expected more sympathy like she had given me the night before, but it was an empty hope. She gave me nothing. In a cold voice, Mother told me to clean myself up and begin my chores. As I heard her march up the stairs, I knew nothing had changed. I was still the bastard of the family.

About three days after the "accident," I continued to feel feverish. I didn't dare ask Mother for even an aspirin, especially since Father was away at work. I knew she was back to her normal self. I thought the fever was due to my injury. The slit in my stomach had opened up more than once since that night. Quietly, so Mother wouldn't hear me, I crept to the garage sink. I picked up the cleanest rag I could find in my heap of rags. I cracked the water faucet open just enough to let a few drops of water spill onto the rag. Then I sat down and rolled up my red, soggy shirt. I touched my wound, flinching from the pain. I took a deep breath and as gently as possible, pinched the slit. The pain was so bad I threw my head back against the cold concrete floor, almost knocking myself out. When I looked at my stomach again, I saw a yellowish-white substance begin to ooze from the red, angry slash. I didn't know much about such things, but I knew it was infected. I started to get up to go upstairs and ask Mother to clean me up. When I was half-standing, I stopped. *"No!"* I told myself. *"I don't need that bitch's help."* I knew enough about basic first-aid training to clean a wound, so I felt confident that I could do it alone. I wanted to be in charge of myself. I didn't want to rely on Mother or give her any more control over me than she already had.

I wet the rag again and brought it down towards my wound. I hesitated before I touched it. My hands were shaking with fear, as tears streamed down my face. I felt like a baby and hated it. Finally I told myself, *"You cry, you die. Now, take care of the wound."* I realized that my injury probably wasn't life-threatening; I brainwashed myself to block out the pain.

I moved quickly before my motivation slipped away. I snatched another rag, rolled it up and stuffed it into my mouth. I focused all my attention on the thumb and first finger of my left hand, as I pinched the skin around my slit. With my other hand I wiped away the pus. I repeated the process until blood seeped through, and I was wiping away only blood. Most of the white stuff was gone. The pain from the pinching and wiping was more than I could stand. With my teeth clamped tightly on the rag, my screaming was muffled. I felt as though I was hanging from a cliff. By the time I finished, a river of tears soaked the neck of my shirt.

Fearing Mother would catch me not sitting at the bottom of the stairs, I cleaned up my mess then half-walked, half-crawled to my assigned place at the foot of the staircase. Before I sat on my hands, I checked my shirt; only small drops of blood escaped from the wound to the rag bandage. I willed the wound to heal. Somehow I knew it would. I felt proud of myself. I imagined myself like a character in a comic book, who overcame great odds and survived. Soon my head slumped forward and I fell asleep. In my dream, I flew through the air in vivid colors. I wore a cape of red . . . I was Superman.

CHAPTER

6

While Father Is Away

*A*fter the knife incident, Father spent less and less time at home and more at work. He made excuses to the family, but I didn't believe him. I often shivered with fear as I sat in the garage, hoping for some reason he might not leave. In spite of all that had happened, I still felt Father was my protector. When he was home, Mother only did about half the things to me that she did when he was gone.

When Father was home, it became his habit to help me with the evening dishes. Father washed and I dried. While we worked, we talked softly so neither Mother nor the other boys could hear us. Sometimes, several minutes would pass without us talking. We wanted to make sure the coast was clear.

Father always broke the ice. "How ya doin', Tiger?" he would say.

Hearing the old name that Father used when I was a little boy, always brought a smile to my face. "I'm okay," I would answer.

"Did you have anything to eat today?" he often asked. I usually shook my head in a negative gesture.

"Don't worry," he'd say. "Some day you and I will both get out of this madhouse."

I knew father hated living at home, and I felt that it was all my fault. I told him that I would be good and that I wouldn't steal food anymore. I told Father I would try harder and do a better job on my chores. When I said these things, he always smiled and assured me that it wasn't my fault.

Sometimes as I dried the dishes, I felt a new ray of hope. I knew

Father probably wouldn't do anything against Mother, but when I stood beside him I felt safe.

Like all good things that happened to me, Mother put an end to Father helping me with the dishes. She insisted that The Boy needed no help. She said that Father paid too much attention to me and not enough to others in the family. Without a fight, Father gave up. Mother now had complete control over everybody in the household.

After awhile, Father didn't even stay home on his days off. He would come in for only a few minutes. After seeing my brothers, he would find me wherever I was doing my chores and say a few sentences, then leave. It took Father no more than 10 minutes to get in and out of the house, and be on his way back to his solitude, which he usually found in a bar. When Father talked to me, he'd tell me that he was making plans for the two of us to leave. This always made me smile, but deep inside I knew it was a fantasy.

One day, he knelt down to tell me how sorry he was. I looked into his face. The change in Father frightened me. He had dark black circles around his eyes, and his face and neck were beet red. Father's once-rigid shoulders were now slumped over. Gray had begun to take over his jet-black hair. Before he left that day, I threw my arms around his waist. I didn't know when I would see him again.

After finishing my chores that day, I rushed downstairs. I had been ordered to wash my ragged clothes and another heap of smelly rags. But that day, Father's leaving had left me so sad that I buried myself in the pile of rags and cried. I cried for him to come back and take me away. After a few minutes of self-comfort, I settled down and began scrubbing my "Swiss cheese" clothes. I scrubbed until my knuckles bled. I no longer cared about my existence. Mother's house had become unbearable. I wished I could somehow manage to escape the place I now called the "Madhouse."

During one period of time when Father was away, Mother starved me for about ten consecutive days. No matter how hard I tried to meet her time limits, I couldn't make it. And the consequence was no food. Mother was completely thorough in making sure I was unable to steal any food. She cleared the dinner table herself, putting the food down the garbage disposal. She rummaged through the garbage can every day before I emptied it downstairs. She locked the freezer in the garage with her key and kept it. I was used to going without food for periods up to three days, but this extended time was unbearable. Water was my only means of survival. When I filled the metal ice cube tray from the refrigerator, I would tip the corner of the tray to my mouth. Downstairs I would creep to the wash basin and crack the faucet tap open. Praying that the pipe would not vibrate and alert Mother, I would carefully suck on the cold metal until my stomach was so full I thought it would burst.

By the sixth day I was so weak when I woke up on my army cot, I could hardly get up. I worked on my chores at a snail's pace. I felt so numb. My thought responses became unclear. It seemed to take minutes for me to understand each sentence Mother yelled to me. As I slowly strained my head up to look at Mother, I could tell that to her it was a game—a game which she thoroughly enjoyed.

"Oh, poor little baby," Mother sarcastically cooed. Then she asked me how I felt, and laughed when I begged for food. At the end of the sixth day, and those that followed, I hoped with all my heart that Mother would feed me something, anything. I was at a point that I didn't care what it was.

One evening, towards the end of her "game," after I had finished my chores, Mother slammed a plate of food in front of me. The cold leftovers were a feast to my eyes. But I was wary; it seemed too good to be true. "Two minutes!" Mother barked. "You have two minutes to eat. That's all." Like lightning I picked up the fork, but the moment before the food touched my mouth, Mother snatched the plate away from me and emptied the food down the garbage disposal. "Too late!" she sneered.

I stood before her dumbstruck. I didn't know what to do or say. All I could think of was *"Why?"* I couldn't understand why she treated me the way she did. I was so close that I could smell every morsel. I knew she wanted me to cave in, but I stood fast and held back the tears.

Alone in the garage, I felt I was losing control of everything. I craved food. I wanted my father. But more than anything, I wanted just an ounce of respect; one little bit of dignity. Sitting there on my hands, I could hear my brothers opening the refrigerator to get their desserts, and I hated it. I looked at myself. My skin had a yellowish tint, and my muscles were thin and stringy. Whenever I heard one of my brothers laugh at a television show, I cursed their names. *"Lucky bastards! Why doesn't she take turns and beat up on one of them for a change?"* I cried to myself as I vented my feelings of hatred.

For nearly ten days I had gone without food. I had just finished the dinner dishes when Mother repeated her "you have two minutes to eat" game. There were only a few bits of food on the plate. I felt she would snatch the plate away again, so I moved with a purpose. I didn't give Mother a chance to snatch it away like she had the past three evenings. So I grabbed the plate and quickly swallowed the food without chewing it. Within seconds, I finished eating all that was on the plate and licked it clean. "You eat like a pig!" Mother snarled. I bowed my head, acting as though I cared. But inside I laughed at her, saying to myself, *"Fuck you! Say what you want! I got the food!"*

Mother had another favorite game for me while Father was away. She sent me to clean the bathroom with her usual time limits. But this time, she put a bucket, filled with a mixture of ammonia and Clorox, in the room with me and closed the door. The first time she did this, Mother informed me she had read about it in a newspaper and wanted to try it. Even though I acted as if I were frightened, I really wasn't. I was ignorant about what was going to happen. Only when Mother closed the door and ordered me not to open it, did I begin to worry. With the room sealed, the air began to quickly change. In the corner of the bathroom I dropped to my hands and knees and stared at the bucket. A fine gray mist swirled towards the ceiling. As I breathed in the fumes, I collapsed and began spitting up. My throat felt like it was on fire. Within minutes it was raw. The gas from the reaction of the ammonia and Clorox mixture made my eyes water. I was frantic about not being able to meet Mother's time limits for cleaning the bathroom.

After a few more minutes, I thought I would cough up my insides. I knew that Mother wasn't going to give in and open the door. To survive her new game, I had to use my head. Lying on the tiled floor I stretched my body and, using my foot, I slid the bucket to the door. I did this for two reasons: I wanted the bucket as far away from me as possible, and in case Mother opened the door, I wanted her to get a snoot full of her own medicine. I curled up in the opposite corner of the bathroom, with my cleaning rag over my mouth, nose and eyes. Before covering my face, I wet the rag in the toilet. I didn't dare turn on the water in the sink for fear of Mother hearing it. Breathing through the cloth, I watched the mist inch its way closer and closer to the floor. I felt as if I were locked in a gas chamber. Then I thought about the small heating vent on the floor by my feet. I knew it turned on and off every few minutes. I put my face next to the vent and sucked in all the air my lungs would hold. In about half an hour, Mother opened the door and told me to empty the bucket into the drain in the garage before I smelled up *her* house. Downstairs I coughed up blood for over an hour. Of all Mother's punishments, I hated the gas chamber game the most.

Towards the end of the summer Mother must have become bored with finding ways to torture me around the house. One day, after I had completed all my morning chores, she sent me out to mow lawns. This wasn't an altogether new routine. During the Easter vacation from school the spring before, Mother had sent me out to mow. She had set a quota on my earnings and ordered me to return the money to her. The quota was impossible for me to meet, so, in desperation, I once stole nine dollars from the piggy bank of a small girl who lived in our neighborhood. Within hours, the girl's father was knocking on the front door. Of course, Mother returned the money and blamed me. After the man left, she beat me until I was black and blue. I only stole the money to try to meet her quota.

The summer mowing plan turned out no better for me than the one during Easter vacation. Going from door to door, I asked people if they cared to have their lawns mowed. No one did. My ragged clothes and my thin arms must have made me a pathetic sight. Out of sympathy, one lady gave me a lunch in a brown bag and sent me on my way. Half a block down the street a couple agreed to have me mow their lawn. When I finished, I started running back to Mother's house, carrying the brown bag with me. I intended to hide it before I turned onto her block. I didn't make it. Mother was out cruising in her car, and she pulled over and caught me with the bag. Before Mother screeched the station wagon to a stop, I threw my hands into the air, as if I were a criminal. I remember wishing that lady luck would be with me just one time.

Mother leaped out of the car, snatched the brown bag in one hand and punched me with the other. She then threw me into the car, and drove to the house where the lady had made the lunch for me. The woman wasn't home. Mother was convinced that I had sneaked into the lady's house and prepared my own lunch. I knew that to be in the possession of food was the ultimate crime. Silently, I yelled at myself for not ditching the food earlier.

Once home, the usual "ten-rounder" left me sprawled on the floor. Mother then told me to sit outside in the backyard while she took "her sons" to the zoo. The section where Mother ordered me to sit was covered with rocks about an inch in diameter. I lost circulation in much of my body, as I sat on my hands in my "prisoner of war" position. I began to give up on God. I felt that He must have hated me. *What other reason could there be for a life like mine?* All my efforts for mere survival seemed futile. My attempts to stay one step ahead of Mother were useless. A black shadow was always over me.

Even the sun seemed to avoid me, as it hid in a thick cloud cover that drifted overhead. I slumped my shoulders, retreating into the solitude of my dreams. I don't know how much time had passed, but later I could hear the distinctive sound of Mother's station wagon returning into the garage. My time sitting on the rocks was over. I wondered what Mother had planned for me next. I prayed it was not another gas chamber session. She yelled from the garage for me to follow her upstairs. She led me to the bathroom. My heart sank. I felt doomed. I began taking huge breaths of fresh air, knowing that soon I would need it.

To my surprise there wasn't any bucket or bottles in the bathroom. *"Am I off the hook?"* I asked myself. This looked too easy. I timidly watched Mother as she turned the cold water tap in the bathtub fully open. I thought it was odd that she forgot to turn on the hot water as well. As the tub began to fill with cold water, Mother tore off my clothes and ordered me to get into the tub. I got into the tub and laid down. A cold fear raced throughout my body. "Lower!" Mother yelled. "Put your face in the water like this!" She then bent over, grabbed my neck with both hands and shoved my head under the water. Instinctively, I thrashed and kicked, trying desperately to force my head above the water so I could breathe. Her grip was too strong. Under the water I opened my eyes. I could see bubbles escape from my mouth and float to the surface as I tried to shout. I tried to thrust my head from side to side as I saw the bubbles becoming smaller and smaller. I began to feel weak. In a frantic effort I reached up and grabbed her shoulders. My fingers must have dug into her because Mother let go. She looked down on me, trying to get her breath. "Now keep your head below the water, or next time it will be longer!"

I submerged my head, keeping my nostrils barely above the surface of the water. I felt like an alligator in a swamp. When Mother left the bathroom, her plan became more clear to me. As I laid stretched out in the tub, the water became unbearably cold. It was as though I was in a refrigerator. I was too frightened of Mother to move, so I kept my head under the surface as ordered.

Hours passed and my skin began to wrinkle. I didn't dare touch any part of my body to try to warm it. I did raise my head out of the water, far enough to hear better. Whenever I heard somebody walk down the hall outside the bathroom, I quietly slid my head back into the cold-ness.

Usually the footsteps I heard were one of my brothers going to their bedroom. Sometimes one of them came into the bathroom to use the toilet. They just glared at me, shook their heads and turned away. I tried to imagine I was in some other place, but I could not relax enough to daydream.

Before the family sat down for dinner, Mother came into the bath-room and yelled at me, telling me to get out of the bathtub and put on my clothes. I responded immediately, grabbing a towel to dry myself. "Oh, no!" she screamed. "Put your clothes on the way you are!" With-out hesitating, I obeyed her command. My clothes were soaked as I ran downstairs to sit in the backyard as instructed. The sun had begun to set, but half the yard was still in direct sunlight. I tried to sit in a sunny area, but Mother ordered me into the shade. In the corner of the backyard, while sitting in my P.O.W. position, I shivered. I wanted only a few seconds of heat, but with every passing minute my chances of drying off were becoming less and less. From the upstairs window I could hear the sound of "the family" passing dishes full of food to each other. Once in a while, a burst of laughter would escape through the window. Since Father was home, I knew that whatever Mother had cooked was good. I wanted to turn my head and look up to see them eating, but I didn't dare. I lived in a different world. I didn't even deserve a glance at the good life.

The bathtub and the backyard treatment soon became routine. At times when I laid in the tub, my brothers brought their friends to the bathroom to look at their naked brother. Their friends often scoffed at me. "What did *he* do *this* time?" they'd ask. Most of the time my brothers just shook their heads, saying, "I don't know."

With the start of school in the fall, came the hope of a temporary escape from my dreary life. Our fourth-grade homeroom class had a substitute teacher for the first two weeks. They told us that our regular teacher was ill. The substitute teacher was younger than most of the other staff, and she seemed more lenient. At the end of the first week, she passed out ice cream to those students whose behavior had been good. I didn't get any the first week, but I tried harder and received my reward at the end of the second week. The new teacher played "pop hits" on 45-rpm records, and sang to the class. We really liked her. When Friday afternoon came, I didn't want to leave. After all the other students had gone, she bent close to me and told me I would have to go home. She knew I was a problem child. I told her that I wanted to stay with her. She held me for a moment, then got up and played the song I liked best. After that I left. Since I was late, I ran to the house as fast as I could and raced through my chores. When I was finished, Mother sent me to the backyard to sit on the cold cement deck.

That Friday, I looked up at the thick blanket of fog covering the sun, and cried inside. The substitute teacher had been so nice to me. She treated me like a real person, not like some piece of filth lying in the gutter. As I sat outside feeling sorry for myself, I wondered where she was and what she was doing. I didn't understand it at the time, but I had a crush on her.

I knew that I wasn't going to be fed that night, or the next. Since Father wasn't home, I would have a bad weekend. Sitting in the cool air in the backyard, on the steps, I could hear the sounds of Mother feeding my brothers. I didn't care. Closing my eyes, I could see the smiling face of my new teacher. That night as I sat outside shivering, her beauty and kindness kept me warm.

By October, my morbid life was in full swing. Food was scarce at school. I was easy prey for school bullies, who beat me up at will. After school I had to run to the house and spill the contents of my stomach for Mother's inspection. Sometimes she would have me start my chores right away. Sometimes she would fill the bathtub with water. If she was *really* in a good mood, she fixed up the gas mixture for me in the bathroom. If she got tired of having me around her house, she sent me out to find some mowing jobs, but not before beating me. A few times she whipped me with the dog's chain. It was very painful, but I just gritted my teeth and took it. The worst pain was a blow to the backs of my legs with the broom handle. Sometimes blows from the broom handle would leave me on the floor, barely able to move. More than once I hobbled down the street, pushing that old wooden lawn mower, trying to earn *her* some money.

There finally came a time when it didn't do me any good for Father to be home because Mother had forbidden him to see me. My hope deteriorated and I began to believe that my life would never change. I thought I would be Mother's slave for as long as I lived. With every passing day, my willpower became weaker. I no longer dreamed of Superman or some imaginary hero who would come and rescue me. I knew that Father's promise to take me away was a hoax. I gave up praying and thought only of living my life one day at a time.

One morning at school, I was told to report to the school nurse. She questioned me about my clothes and the various bruises that spanned the length of both my arms. At first I told her what Mother had instructed me to tell her. But as my trust in her began to grow, I told her more and more about Mother. She took notes and told me I should come to see her anytime I wanted to talk to somebody. I learned later that the nurse became interested in me because of some reports she had received from the substitute teacher, earlier in the school year.

During the last week in October, it was tradition at Mother's house for the boys to carve designs on pumpkins. I had been denied this privilege since I was seven or eight years old. When the night came to carve the pumpkins, Mother filled the tub just as soon as I had finished my chores. Again she warned me about keeping my head under the water. As a reminder, she grabbed my neck and pushed my head under the water. Then she stormed out of the bathroom, turning the light out as she went. Looking to my left, I could see through the small bathroom window that night was beginning to fall. I passed the time by counting to myself. I started at one and stopped at one thousand. Then I started over. As the hours passed, I could feel the water slowly draining away. As the water drained, my body became colder and colder. I cupped my hands between my legs and laid the length of my body against the right side of the bathtub. I could hear the sounds of Stan's Halloween record that Mother had bought for him several years before. Ghosts and ghouls howled, and doors creaked open. After the boys had carved their pumpkins, I could hear Mother in her soothing voice telling them a scary story. The more I heard, the more I hated each and every one of them. It was bad enough waiting like a dog out in the backyard on the rocks while they enjoyed dinner, but having to lay in the cold bathtub, shivering to keep warm while they ate popcorn and listened to Mother's tales made me want to scream.

Mother's tone of voice that night reminded me of the kind of Mommy I had loved so many years ago. Now, even the boys refused to acknowledge my presence in the house. I meant less to them than the spirits that howled from Stan's record. After the boys went to bed, Mother came into the bathroom. She appeared startled to see me still laying in the bathtub. "Are you cold?" she sneered. I shivered and shook my head indicating that I was very cold. "Well, why doesn't my precious little boy get his ass out of the bathtub and warm his hide in his father's bed?"

I stumbled out of the tub, put on my underwear and crawled into Father's bed, soaking the sheets with my wet body. For reasons I didn't understand, Mother had decided to have me sleep in the master bedroom, whether Father was home or not. She slept in the upstairs bedroom with my brothers. I didn't really care as long as I didn't have to sleep on the army cot in the cold garage. That night Father came home, but before I could say anything to him, I fell asleep.

By Christmas, my spirit was drained. I detested being home during the two-week vacation and impatiently awaited my return to school. On Christmas Day I received a pair of roller skates. I was surprised to get anything at all, but as it turned out, the skates were not a gift given in the spirit of Christmas. The skates proved to be just another tool for Mother to get me out of the house and make me suffer. On weekends Mother made me skate outside when the other children were inside because of the chilly weather. I skated up and down the block, without even a jacket to keep me warm. I was the only child outside in the neighborhood. More than once, Tony, one of our neighbors, stepped outside to get his afternoon newspaper and saw me skating. He'd give me a cheerful smile before scurrying back inside to get away from the cold. In an effort to keep warm, I skated as fast as I could. I could see smoke rising from the chimneys of houses that had fireplaces. I wished that I could be inside, sitting by a fire. Mother had me skate for hours at a time. She called me in, only when she wanted me to complete some chores for her.

At the end of March that year, Mother went into labor while we were home from school on Easter vacation. As Father drove her to a hospital in San Francisco, I prayed that it was the real thing and not false labor. I wanted Mother out of the house so badly. I knew that with her gone, Father would feed me. I was also happy to be free from the beatings.

While Mother was in the hospital, Father let me play with my brothers. I was immediately accepted back into the fold. We played "Star Trek," and Ron gave me the honor of playing the role of Captain Kirk. The first day Father served sandwiches for lunch and let me have seconds. When Father went to the hospital to see Mother, the four of us played across the street at the home of a neighbor named Shirley. Shirley was kind to us and treated us as though we were her own children. She kept us entertained with games like ping-pong, or just let us run wild outside. In some ways Shirley reminded me of Mom, in the early days before she started beating me.

In a few days, Mother came home. She presented the family with a new baby brother named Kevin. After a few weeks had passed, things returned to normal. Father stayed away most of the time, and I continued to be the scapegoat upon which Mother vented her frustrations.

Mother rarely spent much time with neighbors, so it was not natural for her when she and Shirley became close friends. They visited each other daily. In Shirley's presence Mother played the role of the loving, caring parent—just as she had when she was a Cub Scout den mother. After several months, Shirley asked Mother why David was not allowed to play with the other children. She was also curious why David was punished so often. Mother had a variety of excuses. David either had a cold or he was working on a school project. Eventually, she told Shirley that David was a bad boy and deserved being grounded for a long, long time.

In time, the relationship between Shirley and Mother became strained. One day, for no apparent reason, Mother broke all ties with Shirley. Shirley's son was not allowed to play with the boys, and Mother ran around the house calling her a bitch. Even though I wasn't allowed to play with the others, I felt a little safer when Shirley and Mother were friends.

One Sunday during the last month of summer, Mother came into the master bedroom where I had been ordered to sit on my hands in my P.O.W. position. She asked me to get up and sit on the corner of the bed. She then told me that she was tired of the life we were living. She told me she was sorry and that she wanted to make up for all the lost time. I smiled from ear to ear, as I jumped into her arms and held her tightly. As she ran her hand through my hair, I began to cry. Mother cried, too, and I began to feel that my bad times were finished. I let go of our hug and looked into Mother's eyes. I had to know for sure. I had to hear her say it again. "Is it really over?" I asked timidly.

"It's over, sweetheart. After this moment, I want you to forget any of it happened at all. You will try to be a good boy, won't you?"

I shook my head.

"Then, I'll try to be a good mother."

After making up, Mom let me take a warm bath and put on the new clothes I had received last Christmas. I had not been allowed to wear them before. Mom then took my brothers and me bowling, while Father stayed home with Kevin. On the way home from the bowling alley, Mom stopped at a grocery store and bought each of us a toy top.

When we got home, Mom said I could play outside with the other boys, but I took the toy top to the corner of the master bedroom and played by myself. For the first time in years, with the exception of holidays when we had guests in the house, I ate with my family at the dinner table. Things were happening too fast, and I felt that somehow it was too good to be true. As happy as I was, I felt as though I were walking on eggshells. I thought for sure Mother would wake up and change back to her old self. But she didn't. I ate all I wanted for dinner, and she let me watch television with my brothers before we went to bed. I thought it was strange that she wanted me to continue to sleep with Father, but she said she wanted to be near the baby.

The next day, while Father was at work, a lady from social services came to our house in the afternoon. Mom shooed me outside to play with my brothers, while she talked to the lady. They talked for more than an hour. Before the lady left, Mom called me into our house. The lady wanted to talk to me for a few minutes. She wanted to know if I was happy. I told her I was. She wanted to know if I got along all right with my mom. I told her I did. Finally, she asked me if Mom ever beat me. Before answering, I looked up at Mother, who smiled politely. I felt as though a bomb had exploded deep in the pit of my stomach. I thought I would throw up. It had suddenly occurred to me why Mother had changed the day before; why she had been so nice to me. I felt like a fool because I had fallen for it. I was so hungry for love that I had swallowed the whole charade.

Mother's hand on my shoulder brought me back to reality. "Well, tell her, sweetheart," Mother said, smiling again. "Tell her that I starve you and beat you like a dog," Mother snickered, trying to get the lady to laugh, too.

I looked at the lady. My face felt flushed, and I could feel the beads of sweat forming on my forehead. I didn't have the guts to tell the lady the truth. "No, it's not like that at all," I said. "Mom treats me pretty good."

"And she never beats you?" the lady asked.

"No . . . uh . . . I mean, only when I get punished . . . when I'm a bad boy," I said, trying to cover up the truth. I could tell by the look Mother gave me that I had said the wrong thing. She had brainwashed me for years, and I had said it badly. I could also tell that the lady had picked up on the communication between Mother and me.

"All right," the lady said. "I just wanted to stop in and say hello." After saying goodbye, Mother walked her visitor to the door.

When the lady was clearly gone, Mother closed the door in a rage. "You little shit!" she screamed. I instinctively covered my face as she began swinging. She hit me several times, then banished me to the garage. After she had fed her boys, she called me up to do my evening chores. As I washed the dishes, I didn't feel all that bad. Deep in my heart I had known Mother was being nice to me for some reason other than wanting to love me. I should have known she didn't mean it, because she acted the same way when somebody like Grandma came over for the holidays. At least I had enjoyed two good days. I hadn't had two good days for a long time, so in an odd way it was worth it. I settled back into my routine and relied on my solitude to keep me going. At least I didn't have to walk on eggshells anymore, wondering when the roof was going to cave in on me. Things were back to normal, and I was the servant for the family again.

Even though I had begun to accept my fate, I never felt as alone, as I did on the mornings that Father went to work. He got out of bed about 5:00 A.M. on workdays. He didn't know it, but I was always awake. I'd listen to him shaving in the bathroom, and I would hear him walking to the kitchen to get something to eat. I knew that when he put on his shoes, he was about ready to leave the house. Sometimes I turned over just in time to see him pick up his dark blue, Pan Am overnight bag. He'd kiss me on the forehead and say, "Try to make her happy and stay out of her way."

I tried not to cry, but I always did. I didn't want him to leave. I never told him, but I am sure he knew. After he closed the front door, I counted the steps that it took him to get to the driveway. I heard him walking on the pathway from the house. In my mind, I could see him turning left down the block to catch the bus to San Francisco. Sometimes, when I felt brave, I hopped out of bed and ran to the window so I could catch a glimpse of Father. I usually stayed in bed and rolled over to the warm place where he had slept. I imagined that I could hear him long after he was gone. And when I accepted the fact that he was truly gone, I had a cold, hollow feeling deep in my soul.

I loved Father so much. I wanted to be with him forever, and I cried inside because I never knew when I was going to see Father again.

The Lord's Prayer

A bout a month before I entered the fifth grade, I came to believe that for me, there was no God.

As I sat alone in the garage, or read to myself in the near darkness of my parents' bedroom, I came to realize that I would live like this for the remainder of my life. No *just* God would leave me like this. I believed that I was alone in my struggle and that my battle was one of survival.

By the time I had decided that there was no God, I had totally disconnected myself from all physical pain. Whenever Mother struck me, it was as if she were taking her aggressions out on a rag doll. Inside, my emotions swirled back and forth between fear and intense anger. But outside, I was a robot, rarely revealing my emotions; only when I thought it would please The Bitch and work to my advantage. I held in my tears, refusing to cry because I didn't want to give *her* the satisfaction of my defeat.

At night I no longer dreamed, nor did I let my imagination work during the day. The once vibrant escapes of watching myself fly through the clouds in bright blue costumes, were now a thing of the past. When I fell asleep, my soul became consumed in a black void. I no longer awoke in the mornings refreshed; I was tired and told myself that I had one day less to live in this world. I shuffled through my chores, dreading every moment of every day. With no dreams, I found that words like *hope* and *faith* were only letters, randomly put together into something meaningless—words only for fairy tales.

When I *was* given the luxury of food, I ate like a homeless dog;

grunting like an animal at Mother's commands. I no longer cared when she made fun of me, as I hurried to devour even the smallest morsel. Nothing was below me. One Saturday while I was washing the morning dishes, Mother scraped some half-eaten pancakes from a plate, into the dogs' dish. Her well-fed pets picked at the food until they wanted no more, then walked away to find a place to sleep. Later, as I put away some pots and pans in a lower cabinet, I crawled on my hands and knees to the dogs' dish and ate what was left of the pancakes. As I ate, I could smell traces of the dogs, but I ate anyway. It hardly bothered me. I fully realized that if The Bitch caught me eating what rightfully belonged to the dogs, I would pay dearly; but getting food any way I could was my only means of existing.

Inside, my soul became so cold I hated everything. I even despised the sun, for I knew I would never be able to play in its warm presence. I cringed with hate whenever I heard other children laughing, as they played outside. My stomach coiled whenever I smelled food that was about to be served to somebody else, knowing it was not for me. I wanted so much to strike out at something every time I was called upstairs to play the role of the family slave, by picking up after those slobs.

I hated Mother most and wished that she were dead. But before she died, I wanted her to feel the magnitude of my pain and my loneliness for all these years. During all the years when I had prayed to God, He answered me only once. One day, when I was five or six years old, Mother had thrashed me from one end of the house to the other. That night before getting into bed, I got down on my knees and prayed to God. I asked Him to make Mother sick so she couldn't hit me any more. I prayed long and hard, concentrating so much that I went to bed with a headache. The next morning, much to my surprise, Mother was sick. She lay on the couch all day, barely moving. Since Father was at work, my brothers and I took care of her as though she were a patient of ours.

As the years passed and the beatings became more intense, I thought about Mother's age and tried to calculate when she might die. I longed for the day when *her* soul would be taken into the depths of hell; only then would I be free of her.

I also hated Father. He was fully aware of the hell I lived in, but he lacked the courage to rescue me as he had promised so many times in the past. But as I examined my relationship with Father, I realized that he considered me part of the problem. I believe he thought of me as a traitor. Many times when The Bitch and Father had heated arguments, Mother involved me. She would yank me from wherever I was and demand that I repeat every vile word Father might have used in their past arguments. I fully realized what her game was, but having to choose between them was not difficult. Mother's wrath was much worse for me. I always shook my head, timidly saying what she wanted to hear. She would then scream for me to repeat the words to her in Father's presence. Much of the time she insisted that I make up the words if I couldn't remember. This bothered me a great deal because I knew that in an effort to avoid a beating, I was biting the hand that often fed me. In the beginning, I tried to explain to Father why I had lied and turned against him. At first he told me that he understood, but eventually I knew he had lost faith in me. Instead of feeling sorry for him, I only hated him more.

The boys who lived upstairs were no longer my brothers. Sometimes in years past, they had managed to encourage me a little. But in the summer of 1972 they took turns hitting me and appeared to enjoy throwing their weight around. It was obvious that they felt superior to the family slave. When they approached me, my heart became hard as stone, and I am sure they saw the hate etched in my face. In a rare and empty victory, I'd sneer the word *"asshole"* under my breath as one of them strutted by me. I made sure they didn't hear me. I came to despise the neighbors, my relatives and anybody else who had ever known me and the conditions under which I lived. Hate was all I had left.

At the core of my soul, I hated myself more than anybody or anything. I came to believe that everything that happened to me or around me was my own fault because I had let it go on for so long. I wanted what others had, but saw no way to get it, so I hated them for having it. I wanted to be strong, but inside I knew I was a wimp. I never had the courage to stand up to The Bitch, so I knew I deserved whatever happened to me. For years, Mother had brainwashed me by having me shout aloud, "I hate myself! I hate myself!" Her efforts paid off. A few weeks before I started the fifth grade, I hated myself so much that I wished I were dead.

School no longer held the exciting appeal that it had years ago. I struggled to concentrate on my work while in class, but my bottled-up anger often flashed at the wrong times. One Friday afternoon in the winter of 1973, for no apparent reason, I stormed out of the classroom, screaming at everyone as I fled. I slammed the door so hard I thought the glass above the door would shatter. I ran to the bathroom, and with my tiny red fist I pounded the tiles until my strength drained away. Afterwards, I collapsed on the floor praying for a miracle. It never came.

Time spent outside the classroom was at least better than Mother's "hell house." Because I was an outcast of the entire school, my classmates at times took over where Mother left off. One of them was Clifford, a school-yard bully who would periodically catch me when I ran to Mother's house after school. Beating me up was Clifford's way of showing off to his friends. All I could do was fall to the ground and cover my head, while Clifford and his gang took turns kicking me.

Aggie was a tormentor of a different sort. She never failed to come up with new and different ways of telling me how much she wished I would simply "drop dead." Her style was absolute snobbery. Aggie made sure she was always the one in charge of a small band of girls. In addition to tormenting me, showing off their fancy clothes seemed to be the main purpose in life for Aggie and her clique. I had always known Aggie didn't like me, but I really didn't learn how much until the last day of school our fourth-grade year. Aggie's mother taught my fourth-grade homeroom, and on the last day of school Aggie came into our room acting as though she were throwing up and said, "David Pelzer-Smellzer is going to be in my homeroom next year." Her day was not complete until she fired off a rude remark about me to her friends.

I didn't take Aggie very seriously; not until a fifth-grade field trip to one of San Francisco's Clipper Ships. As I stood alone on the bow of the ship, looking at the water, Aggie approached me with a vicious smile and said in a low voice, "Jump!" She startled me, and I looked into her face, trying to understand what she meant. Again she spoke, quietly and calmly, "I said you should go ahead and jump. I know all about you Pelzer, and jumping is your only way out."

Another voice came from behind her, "She's right, you know." The voice belonged to John, another classmate, one of Aggie's macho buddies. Looking back over the railing, I stared at the cold green water lapping against the wooden side of the ship. For a moment, I could visualize myself plunging into the water, knowing I would drown. It was a comforting thought that promised an escape from Aggie, her friends and all that I hated in the world. But my better senses returned, and I looked up and fixed my eyes directly on John's eyes and tried to hold my stare. After a few moments, he must have felt my anger because he turned away taking Aggie with him.

At the beginning of my fifth-grade year, Mr. Ziegler, my homeroom teacher, had no idea why I was such a problem child. Later, after the school nurse had informed him why I had stolen food and why I dressed the way I did, Mr. Ziegler made a special effort to treat me as if I were a normal kid. One of his jobs as sponsor of the school newspaper was to form a committee of kids to find a name for the paper. I came up with a catchy phrase, and a week later my entry was among others in a school-wide election to select the best name for the newspaper. My title won by a landslide. Later that day the voting took place, and Mr. Ziegler took me aside and told me how proud he was that my title had won. I soaked it up like a sponge. I hadn't been told anything positive for so long that I nearly cried. At the end of the day, after assuring me that I wasn't in trouble, Mr. Ziegler gave me a letter to take to Mother.

Elated, I ran to Mother's house faster than ever before. As I should have expected, my happiness was short-lived. The Bitch tore the letter open, read it quickly and scoffed, "Well, Mr. Ziegler says I should be so proud of you for naming the school newspaper. He also claims that you are one of the top pupils in his class. Well, aren't you special?" Suddenly, her voice turned ice cold and she jabbed her finger at my face and hissed, "Get one thing straight, you little son of a bitch! There is nothing you can do to impress me! Do you understand me? You are a *nobody!* An *It!* You are nonexistent! You are a bastard child! I hate you and I wish you were dead! *Dead!* Do you hear me? *Dead!*"

After tearing the letter into tiny pieces, Mother turned away from me and returned to her television show. I stood motionless, gazing at the letter which lay like snowflakes at my feet. Even though I had heard the same words over and over again, this time the word *"It"* stunned me like never before. She had stripped me of my very existence. I gave all that I could to accomplish anything positive for *her* recognition. But again, I failed. My heart sank lower than ever before. Mother's words were no longer coming from the booze; they were coming from her heart. I would have been relieved if she had returned with a knife and ended it all.

I knelt down, trying to put the many pieces of the letter back together again. It was impossible. I dumped the pieces of the letter in the trash, wishing my life would end. I truly believed, at that moment, that death would be better than my prospects for any kind of happiness. I was nothing but an *"It."*

My morale had become so low that in some self-destructive way I hoped she would kill me, and I felt that eventually she would. In my mind it was just a matter of when she would do it. So I began to purposefully irritate her, hoping I could provoke her enough that she would end my misery. I began doing my chores in a careless manner. I made sure that I forgot to wipe the bathroom floor, hoping that Mother or one of her royal subjects might slip and fall, hurting themselves on the hard tile floor. When I washed the evening dishes, I left bits of food on the plates. I wanted The Bitch to know I didn't care anymore.

As my attitude began to change, I became more and more rebellious. A crisis erupted one day at the grocery store. Usually I stayed in the car, but for some reason Mother decided to take me inside. She ordered me to keep one hand clamped onto the cart and bend my head towards the floor. I deliberately disobeyed her every command. I knew she didn't want to make a scene in public, so I walked in front of the cart, making sure I was at least an arm's length away from her. If my brothers made any comments to me, I fired back at them. I simply told myself that I wasn't going to take anybody's crap anymore.

Mother knew that other shoppers were watching us and could hear us, so several times she gently took my arm and told me in a pleasant voice to settle down. I felt so alive knowing I had the upper hand in the store, but I also knew that once we were outside, I would pay the price. Just as I thought, Mother gave me a sound thrashing before we reached the station wagon. As soon as we were in the car, she ordered me to lie on the floor of the back seat, where her boys took turns stomping me with their feet for "mouthing off" to them and Mother. Immediately after we entered the house, Mother made a special batch of ammonia and Clorox. She must have guessed I had been using the rag as a mask because she tossed the rag into the bucket. As soon as she slammed the bathroom door, I hurried to the heating vent. It didn't come on. No fresh air came through the vent. I must have been in the bathroom for over an hour because the gray fumes filled the small room all the way to the floor. My eyes filled with tears, which seemed to activate the poison even more. I spat mucus and heaved until I thought I would faint. When Mother finally opened the door, I bolted for the hallway, but her hand seized me by the neck. She tried to push my face into the bucket, but I fought back and she failed. My plan for rebellion also failed. After the longer "gas chamber" incident, I returned to my wimpy self, but deep inside I could still feel the pressure building like a volcano, waiting to erupt from deep inside my soul.

The only thing that kept me sane was my baby brother Kevin. He was a beautiful baby and I loved him. About three and a half months before he was born, Mother allowed me to watch a Christmas cartoon special. After the program, for reasons unclear to me, she ordered me to sit in my brothers' room. Minutes later she stormed into the room, wrapped her hands around my neck and began choking me. I twisted my head from side to side, trying to squirm away from her grip. As I began to feel faint, I instinctively kicked her legs, forcing her away from me. I soon regretted the incident.

About a month after Mother's attempt to choke me, she told me that I had kicked her so hard in the stomach that the baby would have a permanent birth defect. I felt like a murderer. Mother didn't stop with just telling me. She had several different versions of the incident for anybody who would listen. She said she had tried to hug me, and I had repeatedly either kicked or punched her in the stomach. She claimed that I had kicked her because I was jealous of the new baby. She said I was afraid the new baby would get more of her attention. I really loved Kevin, but since I was not allowed to even *look* at him or my brothers, I did not have a chance to show how I felt. I do remember one Saturday, when Mother took the other boys to a baseball game in Oakland, leaving Father to babysit with Kevin while I performed my chores. After I finished my work, Father let Kevin out of his crib. I enjoyed watching him crawl around in his cute outfit. I thought he was beautiful. When Kevin lifted his head and smiled at me, my heart melted. He made me forget my suffering for awhile. His innocence was hypnotic as I followed him around the house; I wiped the drool from his mouth and stayed one step behind him so he wouldn't get hurt. Before Mother returned, I played a game of patty-cake with him. The sound of Kevin's laughter filled my heart with warmth, and later, whenever I felt depressed I thought of him. I smiled inside when I heard Kevin cry out in joy.

My brief encounter with Kevin quickly faded away and my hatred surfaced again. I fought to bury my feelings, but I couldn't. I knew I was never meant to be loved. I knew I would never live a life like my brothers. Worst of all, I knew that it was only a matter of time until Kevin would hate me, just like the others did.

Later that fall, Mother began directing her frustrations in more directions. She despised me as much as ever, but she began to alienate her friends, husband, brother and even her own mother. Even as a small child, I knew that Mother didn't get along very well with her family. She felt that everybody was trying to tell her what to do. She never felt at ease, especially with her own mother who was also a strong-willed person. Grandmother usually offered to buy Mother a new dress or take her to the beauty parlor. Not only did Mother refuse the offers, but she also yelled and screamed until Grandmother left *her* house. Sometimes Grandmother tried to help me, but that only made things worse. Mother insisted that her appearance and the way she raised her family were "nobody else's damn business." After a few of these confrontations, Grandmother rarely visited Mother's house.

As the holiday season approached, Mother argued more and more with Grandmother on the telephone. She called her own mother every vicious name Mother could imagine. The trouble between Mother and Grandmother was bad for me because after their battle, I often became the object of Mother's anger. Once, from the basement, I heard Mother call my brothers into the kitchen and tell them that they no longer had a grandmother or an Uncle Dan.

Mother was equally ruthless in her relationship with Father. When he did come home, either to visit or stay for a day, she started screaming at him the moment he walked through the door. As a result, he often came home drunk. In an effort to stay out of Mother's path, Father often spent his time doing odd jobs outside the house. He even caught her wrath at work. She often telephoned Father at the station and called him names. "Worthless" and "drunken loser" were two of her favorite names for him. After a few calls, the fireman who answered the phone would lay it down and not page Father. This made Mother furious, and again I became the object of her fury.

For awhile Mother banned Father from the house, and the only time we saw him was when we drove to San Francisco to pick up his paycheck. One time, on our way to get the check, we drove through Golden Gate Park. Even though my anger was ever present, I flashed back to the good times when the park meant so much to the whole family. My brothers were also silent that day as we drove through the park. Everybody seemed to sense that somehow the park had lost its glamour, and that things would never be the same again. I think that perhaps my brothers felt the good times were over for them, too.

For a short time Mother's attitude towards Father changed. One

Sunday, Mother piled everybody into the car, and shopped from store to store for a record of German songs. She wanted to create a special mood for Father when he came home. She spent most of that afternoon preparing a feast, with the same enthusiasm that had driven her years before. It took her hours to fix her hair and apply her makeup just right. Mother even put on a dress that brought back memories of the person she once was. I thought for sure that God had answered my prayers. As she paced around the house, straightening anything she thought was out of place, all I could think about was the food. I knew she would find it in her heart to let me eat with the family. It was an empty hope.

Time dragged on into the late afternoon. Father was expected to be home by about 1:00 P.M., and every time Mother heard an approaching car she dashed to the front door, waiting to greet him with open arms. Sometime after 4:00 P.M., Father came staggering in with a friend from work. The festive mood and setting were a surprise to him. From the bedroom I could hear Mother's strained voice as she tried to be extra patient with Father. A few minutes later, Father stumbled into the bedroom. I looked up in wonder. I had never seen him so drunk. He didn't need to speak for me to smell the liquor on him. His eyes were beyond the bloodshot stage, and it appeared to be more of a problem than he could manage to stand upright and keep his eyes open. Even before he opened the closet door, I knew what he was going to do. I knew why he had come home. As he stuffed his blue overnight bag, I began to cry inside. I wanted to become small enough to jump into his bag and go with him.

When he finished packing, Father knelt down and mumbled something to me. The longer I looked at him, the weaker my legs felt. My mind was numb with questions. *Where's my Hero? What happened to him?* As he opened the door to leave the bedroom, the drunk friend crashed into Father, nearly knocking him down. Father shook his head and said in a sad voice, "I can't take it anymore. The whole thing. Your mother, this house, you. I just can't take it anymore." Before he closed the bedroom door I could barely hear him mutter, "I . . . I'm . . . I'm sorry."

That year Thanksgiving dinner was a flop. In some kind of gesture of good faith, Mother allowed me to eat at the table with the family. I sat deep in my chair, quietly concentrating so I wouldn't say or do anything that might set Mother off. I could feel the tension between my parents. They hardly spoke at all, and my brothers chewed their food in silence. Dinner was hardly over when harsh words erupted. After the fight ended, Father left. Mother reached into one of the cabinets for her bottled prize and seated herself at the end of the sofa. She sat alone, pouring glass after glass of alcohol. As I cleared the table and washed the dishes, I could see that this time I wasn't the only one affected by Mother's behavior. My brothers seemed to be experiencing the same fear I had for so many years.

For a short time, Mother and Father tried to be civil to one another. But by Christmas Day, they had both become tired of their charade. The strain of trying to be so nice to each other was more than either could bear. As I sat at the top of the stairs, while my brothers finished opening their gifts, I could hear angry words being exchanged between them. I prayed that they could somehow make up, if only for that special day. While sitting on the basement stairs that Christmas morning, I knew that if God had wanted Mother and Father to be happy, then I would have to be dead.

A few days later, Mother packed Father's clothes in boxes, and drove with my brothers and me to a place a few blocks from the fire station. There, in front of a dingy motel, Father waited. His face seemed to express relief. My heart sank. After years of my useless prayers, I knew it had finally happened—my parents were separating. I closed my fists so tightly I thought my fingers would tear into the palms of my hands. While Mother and the boys went into Father's motel room, I sat in the car, cursing his name over and over. I hated him so much for running out on his family. But perhaps even more, I was jealous of him, for he had escaped and I had not. I still had to live with Mother. Before Mother drove the car away, Father leaned down to the open window where I was sitting, and handed me a package. It was some information he had said he would get me, for a book report that I was doing at school. I knew he was relieved to get away from Mother, but I could also see sadness in his eyes as we pulled away into the downtown traffic.

The drive back to Daly City was solemn. When my brothers spoke, they did so in soft tones that wouldn't upset Mother. When we reached the city limits, Mother tried to humor her boys by treating them to McDonald's. As usual, I sat in the car while they went inside. I looked out the open car window at the sky. A dull gray blanket covered everything, and I could feel the cold droplets of fog on my face. As I stared into the fog, I became terrified. I knew nothing could stop Mother now. What little hope I had was gone. I no longer had the will to carry on. I felt as if I were a man on death row, not knowing when my time would come.

I wanted to bolt from the car, but I was too scared to even move an inch. For this weakness, I hated myself. Rather than running, I clutched the package Father had given me and smelled it, trying to pick up a scent of Father's cologne.

When I failed to pick up any odor at all, I let out a sobbing cry. At that instant, I hated God more than anything else in this or any other world. God had known of my struggles for years, but He had stood by watching as things went from bad to worse. He wouldn't even grant me a trace of Father's Old Spice After Shave. God had completely taken away my greatest hope. Inside I cursed His name, wishing I had never been born.

Outside, I could hear the sounds of Mother and the boys approaching the car. I quickly wiped my tears and returned to the inner safety of my hardened shell. As Mother drove out of the McDonald's parking lot, she glanced back at me and sneered, "You are all mine now. Too bad your father's not here to protect you." I knew all my defenses were useless. I wasn't going to survive. I knew she was going to kill me, if not today, tomorrow. That day I wished Mother would have mercy and kill me quickly.

As my brothers wolfed down their hamburgers, without them knowing I clasped my hands together, bent my head down, closed my eyes and prayed with all my heart. When the station wagon turned onto the driveway, I felt that my time had come. Before I opened the car door, I bowed my head and with peace in my heart, I whispered, ". . . and deliver me from evil."

"Amen."

*E*pilogue
Sonoma County,
California

I'm so alive.

As I stand facing the beauty of the never-ending Pacific Ocean, a late afternoon breeze blows down from the hills behind. As always, it is a beautiful day. The sun is making its final descent. The magic is about to begin. The skies are ready to burn with brilliance, as it turns from a soft blue to a bright orange. Looking towards the west, I stare in awe at the hypnotic power of the waves. A giant curl begins to take form, then breaks with a thundering clap as it crashes on the shore. An invisible mist hits my face, moments before the white foamy water nearly drowns my feet. The bubbling foam quickly recedes to the power of the surf. Suddenly, a piece of driftwood washes onto the shore. It has an odd, twisted shape. The wood is pitted, yet smoothed and bleached from its time in the sun. I bend down to pick it up. As my fingers begin to reach out, the water catches hold dragging the wood back out to sea. For a moment, it looks as if the wood is struggling to stay ashore. It leaves a trail behind before reaching the waters, where it bobs violently before giving in to the ocean.

I marvel at the wood, thinking how it reminds me of my former life. My beginning was extremely turbulent, being pushed and pulled in every direction. The more grisly my situation became, the more I felt as if some immense power were sucking me into some giant undertow. I fought as hard as I could, but the cycle never seemed to end. Until suddenly, without warning, I broke free.

I'm so lucky. My dark past is behind me now. As bad as it was, I knew even back then, in the final analysis, my way of life would be up to me. I made a promise to myself that if I came out of my situation alive, I had to make something of myself. I would be the best person that I could be. Today I am. I made sure I let go of my past, accepting the fact that that part of my life was only a small fraction of my life. I knew the black hole was out there, waiting to suck me in and forever control my destiny—but only if I let it. I took positive control over my life.

I'm so blessed. The challenges of my past have made me immensely strong inside. I adapted quickly, learning how to survive from a bad situation. I learned the secret of internal motivation. My experience gave me a different outlook on life, that others may never know. I have a vast appreciation for things that others may take for granted. Along the way I made a few mistakes, but I was fortunate enough to bounce back. Instead of dwelling on the past, I maintained the same focus that I had taught myself years ago in the garage, knowing the good Lord was always over my shoulder, giving me quiet encouragement and strength when I needed it most.

My blessings also mean having the opportunity to meet so many people who had a positive impact on my life. The endless sea of faces, prodding me, teaching me to make the right choices, and helping me in my quest for success. They encouraged my hunger to prevail. Branching out on a different level, I enlisted in the United States Air Force, discovering historical values and an instilled sense of pride and belonging that until then, I had never known. After years of struggle, my purpose became clear; for above all, I came to realize that America was truly the land where one could come from less than humble beginnings, to become a winner from within.

An explosive pounding of the surf brings me back to reality. The piece of wood I've been watching, disappears into the swirling waters. Without further hesitation, I quickly turn away and head back towards my truck. Moments later, I race my Toyota through the snake-like turns driving to my secret utopia. Years ago when I lived in the dark, I used to dream about my secret place. Now, whenever I can get away, I always return to the river. After stopping to pick up my precious cargo at the Rio Villa in nearby Monte Rio, I'm back on the single-lane black top. For me, it is a race against time, for the sun is about to set and one of my lifetime dreams is about to come true.

As I enter the serene city of Guerneville, the 4-Runner truck goes from a Mach-like speed to that of a snail. I tap on the brakes before turning right, onto Riverside drive. With the windows rolled down, I fill my lungs full of sweet, purified air from the towering redwoods that gently sway back and forth.

I bring the white Toyota to a stop, in front of the same home where a lifetime ago my family and I stayed during our summer vacations. 17426 Riverside Drive. Like many things, the house too has changed. Years ago, two tiny bedrooms were added behind the fireplace. A vague attempt of expanding the tiny kitchen was made before the flood of 1986. Even the mighty tree stump, where years ago my brothers and I spent endless hours climbing on, is now in decay. Only the cabin's darkened cedar ceiling and the river-stone fireplace have been left unchanged.

I feel a little sad as I turn away, strolling across the small gravel road. Then, making sure not to disturb anyone, I lead my son, Stephen, through a tiny passage beside the same house that my parents led my brothers and me through, years ago. I know the owner and I am sure he wouldn't mind. Without saying a word, my son and I gaze westward. The Russian River is the same as it always was, dark green and as smooth as glass, as it flows ever so gently to the mighty Pacific. Blue Jays call to each other as they glide through the air, before disappearing into the redwoods. The sky above is now bathed with streaks of orange and blue. I take another deep breath and close my eyes, savoring the moment like I did years ago.

As I open my eyes, a single tear rolls down the side of my cheek. I kneel down wrapping my arms around Stephen's shoulders. Without hesitation, he leans his head back and gives me a kiss. "Love you, Dad."

"Love you, too," I reply.

My son gazes up at the darkening sky. His eyes grow wide as he strains to capture the disappearing sun. "This is my favorite place in the whole world!" Stephen announces.

My throat becomes tight. A small stream of tears begins to fall. "Mine, too," I reply. "Mine, too."

Stephen is at that magical age of innocence, but yet is wise beyond his years. Even now, as salty tears run down my face, Stephen smiles, letting me maintain my dignity. But he knows why I'm crying. Stephen knows my tears are tears of joy.

"*Love you, Dad.*"

"*Love you, too, son.*"

I'm free.

*P*erspectives on Child Abuse

Dave Pelzer
Survivor

As a child living in a dark world, I feared for my life and thought I was alone. As an adult I know now that I was not alone. There were thousands of other abused children.

Sources of information vary, but it is estimated that one in five children are physically, emotionally or sexually abused in our country. Unfortunately, there are those among the uninformed public who believe that most abuse is nothing more than parents exerting their "right" to discipline their children and letting it get a little out of hand. These same people may believe that over-discipline is not likely to follow the child into adulthood. They are tragically misinformed.

On any given day, some adult who is the victim of a dark past of child abuse may vent his or her pent-up frustrations on society or on those he or she may love. The public is well informed about the most uncommon cases. Unusual incidents attract the media and boost ratings. We heard about the lawyer father who struck out with his fist and left the child unconscious on the floor before retiring to bed. We heard about the father who dunked the small child in the toilet. Both children died. In a more bizarre case both a mother and a father each killed a child and hid their bodies for a period of four years. There are other high profile stories, like the abused child who grew into the man who went on a killing spree at a McDonald's, gunning down helpless victims until the police took his life.

More common are the unknowns who disappear, like the homeless boy who sleeps under a freeway bridge and calls a cardboard box his home. Each year thousands of abused girls run away from home and sell their bodies in order to survive. Others strike out by joining gangs who are totally committed to violence and destruction.

Many child abuse victims hide their past deep inside, so deep that the possibility of becoming an abuser themselves is unthinkable. They live normal lives, becoming husbands and wives, raising families and building careers. But the ordinary problems of everyday life often force the former abuse victim to behave as they were taught as children. Spouses and children then become the object of their frustration, and they unknowingly come the full circle, completing the never-ending cycle of rage.

Some child abuse victims stay quietly locked in their shells. They look the other way, believing that by not acknowledging their past it will go away. They seem to believe that above all Pandora's Box must stay closed.

Each year, millions of dollars are poured into child protection agencies in our country. These dollars go to local facilities like foster homes and juvenile halls. There are dollar grants to thousands of private organizations whose mission includes basic child abuse prevention, the counseling of abusive parents and the victims. Every year the number grows larger. In 1990 over 2.5 million child abuse cases were reported in the United States. In 1991 the number increased to more than 2.7 million. As of this writing, the estimate is over 3 million.

Why? What causes the tragedy of child abuse? Is it really as bad as they say? Can it be stopped? And perhaps the most important of all questions, what is abuse like through the eyes of the child?

What you have just read is a story of an ordinary family that was devastated by their hidden secret. The story has two objectives: the first is to inform the reader how a loving, caring parent can change to a cold, abusive monster venting frustrations on a helpless child; the second is the eventual survival and triumph of the human spirit over seemingly insurmountable odds.

Some readers will find the story unreal and disturbing, but child abuse is a disturbing phenomenon that is a reality in our society. Child abuse has a domino effect that spreads to all who touch the family. It takes its greatest toll on the child and spreads into the immediate family to the spouse, who is often torn between the child and their mate. From there it goes to other children in the family who do not understand and also feel threatened. Also involved are neighbors who hear the screams but do not react, teachers who see the bruises and must deal with a child too distracted to learn, and relatives who want to intervene but do not want to risk relationships.

This is more than a story of survival. It is a story of victory and celebration. Even in its darkest passages, the heart is unconquerable. It is important that the body survives, but it is more meaningful that the human spirit prevails.

This is my story and mine alone. For years I was confined to the darkness of my own mind and heart, being alone and a pitiful "loser." At first I wanted nothing more than to be like others, but that motivation grew. I wanted to become a "winner." For over 13 years I served my country in the military. I now serve my country giving seminars and workshops to others in need, helping them to break their chains. From one who has been there, I bring a message to abused children and those who work with them. I bring a perspective born in the brutal reality of child abuse and nurtured in hope for a better tomorrow. Most importantly, I broke the cycle and became a father whose only guilt is that of spoiling his son with love and encouragement.

Today there are millions in our country in desperate need of help. It is my mission to assist those in need of a helping hand. I believe it is important for people to know that no matter what lies in their past, they can overcome the dark side and press on to a brighter world. It is perhaps a paradox that without the abuse of my past, I might not be what I am today. Because of the darkness in my childhood, I have a deep appreciation for life. I was fortunate enough to turn tragedy into triumph. This is my story.

Perhaps at no time in the history of our country has the family been under more stress. Economic and social changes have pushed the family to its limit and made child abuse more likely. If society is to come to grips with the problem, it must be exposed. Once exposed, the causes of child abuse can be understood and support can truly begin. Childhood should be carefree, playing in the sun; not living a nightmare in the darkness of the soul.

Steven E. Ziegler
Teacher

September, 1992, began as a typical back-to-school month for me. In my 22nd year of teaching, I found the usual hectic, non-stop confusion. There were close to 200 new students who had names for me to learn and several new faculty members to welcome aboard. It was goodbye to summer vacation and hello to additional responsibilities, and the annual doom and gloom from Sacramento regarding money for schools. Nothing had seemingly changed about the beginning of school, until a telephone message arrived on the 21st that rather painfully jolted me back 20 years: "A David Pelzer would like you to contact his agent, regarding some child abuse reports you were associated with 20 years ago." The past came back all too quickly.

Oh, yes, how well I remember David Pelzer. I was a recent college graduate, a new teacher; and as I look back, I knew little about the real world of my chosen career. And the thing I knew least about was child abuse. In the early 1970s I didn't know if child abuse actually existed. If it did, it remained very much in the "closet" as did so many unmentionable lifestyles and behaviors back then. We have learned so much; yet we have so far to go.

My mind returned to the Thomas Edison School in Daly City, California, September, 1972. Enter little David Pelzer as one of my fifth-grade students. I was naive back then, but I was blessed with a sensitivity that told me there was something terribly wrong in David's life. Food missing from other students' lunches was traced to this thin, sad boy. Questionable bruises appeared on exposed parts of his body. Everything began to point to one thing: this kid was being beaten and punished in ways far beyond normal parental practice. It was several years later when I learned that what I was witnessing in my classroom was the third-worst case of child abuse on record in the entire state of California.

It is not for me to tell again all the graphic details my colleagues and I witnessed and reported to the authorities so many years ago. That account remains David's privilege and opportunity in this book. But what a wonderful opportunity it is for this young man to come forward and tell his story so that other children may not suffer. I deeply admire his courage in doing so.

My very best to you, David. There is absolutely no doubt in my mind how far you have truly come.

Valerie Bivens
Social Worker

As a Social Worker for Child Protective Services in California, I am all too aware of the frequency and severity of crimes against children. This book is the account of one child's unthinkable abuse. We see the child's perception as he moves through a horrifying continuum, from an idealistic family life to becoming a "prisoner of war" in his own home. This story is shared with the reader by a survivor, a man of extreme courage and fortitude.

Unfortunately, the general public is unaware of the extent of child abuse. These children, victims of outrageous crimes, too often are unable to speak about or against their abusers. Their rage and pain is then turned on themselves or others close to them, and the cycle continues.

We are beginning to hear more about child abuse. Movies and magazine articles on the subject are becoming more frequent, but cases are often sensationalized, and we are too far removed to understand the virtual reality and pain of the victim child. This book enlightens and educates. As we move with David through fear, loss, isolation, pain and rage to eventual hope, the dark world of the abused child becomes painfully clear. We become aware of the child's cry through David Pelzer's eyes, ears and body. We also feel the victim's heart as it moves from unbearable aching to eventual triumph.

Glenn A. Goldberg
Former Executive Director of the
California Consortium for the
Prevention of Child Abuse

David Pelzer's story must be told so that we can mobilize Americans to create a country where it won't hurt to be a child. Millions of our children, our most precious natural resource, are being victimized by a tragic and unconscionable epidemic of child abuse and neglect. Both the level and intensity of child maltreatment have increased dramatically in the last decade. David's story will help people understand that our child abuse crisis goes far beyond excessive spanking. Each year hundreds of thousands of helpless children are being brutalized and tortured physically, emotionally and sexually.

Each act of child abuse reverberates into the future; when a child gets hurt, we may all suffer the consequences. David Pelzer is a triumphant survivor of his childhood abuse, and his story is an inspiration to all of us. We must never forget, however, the tens of thousands of other children who didn't survive their ordeals, and the millions who are still suffering. The only cure for child abuse is its prevention; and it is my fervent hope that this book will help build our growing movement of people working to prevent child abuse in all its forms.

I Never Knew

I never knew how bad it was;
I heard it did exist.
I was appalled at this crime
That robbed youth
Of their "special" time.

I never knew how bad it hurt;
The bruises and scars aren't seen.
And why somewhere along life's way,
The brutality of abuse
Has made you pay.

I never knew how you felt;
Your self-esteem so low.
I only knew you crept away,
And never let your feelings show.

I never knew what I could do;
That I could help somehow.
That all you needed was a friend;
Just someone to be your pal.

But now I know that I can help;
I can make a difference, too.
I'll stand with you; I'll shout with you,
And the rest can't say, "I never knew."

Cindy M. Adams

Resources for Help

Child Help USA offers a 24-hour crisis hot line, national information and referral network for support groups and therapists, and for reporting suspected abuse.
6463 Independence Avenue
Woodland Hills, CA 91367
(800) 422-4453

Child Welfare League of America headquartered in Washington, DC, the Child Welfare League of America is a 75-year-old association of nearly 800 public and private, non-profit agencies that serve abused, neglected, and abandoned children, youth and their families. CWLA plays a major advocacy role on Capitol Hill, develops model guidelines for the provision of child welfare services, conducts research and training, and is the world's largest publisher of child welfare materials.
440 First Street, NW, Suite 310
Washington, DC 20001-2085
(202) 638-2952

The National Committee to Prevent Child Abuse (NCPCA), headquartered in Chicago, is a not-for-profit organization with the goal of preventing child abuse in all its forms. NCPCA promotes public education through its national media campaign, a catalog of publications, and training and technical assistance. Chapters of the national organization are located throughout the United States.

P.O. Box 2866
Chicago, IL 60690
(800) 556-2722

The Lost Boy

To the teachers and staff who rescued me
Steven Ziegler
Athena Konstan
Joyce Woodworth
Janice Woods
Betty Howell
Peter Hansen
the school nurse of
Thomas Edison Elementary School
and the Daly City police officer

To the angel of social services
Ms. Pamela Gold

To my foster parents
Aunt Mary
Rudy and Lillian Catanze
Michael and Joanne Nulls
Jody and Vera Jones
John and Linda Walsh

To those with a firm but gentle guiding hand
Gordon Hutchenson
Carl Miguel
Estelle O'Ryan
Dennis Tapley

To friends and mentors
David Howard
Paul Brazell
William D. Brazell
Sandy Marsh
Michael A. Marsh

In memory of Pamela Eby
who gave her life to saving the
children of Florida

To MY PARENTS, who always knew
Harold and Alice Turnbough

And finally, to MY SON, Stephen,
whose unconditional love for who I am
and what I do keeps me going.
I love you with all my heart and soul.

Bless you all, for,
"It takes a community to save a child."

Contents

Contents

A cknowledgments

This book would not have been possible without the tenacious devotion of Marsha Donohoe—editor extraordinaire—of *Donohoe Publishing Projects*. It was Marsha who not only edited the entire text from the original, dismayed *printed* version, but who also typeset, copyedited and proofread the tome to simplify the publication process. And, more important, she maintained the rigid, chronological perspective of the continuing journey through the eyes of a bewildered child. For Marsha, it was a matter of ". . . *If I Could.*"

Thank you to Christine Belleris, Matthew Diener and Allison Janse of the editorial department for their professionalism throughout the production of this book. And a special thank you to Matthew for handling all of our needs and last-minute requests with a smile, and expertly following through on everything.

To Irene Xanthos and Lori Golden of the sales department of Health Communications, Inc., for their undying genuine sincerity. And to Doreen Hess for all her kindness.

A gargantuan thank you to Laurel Howanitz and Susy Allen of *Hot Guests*, for their unyielding dedication and promotion. Thanks for believing.

To Cindy Edloff, for her efforts and time.

A special thank you to the owners and staff of *Coffee Bazaar* in Guerneville, California, for keeping the raspberry mochas coming, for allowing Marsha and me to plug in and camp out, and for providing us with "The Big Table"—enabling us to spread out, take over and promote chaos within the quiet confines of this serene setting.

*A*uthor's Notes

Some of the names in this book have been changed in order to protect the dignity and privacy of others.

As in the first part of the trilogy, *A Child Called "It,"* this second part depicts language that was developed from a child's viewpoint. The tone and vocabulary reflect the age and wisdom of the child at that particular time.

The perspective of *A Child Called "It"* was based on the child's life from ages 4 to 12; the perspective of this book is based on life from ages 12 to 18.

CHAPTER 1

The Runaway

*W*inter 1970, Daly City, California—*I'm alone. I'm hungry and I'm shivering in the dark. I sit on top of my hands at the bottom of the stairs in the garage. My head is tilted backward. My hands became numb hours ago. My neck and shoulder muscles begin to throb. But that's nothing new—I've learned to turn off the pain.*

I'm Mother's prisoner.

I am nine years old, and I've been living like this for years. Every day it's the same thing. I wake up from sleeping on an old army cot in the garage, perform the morning chores, and if I'm lucky, eat leftover breakfast cereal from my brothers. I run to school, steal food, return to "The House" and am forced to throw up in the toilet bowl to prove that I didn't commit the crime of stealing any food.

I receive beatings or play another one of her "games," perform afternoon chores, then sit at the bottom of the stairs until I'm summoned to complete the evening chores. Then, and only if I have completed all of my chores on time, and if I have not committed any "crimes," I may be fed a morsel of food.

My day ends only when Mother allows me to sleep on the army cot, where my body curls up in my meek effort to retain any body heat. The only pleasure in my life is when I sleep. That's the only time I can escape my life. I love to dream.

Weekends are worse. No school means no food and more time at "The House." All I can do is try to imagine myself away—somewhere, anywhere—from "The House." For years I have been the outcast of "The Family." As long as I can remember I have always been in trouble and have "deserved" to be punished. At first I thought I was a bad boy. Then I thought Mother was sick because she only acted differently when my brothers were not around and my father was away at work. But somehow I always knew Mother and I had a private relationship. I also realized that for some reason I have been Mother's sole target for her unexplained rage and twisted pleasure.

I have no home. I am a member of no one's family. I know deep inside that I do not now, nor will I ever, deserve any love, attention or even recognition as a human being. I am a child called "It."

I'm all alone inside.

Upstairs the battle begins. Since it's after four in the afternoon, I know both of my parents are drunk. The yelling starts. First the name-calling, then the swearing. I count the seconds before the subject turns to me—it always does. The sound of Mother's voice makes my insides turn. "What do you mean?" she shrieks at my father, Stephen. "You think I treat 'The Boy' bad? Do you?" Her voice then turns ice cold. I can imagine her pointing a finger at my father's face. "You . . . listen . . . to . . . me. You . . . have no idea what 'It's' like. If you think I treat 'It' that bad . . . then . . . 'It' can live somewhere else."

I can picture my father—who, after all these years, still tries somewhat to stand up for me—swirling the liquor in his glass, making the ice from his drink rattle. "Now calm down," he begins. "All I'm trying to say is . . . well . . . no child deserves to live like that. My God, Roerva, you treat . . . dogs better than . . . than you do The Boy."

The argument builds to an ear-shattering climax. Mother slams her drink on the kitchen countertop. Father has crossed the line. No one ever tells Mother what to do. I know I will have to pay the price for her rage. I realize it's only a matter of time before she orders me upstairs. I prepare myself. Ever so slowly I slide my hands out from under my butt, but not too far—for I know sometimes she'll check on me. I know I am never to move a muscle without her permission.

I feel so small inside. I only wish I could somehow . . .

Without warning, Mother opens the door leading to the downstairs garage. "You!" she screams. "Get your ass up here! Now!"

In a flash I bolt up the stairs. I wait a moment for her command before I timidly open the door. Without a sound I approach Mother and await one of her "games."

It's the game of address, in which I have to stand exactly three feet in front of her, my hands glued to my side, my head tilted down at a 45-degree angle and my eyes locked onto her feet. Upon the first command I *must look above her bust, but below her eyes. Upon the second command I must look into her eyes, but never, never may I speak, breathe or move a single muscle unless Mother gives me permission to do so. Mother and I have been playing this game since I was seven years old, so today it's just another routine in my lifeless existence.*

Suddenly Mother reaches over and seizes my right ear. By accident, I flinch. With her free hand Mother punishes my movement with a solid slap to my face. Her hand becomes a blur, right up until the moment before it strikes my face. I cannot see very well without my glasses. Since it is not a school day, I am not allowed to wear them. The blow from her hand burns my skin. "Who told you to move?" Mother sneers. I keep my eyes open, fixing them on a spot on the carpet. Mother checks for my reaction before again yanking my ear as she leads me to the front door.

"Turn around!" she yells. "Look at me!" But I cheat. From the corner of my eye I steal a glance at Father. He gulps down another swallow from his drink. His once rigid shoulders are now slumped over. His job as a fireman in San Francisco, his years of drinking and the strained relationship with Mother have taken their toll on him. Once my superhero and known for his courageous efforts in rescuing children from burning buildings, Father is now a beaten man. He takes another swallow before Mother begins. "Your father here thinks I treat you bad. Well, do I? Do I?"

My lips tremble. For a second I'm unsure whether I am supposed to answer. Mother must know this and probably enjoys "the game" all the more. Either way, I'm doomed. I feel like an insect about to be squashed. My dry mouth opens. I can feel a film of paste separate from my lips. I begin to stutter.

Before I can form a word, Mother again yanks on my right ear. My ear feels as if it were on fire. "Shut that mouth of yours! No one told you to talk! Did they? Well, did they?" Mother bellows.

My eyes seek out Father. Seconds later he must have felt my need. "Roerva," he says, "that's no way to treat The Boy."

Again I tense my body and again Mother yanks on my ear, but this time she maintains the pressure, forcing me to stand on my toes. Mother's face turns dark red. "So you think I treat him badly? I . . ." Pointing her index finger at her chest, Mother continues. "I don't need this. Stephen, if you think I'm treating It badly . . . well, It can just get out of my house!"

I strain my legs, trying to stand a little taller, and begin to tighten my upper body so that when Mother strikes I can be ready. Suddenly she lets go of my ear and opens the front door. "Get out!" she screeches. "Get out of my house! I don't like you! I don't want you! I never loved you! Get the hell out of my house!"

I freeze. I'm not sure of this game. My brain begins to spin with all the options of what Mother's real intentions may be. To survive, I have to think ahead. Father steps in front of me. "No!" he cries out. "That's enough. Stop it, Roerva. Stop the whole thing. Just let The Boy *be."*

Mother now steps between Father and me. "No?" Mother begins in a sarcastic voice. "How many times have you told me that about The Boy? The Boy *this,* The Boy *that.* The Boy, The Boy, The Boy. *How many times, Stephen?" She reaches out, touching Father's arm as if pleading with him; as if their lives would be so much better if I no longer lived with them—if I no longer existed.*

Inside my head my brain screams, Oh my God! Now I know!

Without thinking, Father cuts her off. "No," he states in a low voice. "This," he says, spreading his hands, "this is wrong." I can tell by his trailing voice that Father has lost his steam. He appears to be on the verge of tears. He looks at me and shakes his head before looking at Mother. "Where will he live? Who's going to take care of . . . ?"

"Stephen, don't you get it? Don't you understand? I don't give a damn what happens to him. I don't give a damn about The Boy."

Suddenly, the front door flies open. Mother smiles as she holds the doorknob. "Okay. All right. I'll leave it up to The Boy." *She bends down, just inches in front of my face. Mother's breath reeks of booze. Her eyes are ice cold and full of pure hatred. I wish I could turn away. I wish I were back in the garage. In a slow, raspy voice, Mother says, "If you think I treat you so badly, you can leave."*

I snap out of my protective mold and take a chance by looking at Father. He misses my glance as he sips another drink. My mind begins to tumble. I don't understand the purpose of her new game. Suddenly I realize that this is no game. It takes a few seconds for me to understand that this is my chance—my chance to escape. I've wanted to run away for years, but some invisible fear kept me from doing it. But I tell myself that this is too easy. I so badly want to move my legs, but they remain rigid.

"Well?" Mother screams into my ear. "It's your choice." Time seems to stand still. As I stare down at the carpet, I can hear Mother begin to hiss. "He won't leave. The Boy *will never leave. It* hasn't *the guts to go."*

I can feel the inside of my body begin to shake. For a moment I close my eyes, wishing myself away. In my mind I can see myself walking through the door. I smile inside. I so badly want to leave. The more I

envision myself walking through the door, the more I begin to feel a
warmth spread through my soul. Suddenly, I can feel my body moving.
My eyes pop open. I look down at my worn-out sneakers. My feet are
stepping through the front door. Oh my God, *I say to myself,* I can't
believe I'm doing this! *Out of fear, I dare not stop.*

"There," *Mother triumphantly states.* "The Boy *did it. It's his decision.*
I didn't force him. Remember that, Stephen. I want you to know I didn't
force him."

I step through the front door, knowing full well that Mother will reach
out and yank me back in. I can feel the hairs on the back of my neck
stand up. I quicken my pace. After stepping past the door, I turn right and
walk down the red steps. From behind me I can hear the sounds of
Mother and Father straining themselves as they lean outside. "Roerva,"
Father says in a low voice, "this is wrong."

"No!" *she replies in a flat voice.* "And remember, it was his decision.
Besides, he'll be back."

I'm so excited that I nearly trip on my own feet and stumble down the
stairs. I grab on to the handrail to stabilize myself. I make it to the
walkway, and I fight to control my breathing. I turn right and walk up the
street until I'm sure no one can see me past The House, then I break into
a run. I make it halfway up the street before stopping, only for a moment,
to look back down at The House.

With my hands on my knees I bend down panting. I try to strain my
ears for the sounds of Mother's station wagon. Somehow, Mother's letting
me go seems all too easy. I know she'll be after me in a few moments.
After catching my breath, I again quicken my pace. I reach the top of
Crestline Avenue and stare down at the small green house. But there's no
station wagon racing out of the garage. No one running after me. No
yelling, screaming or hitting. I'm not sitting at the bottom of the stairs in
the garage, not being beaten in the back of the knees with a broomstick
and not getting locked in the bathroom with another concoction of am-
monia and Clorox.

I spin around at the sound of a passing car. I wave.

Even though I'm wearing ragged pants, a torn, thin, long-sleeved shirt
and a pair of worn-out tennis shoes, I feel happy inside. I'm warm. I tell
myself I'm never going back. After years of living in fear, surviving tortur-
ous beatings and eating out of garbage cans, I now know I will somehow
survive.

I have no friends, no place to hide, nothing to turn to. But I know
exactly where I'm going—the river. Years ago, when I was a member of

The Family, for every summer vacation we would drive up to the Russian River in Guerneville. The best times in my life were the days spent learning to swim at Johnson's Beach, riding down the Super Slide, going on hayrides at sunset and playing with my brothers on the old tree stump by our cabin. Remembering the smell of the giant redwood trees and the beauty of the dark green river makes me smile.

I'm not sure exactly where Guerneville is, but I do know it lies north of the Golden Gate Bridge. I'm sure it will take me a few days to get there, but I don't care. Once I'm there I can survive by stealing loaves of French bread and salami from the local Safeway supermarket, and sleep on Johnson's Beach while listening to the sounds of the cars rumbling across the old evergreen Parker truss bridge that leads into the city. Guerneville was the only place I ever felt safe. Ever since I was in kindergarten, I knew it was where I wanted to live. And once I make it there, I know I will live in Guerneville for the rest of my life.

I begin walking down Eastgate Avenue when a cold chill whistles through my body. The sun has set and the evening fog begins to roll in from the nearby ocean. I clamp my hands inside my armpits and make my way down the street. My teeth begin to chatter. The thrill of the great escape begins to wear off. I begin to think that maybe, maybe, *Mother was right. As much as she beat me and yelled at me, at least the garage was warmer than out here.* Besides, I tell myself, I do *lie and steal food.* Maybe I do *deserve to be punished. I stop for a second to rethink my plan. If I turn back now, right now, she'll yell and beat me-but I'm used to that. If I'm lucky, tomorrow she may feed me some leftover scraps from dinner. Then I can steal food from school the next day. Really, all I have to do is go back. I smile to myself. I've survived worse from Mother before.*

I stop midstride. The thought of returning to The House doesn't sound half bad. Besides, I tell myself, I could never find the river anyway. *I turn around. She was right.*

I picture myself sitting at the bottom of the stairs, shaking with fear, frightened of every sound I may hear from above. Counting the seconds and being terrified by every set of commercials; then waiting for the sound of the floor to creak upstairs when Mother gets up from the couch, strolls into the kitchen to pour herself a drink and then screeches for me to come upstairs—where she'll beat me until I can no longer stand. I may be unable to crawl away.

I hate commercials.

The sound of a nearby cricket rubbing its wings brings me back to reality. I try to find the insect and stop for a moment when I think I'm close. The chirping stops. I remain perfectly still. If I catch it, maybe I could put the cricket in my pocket and make it my pet. I hear the cricket again. As I bend over to reach out, I hear the rumbling sounds of Mother's car from behind me. I dive beside a nearby car the moment before the headlights spot me. The car creeps down the street. The sound of Mother's squeaky brakes pierces through my ears. She's searching for me. I begin to wheeze. I clamp my eyes closed as her headlights inch their way toward me. I wait for the sound of Mother's car to grind to a halt, followed by her leaping from the car, then throwing me back into her station wagon. I count the seconds. I open my eyes slowly, turning my head to the left just in time to see the rear brakes light up before the brakes squeal. It's over! She's found me! In a way, I'm relieved. I would have never made it to the river. The anticipation drained me. Come on, come on, *I say to myself.* Just do it. Come on.

The car cruises past me.

I don't believe it! I jump up from behind the car and stare at a shiny two-door sedan tapping its brakes every few seconds. Suddenly I feel lightheaded. My stomach tightens up. A surge of fluid climbs up my throat. I stumble over to someone's grass and try to throw up. After a few seconds of dry heaves because of my empty stomach, I glance up at the stars. I can see patches of clear sky through the foggy mist. Bright silver stars twinkle above me. I try to remember how long it's been since I've been outside like this. I take a few deep breaths.

"No!" I yell. "I'm not going back! I'm never going back!" *I turn around and walk back down the street, north toward the Golden Gate Bridge. After a few seconds I walk past the car, which is now parked in someone's driveway. I can see a couple standing at the top of the steps being greeted by the host. The sound of laughter and music escape through the open door. I wonder what it would be like to be welcomed in a home. As I make my way past a house, my nose detects the smell of food, and the thought of wolfing down something to eat possesses me. It's Saturday night—that means I haven't eaten anything since Friday morning at school.* Food, *I think to myself.* I have to find some food.

Sometime later I make my way to my old church. Years ago, Mother sent my two brothers, Ron and Stan, and me to afternoon catechism classes for a few weeks. I haven't been to the church since I was seven. I gently open the door. Immediately I can feel the heat seep through the holes in my pants and my paper-thin shirt. As quietly as I can, I close the door behind me. I can see the priest picking up books from the pews. I hide beside the door, hoping he won't see me. The priest makes his way to the back pews toward me. I so badly want to stay, but . . . I close my eyes, trying to absorb the heat for a moment, before my hand again reaches for the door.

Once outside I cross the street, where I can see a row of stores. I stop in front of a doughnut shop. One early morning, years ago, Father stopped to pick up some doughnuts before he drove the family to the Russian River. It was a magical time for me. Now I stare through the glass, then up at the fat, jolly, animated cartoon characters that were painted on the wall and going through the various stages of making doughnuts.

From my left the smell of pizza makes my head turn. I stumble past a few stores until I stop in front of a pizza bar. My mouth waters. Without thinking I open the door and make my way, in a daze, to the back of the room. My eyes take a few minutes to adjust. I can make out a pool table, the sounds of beer mugs clashing together and laughter. I can feel stares from above me, and I stop at the far corner of the bar. My eyes dart around in search of abandoned food. Finding none, I make my way to the pool table, where two men have just finished a game. I find a quarter on the table and slowly cover it with my fingers. I look around before dragging the quarter over the edge of the pool table and into my hand. The coin feels warm. As casually as possible I stroll back to the bar. A voice explodes above me. I try to ignore the sound. From behind, someone grabs my left shoulder. Instantly I tighten my upper body, waiting for a blow to my face or stomach. "Hey kid, what are you doing?"

I spin around toward the voice, but I refuse to look up.

"I said, what are you doing?" the voice again asks.

I look up at a man wearing a white apron covered with red pizza sauce. He places his hands on his hips, waiting for a reply. I try to answer, but I begin to stutter. "Uhm. Noth . . . nothing . . . sir."

The man places his hand on my shoulder and leads me to the end of the bar. He then stops and bends down. "Hey kid, you need to give me the quarter."

I shake my head no. Before I can tell him a lie, the man says, "Hey, man, I saw you do it. Now give it back. Those guys over there need it to play pool." I clench my fist. That quarter can buy me some food, maybe even a piece of pizza. The man continues to stare at me. Slowly I uncurl my fingers and drop the coin into the man's hand. He flicks the quarter over to a pair of men holding pool sticks. "Thanks, Mark," one of them yells.

"Yeah, man, no problem." I try to turn away, looking for the front

door, when Mark grabs me. "What are you doing here? Why'd you steal that quarter?"

I retreat inside my shell and stare at the floor.

"Hey, man," Mark raises his voice, "I asked you a question."

"I didn't steal anything. I . . . I just thought that . . . I mean, I just saw the quarter and . . . I . . ."

"First off, I saw you steal the quarter, and secondly, the guys need it so they can play pool. Besides, man, what were you going to do with a quarter anyway?"

I could feel an eruption of anger surge through me. "Food!" I blurt out. "All I wanted was to buy a piece of pizza! Okay?"

"A piece of pizza?" Mark laughs. "Man, where are you from . . . Mars?"

I try to think of an answer. I can feel myself lock up inside. I empty my lungs of breath and shrug my shoulders.

"Hey, man, calm down. Here, pull up a stool," Mark says in a soft voice. "Jerry, give me a Coke." Mark now looks down at me. I try to pull my arms into my sleeves—to hide my slash marks and bruises. I try to turn away from him. "Hey, kid, are you all right?" Mark asks.

I shake my head from side to side. No! I say to myself. I'm not all right. Nothing's right! I so badly want to tell him, but . . .

"Here, drink up," Mark says as he slides over the glass of Coke. I grab the red plastic glass with both hands and suck on the paper straw until the soda is gone.

"Hey, kid," Mark asks, "what's your name? You got a home? Where do you live?"

I'm so ashamed. I know I can't answer. I act as if I did not hear him.

Mark nods his head in approval. "Don't move," he states as he grabs my glass. From behind the bar I can see him fill up the glass as he grabs the phone. The phone cord stretches to its limit as Mark strains to give me another Coke. After he hangs up the phone, Mark sits back down. "You want to tell me what's wrong?"

"Mother and I don't get along," I mumble, hoping no one can hear me. "She . . . ah . . . she . . . told me to leave."

"Don't you think she's worried about you?" he asks.

"Right! Are you kidding?" I blurt out. Oops, I say to myself. Keep your mouth shut! I tap my finger on the bar, trying to turn away from Mark. I glance at the two men playing pool and the others beside them—laughing, eating, having a good time.

I wish I were a real person.

I suddenly feel sick again. As I slide down the stool, I turn back to Mark. "I gotta go."

"Where ya going?"

"Uhm, I just gotta go, sir."

"Did your mother really tell you to leave?"

Without looking at him, I nod my head yes.

Mark smiles. "I bet she's really worried about you. What do you think? I tell you what. You give me her number, and I'll give her a call, okay?"

I can feel my blood race. The door, *I tell myself.* Just get to the door and run. *My head frantically swivels from side to side in search of an exit.*

"Come on now. Besides," Mark says, raising his eyebrows, "you can't leave now. I'm making you a pizza . . . with the works!"

My head snaps up. "Really?" I shout. "But . . . I don't have any . . ."

"Hey, man, don't worry about it. Just wait here." Mark gets up and makes his way to the front. He smiles at me through an opening from the kitchen. My mouth begins to water. I can see myself eating a hot meal— not from a garbage can or a piece of stale bread, but a real meal.

Minutes pass. I sit upright waiting for another glance from Mark.

From the front door a policeman in a dark blue uniform enters the shop. I don't think anything of it until Mark walks toward the officer. The two men talk for a few moments, then Mark nods his head and points toward me. I spin around, searching for a door in the back of the room. Nothing. I turn back toward Mark. He's gone, and so is the police officer. I twist my head from side to side as I strain my eyes, hunting for the two men. They're both gone. False alarm. My heart begins to slow down. I begin to breathe again. I smile.

"Excuse me, young man." I raise my head up to a police officer smiling down at me. "I think you need to come with me."

No! *I say to myself.* I refuse to move! *The tips of my fingers dig into the bottom of the stool. I try to find Mark. I can't believe he called the police. He seemed so cool. He had given me a Coke and promised me some food. Why did he do this? As much as I hate Mark now, I hate myself more. I knew I should have just kept on walking down the street. I should have never, never come into the pizza bar. I knew I should have gotten out of town as soon as I could. How could I have been so stupid!*

I know I've lost. I feel whatever strength I had now drain. I so badly want to find a hole to curl up into and fall asleep. I slide off the bar stool. The officer walks behind me. "Don't worry," he says. "You're going to be all right." I barely hear what he is saying. All I can think about is that somewhere out there, she is waiting for me. I'm going back to The House—*back to* The Mother. *The police officer walks me to the front door. "Thanks for giving us a call," the officer says to Mark.*

I stare down at the floor. I'm so angry. I refuse to look at Mark. I wish I were invisible.

"Hey, kid," Mark smiles as he shoves a thin white box into my hands, "I told you I'd give you a pizza."

My heart sinks. I smile at him. I begin to shake my head no. I know I'm not worthy. I push the box back toward Mark. For a second, nothing else in my world exists. I look into his heart. I know he understands. Without a word, I know what he is telling me. I take the box. I look deeper into his eyes, "Thank you, sir." Mark runs his hand through my hair. I suck in the scent from the box.

"It's the works. And kid . . . hang tough. You'll be fine," Mark says as I make my way out the door, holding my prize. The pizza box warms my hands. Outside a gray swirling fog covers the street where the police car is parked in the middle of the road. I hug the box close to my chest. I can feel the pizza slide down to the bottom of the box as the officer opens the front door of his car for me. I can hear a faint humming sound from the heat pump of the floorboard. I wiggle my toes to warm myself. I watch the officer as he makes his way to the driver's side. He slides into the car, then picks up a microphone. A soft, female voice answers his call. I turn away, looking back toward the pizza bar. Mark and a group of adults shiver as they stand together outside. As the police car slowly rumbles away, Mark raises his hand, forms a peace sign, then waves good-bye. One by one, the others smile as they join him.

My throat tightens. I can taste the salt as tears run down my face. Somehow I know I'll miss Mark. I stare down at my shoes and wiggle my toes. One of them pops through a hole.

"So," the officer says, "first time in a police car?"

"Yes, sir," I reply. "Am I . . . uhm . . . I mean, am I in trouble, sir?"

The officer smiles. "No. We're just concerned. It's kinda late, and you're a little young to be out here alone. What's your name?"

I glance down at my dirty toe.

"Come on, now. There's no harm in telling me your name."

I clear my throat. I don't want to talk to the officer. I don't want to talk to anybody. I know every time I open my mouth, I'm one step closer to Mother's evil clutches. But, I tell myself, what can I do? I know whatever chances I had of escaping to the river are now gone. I don't care. As long as I don't have to return to her. After a few seconds I answer the officer, "Da . . . Da . . . David, sir," *I stutter.* "My name is David."

The officer chuckles. I smile back. He tells me I'm a good-looking boy. "How old are you?"

"Nine, sir."

"Nine? Kinda small, aren't you?"

We begin to talk back and forth. I can't believe how much the officer is interested in me. I feel he actually likes me. He parks the car in front of the police station and leads me downstairs to an empty room with a pool table in the middle. We sit beside the pool table, and the officer says, "Hey, David, let's say we get to that pizza before it gets cold."

My head bounces up and down. I rip open the box. I bend down and suck in the aroma. "So, David," *the officer asks,* "where did you say you live?"

I freeze. The toppings from my piece of pizza slide off. I turn away. I was hoping he would somehow forget why he picked me up.

"Come on now, David. I'm really concerned about you." *His eyes lock onto mine. I can't turn away. I gently replace my piece of pizza in the box. The officer reaches out to touch my hand. By reflex, I flinch. Before the officer tries again, I stare him down. Inside my head I scream,* Don't you understand? Mother doesn't want me, doesn't love me, doesn't give a damn about me! All right? So . . . if you can just leave me alone, I can be on my way. Okay?!

The officer backs his chair away from the table before he begins in a soft voice. "David, I'm here to help you. You have to know that, and I'm going to stay here with you as long as it takes." *He leans over and lifts my chin with his finger. Tears roll down my eyes. My nose is runny. I know now there is no escape for me. I don't have the guts to look the policeman in the eyes.*

"Crestline Avenue, sir," *I say in a low voice.*

"Crestline Avenue?" *the officer asks.*

"Yes, sir . . . 40 Crestline Avenue."

"David, you did the right thing. Whatever the problem is, I'm sure we can work it out."

I tell him the phone number and the officer disappears for a few moments. After he returns, he again attacks the pizza.

I pick up the same piece of pizza. It's cold and soggy. I so badly want to eat, but my mind is a million miles away. The policeman reassures me with a smile. "Everything's going to be okay."

Right! *I tell myself.* The only time I ever felt secure, safe and wanted was when I was a tiny child. *I was five that day when The Family waited for me as I raced up the small hill on the last day of kindergarten. I can still see Mommy's face glowing with love as she shouted, "Come on, sweetheart. Come on now, David!" She opened the door for me after giving me a tight hug. Then she shut the door before Father sped away. Destination: the river. That summer Mommy taught me how to float on my back. I was scared, but Mommy stayed with me until I learned to float all by myself. I was so proud as I showed off to her, proving to Mommy I was a big boy, worthy of her attention and praise. That summer was the best time of my life. But now, as I sit in front of the policeman, I know nothing will ever be like it was back then. My good times are now only memories.*

The officer looks up. I turn my shoulders to find my father in one of his red cotton shirts standing behind me. Another police officer nods at the policeman sitting with me. "Mr. Pelzer?" the officer near me asks.

My father nods yes. The two of them disappear into an office. The policeman closes the door. I wish I could hear what they're saying. I'm sure it's about me and how I'm always in trouble with Mother. I'm only relieved that she didn't come, but somehow I know that she would never dare risk exposing herself to anyone of authority. I know she always uses Father for her dirty work. She controls Father—the same as she tries to control everyone. Above all, I know she must hide the secret. No one must ever know about our private relationship. But I know she's slipping. She's losing control. I try to think what this means. To survive, I must think ahead.

Minutes later the door from the office creaks. Father steps out from the room, shaking the policeman's hand. The officer approaches me. He bends down. "David, it was just a small misunderstanding. Your father here tells me that you became upset when your mother wouldn't let you ride your bike. You didn't need to run away for something like that. So, you go home with your father now, and you and your mother work this thing out. Your father here says she's worried sick over you." He then changes the tone of his voice as he points a finger at me. "And don't you ever put your parents through that again. I hope you've learned your lesson. It can be pretty scary out there, right?" the officer asks, while gesturing to the outside of the building.

I stand in front of the officer in total disbelief. I can't believe what I'm hearing. Ride my bike? I don't even have one! I've never even ridden on one before! I want to spin around to see if he is talking to some other kid.

From behind, Father looks down at me. His eyes are blank. I realize this is just one of Mother's cover stories. It figures.

"And David," the officer states, "treat your parents with dignity and respect. You don't know how lucky you are."

My mind becomes foggy. All I can hear inside my head is, " how lucky you are . . . how lucky you are . . . ," over and over and over again. I shudder when Father slams the door from the driver's side of the station wagon. He exhales deeply before leaning over to me. "Jesus H. Christ, David!" he begins as he turns the ignition and pumps the gas pedal. "What in the hell were you thinking? Do you have any idea what you did? Do you know what you put your mother through?"

My head snaps toward Father. Put *her* through? What about me? Doesn't anyone care about me? But . . . *I tell myself,* maybe she broke down. Maybe she's really concerned about me. Is it possible she knows she went too far? *For a moment I can imagine Mother sobbing in Father's arms, wondering where I am, whether I'm alive. Then I can see my mommy running up to me with tears in her eyes as she wraps me in love, showering me with kisses, tears rolling down her face. I can almost hear my mommy say the three most important words I long to hear. And I'll be ready to say the four most important words: I love you, too!*

"David!" Father grabs my arm. I jump up, striking my head against the top of the car. "Do you have any idea what your mother's been doing? I can't get a moment of peace in that house. For Christ's sake, it's been nothing but hell since you left. Jesus, can't you just stay out of trouble? Can't you just try and make her happy? Just stay out of her way and do whatever she wants. Can you do that? Can you do that for me? Well?" Father yells, raising his voice so loud I can feel my skin crawl.

Slowly I nod my head yes. I don't dare make a sound as I cry deep inside. I know I'm wrong. And, as always, it's all my fault. I turn to Father while shaking my head up and down. He reaches over to pat my head.

"All right," he says in a softer tone, "all right. That's my Tiger. Now let's go home."

As Father drives the car up the same street I walked down hours ago, I sit at the far side of the car, resting the weight of my body on the door. I feel like a trapped animal who wants to claw its way through the glass. The closer we get to The House, the more I can feel myself quiver inside. I need to go to the bathroom. Home, *I say to myself. I stare down at my hands. My fingers tremble from fear. I know in a few moments I'll be back where it all started. In all, nothing's changed, and I know nothing will. I wish I were someone, anyone but who I am. I wish I had a life, a family, a home.*

Father drives into the garage. He turns to me before opening his door. "Well, here we are," he states with a false smile. "We're home."

I look right through him, hoping, praying he can feel my fear, my pain from inside of me. Home? *I say to myself.*

I have no home.

An Angel Named Ms. Gold

*O*n March 5, 1973, I received the long-awaited answer to my prayers. I was rescued. My teachers and other staff members at Thomas Edison Elementary School intervened and notified the police.

Everything happened with lightning speed. I cried with all my heart as I said my final good-byes to my teachers. I somehow knew I would never see them again. By the tears in their eyes I realized they understood the truth about me—the *real* truth. Why I was so different from the other children; why I smelled and dressed in rags; why I climbed into garbage cans to hunt for a morsel of food.

Before I left, my homeroom teacher, Mr. Ziegler, bent down to say good-bye. He shook my hand and told me to be a good boy. He then whispered to me that he would tell my homeroom class the truth about me. Mr. Ziegler's statement meant the world to me. I so badly wanted to be liked, to be accepted by my class, my school—by everyone.

The police officer had to nudge me through the door of the school office. "Come on, David, we gotta go." I wiped my nose before I stepped through the door. A million thoughts raced through my mind, all of them bad. I was terrified of what the consequences would be when Mother found out. No one had ever crossed The Mother like this before. When she found out, I knew there would be hell to pay.

As the police officer led me to his car, I could hear the sounds of all the schoolchildren playing in the yard during their lunch break. As we drove off, I twisted around in my seat to catch a glimpse of the schoolyard one last time. I left Thomas Edison Elementary School without having a single friend. But my only regret was that I did not have a chance to say good-bye to my English teacher, Mrs. Woodworth, who was ill that day. During the time I was Mother's prisoner, Mrs. Woodworth, without knowing, helped me escape my loneliness through the use of books. I had spent hundreds of hours in the dark, reading books of high adventure. This somehow eased my pain.

After filling out some forms at the police station, the officer called Mother to inform her that I was not coming home that afternoon, and that she could call the county's juvenile authorities if she had any questions. I sat like a statue, feeling both horror and excitement as the officer spoke on the phone. I could only imagine what was going through Mother's head. As the policeman spoke with a dry voice on the phone, I could see beads of sweat cover his forehead. After he hung up the phone, I wondered for a moment if anyone else had ever had the same experience after talking to Mother. It seemed to be very important to the officer that we leave the station right away. I didn't help matters by pestering him over and over again as I jumped up and down and asked, "What'd she say? What'd she say?" The officer refused to answer. He seemed to breathe easier once we drove past the city limits. He then bent down and said, "David, you're free. Your mother is never going to hurt you again."

I didn't fully understand the weight of his statement. I had hoped that he was taking me to some kind of jail, with all the other bad children—as Mother had programmed into me for so many years. I had decided long ago that I'd rather live in jail than live one more minute with *her*. I turned away from the sun. A single tear rolled down my face.

As long as I could remember, I had always wiped my tears and retreated inside my shell. This time I refused to wipe the tear away. I could feel the tear reach my lips, tasted the salt and let the tear dry on my skin as the rays from the sun baked through the windshield. I wanted to remember that tear not as a tear of fear, anger or sorrow, but as one of joy and freedom. I knew that from that moment on, everything in my life was new.

The officer drove me to the county hospital. Immediately, I was taken into an examination room. The nurse seemed shocked by my appearance. As gently as possible, she bathed my entire body from head to toe with a sponge before the doctor examined me. I couldn't look at her. I felt so ashamed as I sat on top of the cold metal examination table, wearing only my soiled underwear briefs filled with holes. As she washed my face, I turned away and kept my eyelids closed as tightly as I could. When the nurse finished, I gazed at the yellow-colored room filled with Snoopy cartoon characters. I looked down at different parts of my body. My legs and arms were a combination of yellow and brown. Dark circles of purple bruises faded on top of fresh rings of blue bruises—where I was either grabbed, punched or slammed down on the kitchen floor. When the doctor came into the room he seemed very concerned about my hands and arms. My fingers were dry, raw and red from all the years of using the combinations of cleaning chemicals used to complete my household chores. The doctor pinched the tips of my fingers, asking me if I could feel the pressure. I shook my head no. I hadn't been able to feel the tips of my fingers for some time now. He shook his head, claiming it was nothing to worry about, so I didn't think anything more of it.

Afterward, the police officer kindly led me through the maze of corridors as we made our way from room to room for lots of examinations, tests, blood samples and X rays. I found myself moving in a daze. I felt as if I were watching someone else's life through my own eyes. I became so scared that I first asked, then begged the policeman to check around every corner and enter every room before I did. I knew that somewhere out there Mother was poised, ready to snatch me away. At first the officer refused, and only after I became so petrified that I couldn't breathe or move did the policeman humor me and follow my requests. I knew deep inside my heart that things were happening too fast—it was too easy for me to escape Mother.

Hours later we ended up with the same nurse who bathed me. She bent down to say something. I waited. She stared into my eyes, then after a few moments, she turned away. I could hear her sniffle. The doctor walked up behind me, patted my shoulder and gave me a bag containing cream for my hands. He then instructed me to keep my arms as clean as possible and said that it was too late to cover them. I looked at the officer, then down at my arms. I didn't understand. To me, my arms seemed the same as they always did—dark red with little skin. Both arms itched quite a bit, but that was normal for me. Before the policeman and I left, the doctor reached over and said to the officer, "Make sure David gets plenty of food. And make sure he gets lots of time in the sun." Then the doctor bent a little closer to him and asked, "Where is she? You're not sending him back to his . . . ?"

The policeman locked eyes with the doctor. "Not to worry, Doc. I gave this kid my word. His mother is *never* going to hurt him again."

From that moment on, I knew I was safe. Standing near the officer, I wanted to hug his leg, but I knew I shouldn't. My eyes gleamed with joy. The police officer became my hero.

A few minutes after we left the hospital, he slowed his car as he drove through the hills on the narrow one-lane roads. I rolled down my window and stared in amazement at the sloping brown hills and tall redwood trees. Moments later the officer parked the car. "Well, David, here we are." I gazed down below me at the prettiest home I had ever seen. The officer explained that I would live here for a while and that this would be my new foster home. I had never heard the words *foster* home before, but I knew I would love the home. To me it seemed like a giant log cabin with lots of open windows. I could see that behind the home was a huge backyard, where sounds of screeching and laughter echoed by the tiny creek.

The elderly woman who ran the temporary foster home introduced herself as "Aunt Mary" and greeted me at the kitchen door. I thanked the police officer with the strongest handshake I could. I felt bad that he had worked overtime for me. He knelt down and said in a deep voice, "David, it's kids like you that made me want to become a policeman." Without thinking, I grabbed his neck. The moment I did, my arms felt as if they were on fire. I didn't care. "Thank you, sir."

"Hey, kid, not a problem," he replied. He then strolled up the curved walkway and saluted me from his car before driving off. I didn't even know his name.

After Aunt Mary fed me a delicious dinner of filet of sole, she introduced me to the seven other children who, like myself, for one reason or another no longer lived with their parents. I stared into every one of their faces. Some eyes were hollow, some full of worry, others full of confusion. I had no idea there were other unwanted children, too; for years I had felt I was all alone. At first I acted shy, but after a few questions from the other children, I opened up. "What are you in for?" they asked. "What happened to you?"

I bent my head down before replying that my mother didn't like me because I was always in trouble. I felt ashamed. I didn't want to tell them the secret about Mother and me. But none of that mattered to any of them, for I was just another face in the crowd. I was instantly accepted. I felt a surge of energy erupt from inside. From that moment on I became a wild child. I blitzed through the home as if my pants were on fire. I joked, laughed and screamed with joy, releasing years of solitude and silence.

I was uncontrollable. I ran from room to room, jumping on every mattress in the home. I bounced so high my head banged again and again against the ceiling. I didn't stop until I saw stars. I didn't care. The other children clapped their hands, egging me on. Their laughs were not cold, like the snide remarks reserved for me back at school, but were full of delight and approval.

My frolicking ended suddenly when I ran through the living room, nearly knocking over a lamp. By reflex, Aunt Mary grabbed my arm. She was about to scold me until she looked down at me. I covered my face, and my knees began to shake. Aunt Mary was a strict, elderly woman who stood her ground, but she didn't yell as she was known to do. For that evening my hyperactivity ended as quickly as air could escape a balloon. Aunt Mary released her grip and knelt down, asking, "What did she do to you?"

"I'm sorry," I stuttered in a low voice. I was still unsure of Aunt Mary's intentions. I retreated into my protective position. "I was a bad boy, and I deserved what I got!"

Later that evening Aunt Mary tucked me into bed. I began to cry, explaining to her that I was afraid Mother would come and take me away. She assured me I was safe and stayed with me until I felt secure. I stared up at the dark cedar ceiling. It reminded me of the old cabin in Guerneville. I fell asleep knowing that Mother was out there, somewhere, waiting to get me.

Alone in my dreams I found myself standing at the end of a long, dark hallway. A shadowy figure emerged at the opposite end. The figure transformed into *The Mother*. She began to march toward me. For some reason, I stood still. I couldn't move; I didn't even try. The closer The Mother came, the more her red face, filled with hatred, came into focus. The Mother held a shiny knife above her, poised and ready to strike me down. I turned and ran down the endless hallway. With all my strength I pumped my legs as fast as I could, searching for a light. I ran forever. The hallway twisted and turned as I hunted for an escape. I could feel The Mother's rancid breath on my neck and hear her cold voice chanting that there was no escape and that she would never let me go.

I snapped out of my dream. My face and chest were covered with a cold, sticky sweat. Not knowing if I was still dreaming, I covered my face. After my breathing began to slow down, I frantically looked all around. I was still in the cedar room. I still had on a pair of pajamas that Aunt Mary had loaned me. I patted myself, feeling for any wounds. *A dream,* I told myself. *A bad dream, that's all.* I tried to control my breathing but couldn't shake the vision. The Mother's words echoed in my mind: *"I will never let you go. Never!"*

I jumped out of bed and scrambled around in the darkness to throw on my clothes. I returned to the head of the bed and held my knees close to my chest. I couldn't go back to sleep. That's where The Mother now lived—in my dreams. I felt it was a mistake that I was taken away, and I knew I would soon be returned to her. That night, and those to follow, while everyone slept, I held on to my knees as I rocked backed and forth, humming to myself. I would stare through the window and listen to the trees sway in the evening breeze. I told myself that I would never fall into the nightmare again.

My first encounter with the county's Child Protective Service agency came in the form of an angel named Ms. Gold. Her long, shiny blond hair and bright face matched her name. "Hi," she smiled. "I'm your social worker." And so began the long and drawn-out sessions in which I had to explain things I did not totally understand. In the beginning of our first session, I huddled at the far end of the couch while Ms. Gold sat at the other end. Without my knowing, she slowly inched her way toward me until she was close enough to hold my hand. At first I was too scared to have her touch me. I did not deserve her kindness. But Ms. Gold held on to my hand, caressing my palm, assuring me that she was there to help me. That day she stayed with me for over five hours.

The other visits were just as long. At times I was too scared to talk and long moments of silence followed. Other times, for no apparent reason and not understanding why, I'd burst into tears. Ms. Gold didn't care. She simply held me tight and rocked me back and forth, whispering in my ear that everything was going to be all right. Sometimes we would lie at the end of the couch, and I would talk about things that were of no relation to my bad past. During those times I would play with the long strands of Ms. Gold's shiny hair. I'd lie in her arms and breathe in the fragrance of her flowery perfume. I soon began to trust Ms. Gold.

She became my best friend. After school, whenever I saw her car, I'd sprint down the walkway and burst into Aunt Mary's home, knowing Ms. Gold had come to see me. We always ended our sessions with a long hug. She would then bend down and assure me that I did not deserve to be treated the way I was and that what my mother did to me was not my fault. I had heard Ms. Gold's words before, but after years of brainwashing I wasn't so sure. So much had happened so fast. One time I asked Ms. Gold why she needed all of this information on Mother and me. To my horror, she told me that the county was going to use it against my mother. "No!" I pleaded. "She must never know I told you! *Never!*"

Ms. Gold assured me that I was doing the right thing, but when she left me alone to think, I came to a different conclusion. As long as I could remember, I had always been in trouble. I was always being punished for one thing or another. Whenever my parents had fought, my name was always thrown into the ring. Was it really Mother's fault? Maybe I deserved everything I got over the years. I did lie and steal food. And I knew I was the reason why Mother and Father no longer lived together. Would the county throw Mother in jail? Then what would happen to my brothers? That day after Ms. Gold left, I sat alone on the couch. My mind raced with questions. I felt my insides turn to jelly. *My God! What have I done?*

Days later, on a Sunday afternoon, while I was outside learning to play basketball, I heard the old familiar sound of Mother's station wagon. My heart felt as though it stopped beating. I closed my eyes, thinking I was daydreaming. When my brain responded, I turned and ran inside Aunt Mary's home and smashed into her. "It's . . . it's my . . ." I stuttered.

"Yes, I know," Aunt Mary gently spoke as she held me. "You're going to be all right."

"No! You don't under . . . she's going to take me away! She found me!" I yelled. I tried to squirm myself away from Aunt Mary's grip so I could run outside and find a safe place to hide.

Aunt Mary's grip didn't budge. "I didn't want to upset you," Aunt Mary said. "She's just going to drop off some clothes. You're going to court this Wednesday, and your mother wants you to look nice."

"No!" I cried. "She's going to take me! She's going to take me back!"

"David, be still! I'll be right here if you need me. Now, please, be still young man!" Aunt Mary did her best to calm me down. But my eyes nearly popped out as I watched The Mother stroll down the walkway with *her* four boys in tow.

I sat by Aunt Mary's side. Greetings were exchanged, and like a trained dog I became my old self—the child called "It." In an instant I went from an enthusiastic boy to Mother's invisible house slave.

Mother didn't even acknowledge my presence. Instead, she turned to Aunt Mary. "So, tell me, how is *The Boy?*"

I looked up at Aunt Mary's face. She seemed startled. Her eyes flickered for just a second. "*David?* David is quite fine, thank you. He's right here, you know," Aunt Mary responded, holding me a little tighter.

"Yes," Mother said in a dry voice, "I can see that." I could feel Mother's hate burn through me. "And how does he get along with the other children?"

Aunt Mary cocked her head to one side. "Quite fine. *David* is very polite and extremely helpful around the home. He's always looking to help out," she answered, knowing that Mother had no intention of talking to me directly.

"Well . . . you should be careful," Mother warned. "He's tried to hurt other children. He does not get along well with others. *The Boy* is violent. He needs special attention, discipline that only I know how to instill. You don't know *The Boy.*"

I could feel the muscles on Aunt Mary's arm become tight as a drum. She leaned forward, giving Mother her best smile—the kind of smile that Aunt Mary would like to slap Mother silly with. "*David* is a fine young man. *David* may be a bit rambunctious . . . but that's to be expected considering what *David's* been put through!"

Suddenly I realized what was happening. Mother was trying to gain control over Aunt Mary, and Mother was losing. On the outside my shoulders slumped forward, and I gave Mother my timid puppy dog look as I stared down at the carpet. But on the inside my ears became like radar, picking up every phrase, every syllable of the conversation. *Finally,* I said to myself. *Someone has finally put Mother in her place. Yes!*

The more I heard Aunt Mary's tone change toward Mother, the more my face lit up. I was enjoying this. I slowly lifted my head up. I looked right into Mother's eyes. Inside I smiled. *Well, isn't this nice. It's about time,* I said to myself. As I listened to them, my head began to weave from left to right, then back again, as if I were watching a tennis match. Aunt Mary tried again to have Mother acknowledge me. I nodded my head at Mother as I openly agreed with Aunt Mary.

I began to feel extremely confident. *I* am *someone. I* am *somebody,* I told myself. I could feel parts of my body begin to relax. I was no longer scared. For once, everything was fine—right up until the moment I heard the phone ring. My head snapped to the right as the kitchen phone shrilled. I counted the rings, hoping someone would hang up. I became tense after the 12th ring. Aunt Mary turned toward the kitchen. I grabbed her arm. *Come on,* I said to myself. *No one's home. Just hang up.* But the phone kept ringing—16, 17, 18 times. *Just hang up! Just hang up!* I could feel Aunt Mary lean forward to get up. I kept my hand on her arm, trying to force her to stay. When she stood up, I followed. My right hand clamped onto her left arm. She stopped midstride and pried my hand off, finger by finger. "David, please. It's just the phone. For goodness sake, don't be rude. Now go back in there." I stood still. I locked onto Aunt Mary's eyes for a brief moment. Aunt Mary understood. She nodded her head. "Okay," she said in a low voice. "Come on, you can stay with me."

I let out a sigh of relief as I followed her feet to the kitchen. Suddenly, I felt my left arm being yanked backwards. I nearly lost my footing. I fought to regain my balance. I closed my eyes as I bit my lip. My legs began to shake. Inches in front me sat Mother. Her heavy, raspy breathing made me quiver. Mother's face was dark red. I could tell that from behind her glasses her eyes were on fire. I tried to search for my savior, but Aunt Mary had already turned into the kitchen.

I stared down at the carpet, wishing her away. Mother squeezed my arm tighter. "Look at me!" she hissed. I became frozen. I wanted to yell, but my voice became mute. Her evil eyes locked onto mine. I closed my eyes as I felt Mother's head inch its way toward my face. Mother's monotone voice became vicious. "Cocky little bastard, aren't you? Well, you don't look so tall now. Do you? What's the matter? Has your little Aunt Mary left you?" she said in a sarcastic, whining voice. Mother then yanked me so close to her face that I could smell her breath and feel droplets of saliva spray on my face. Mother's voice turned ice cold. "Do you know what in the hell you've done? Do you?! The questions they've asked me? Do you realize the embarrassment you've cost *This Family?*" Mother asked, as she spread her left hand at my brothers sitting beside her.

My knees began to buckle. I wanted to go to the bathroom and throw up. Mother smiled, showing me her dark yellow teeth. "They think I tried to hurt you. Now why would I do that?"

I tried to turn my head toward the kitchen. I could barely make out Aunt Mary's voice on the phone.

"Child!" Mother hissed, "Boy . . . get this straight! I don't care what they say! I don't care what they do! You're not out of this yet! I'll get you back! You hear me? *I'll get you back!*"

When she heard Aunt Mary hang up the phone, Mother released my arm and pushed me away. I sat back in the wide chair and watched my savior stroll back into the living room and sit down beside me. "I'm sorry about that," Aunt Mary said.

Mother batted her eyes and waved her hand. Suddenly she became regal. The act was on. "That? Oh, the phone? No problem. I have to . . . I mean, we have to get going anyway."

I stole a glance at my brothers. Their eyes were hard and fixed. I gazed at them, wondering what they thought of me. Except for Kevin, who was still a toddler, the three of them seemed as if they wanted to throw me outside and stomp on me. I knew they hated me, and I felt I deserved it. For I had exposed the family secret.

I tried to imagine what it must be like for them to live with Mother now. I prayed that somehow my brothers would forgive me. I felt like a deserter. I also prayed that the cycle of hate had not moved on to one of them. I felt sorry for them. They had to live in total hell.

After another round of pleasantries and final warnings from Mother to Aunt Mary, *The Family* departed. As I heard the sound of Mother's tires from her station wagon mash down on the rocks as she drove away, I remained glued to the chair. I sat in the living room for the rest of the afternoon, rocking back and forth, repeating Mother's pledge over and over again, *"I'll get you back. I'll get you back."*

That evening I couldn't eat. In bed I rolled back and forth until I sat up clutching my knees. The Mother was right. I knew in my heart she would get me back. I stared out the window of my room. I could hear the wind howl through the tops of trees and the branches rub against each other. My chest began to tighten. I cried. I knew at that moment there was no escape for me.

At school the next day I couldn't concentrate on my work. I strolled around the schoolyard like a zombie. Later that afternoon I met Ms. Gold at Aunt Mary's home. "David, we're going to court in two days. I need to ask you just a few questions to clarify our case. Okay, honey?" she asked with a bright smile.

I refused to speak and sat rigidly at the far end of the couch. I couldn't look at Ms. Gold. To her dismay I muttered, "I don't think I should say anything."

Ms. Gold's mouth nearly fell to the carpet. She began to speak, but I raised my hand, cutting her off. I then retracted as many statements as I could, claiming that I had lied about everything. I had caused all of the household problems. I told her that I had fallen down the stairs. I had run into doorknobs. I had beaten myself. I had stabbed myself. I then cried to Ms. Gold that my mommy was a beautiful, kind woman, with the perfect flower garden, the perfect home, the perfect family, and that I craved her attention because of my other brothers. And everything was all my fault.

Ms. Gold became speechless. She scooted over to where I sat. She tried several times to reach out and hold my hand. I brushed her delicate fingers away. She became so frustrated that she began to cry. After several hours and many attempts, Ms. Gold looked at me with dried streaks of tears and blotches of black eyeliner running down her face. "David, honey," she sniffled, "I don't understand. Why won't you talk to me? Please, honey."

Then she tried to switch tactics. She stood up and pointed her finger at me. "Don't you know how important this case is? Don't you know that all I talk about in my office is a cute little boy who is brave enough to tell me his secret?"

I looked through Ms. Gold and tuned her out. "I don't think I should say anything else," I coldly replied.

Ms. Gold bent over, trying to force me to look into her face. "David, please . . ." she begged.

But to me, she just wasn't there. I knew that my social worker was trying everything in her power to help me, but I feared Mother's wrath more than Ms. Gold's. From the moment Mother stated "I'll get you back," I knew everything in my new world was lost.

Ms. Gold reached out to hold my hand. I slapped her fingers away. I turned my back to her. "David James Pelzer!" she barked. "Do you have any idea what you're saying? Do you understand what you're doing? You had better get your story straight! You're going to have to make a major decision pretty soon, and you better be ready for it!"

Ms. Gold sat back down, wedging me between her knees and the end of the couch. "David, you have to understand that in a person's life there are a few precious moments in which decisions, choices that you make now, will affect you for the rest of your life. I can help you, but only if you let me. Do you understand?"

I again turned away. Suddenly Ms. Gold sprang up from the couch. Her face became bright red and her hands were shaking. I tried to hold back my feelings, but a surge of anger erupted. "No!" I cried out. "Don't you get it? Don't you understand? She'll get me back. She'll win. She always wins. No one can stop The Mother. Not you, not anyone! She'll get me back!"

Her face went blank. "Oh my God!" Ms. Gold exclaimed as she bent down to hold me. "Is that what she said to you? David, honey . . ." Her arms stretched out to embrace me.

"No!" I yelled. "Won't you just leave me alone? Just . . . go . . . away!"

Ms. Gold stood over me for a few moments, then turned on her heels and stormed out of the room. A few seconds later I could hear the sound of the screen door slamming in the kitchen. Without thinking, I ran into the kitchen, but I stood frozen behind the door. Through the screen I could see Ms. Gold stumbling up the steep walkway. She lost her grip on her papers and tried to catch some of them in midair. "Shit!" she cried out. The papers scattered as she desperately tried to gather them into one pile. As soon as she stood up, she fell down, scraping her right knee. I could see the frustration on her face as she clamped her hand over her mouth. Ms. Gold tried again to stand up, but this time with more caution as she made her way to the county car. She slammed the car door shut and bent her head against the steering wheel. As I stood behind the screen door, I could hear Ms. Gold—my angel—sobbing uncontrollably. After several minutes she finally started her car and sped off.

I stayed behind the kitchen screen and cried inside. I knew I could never forgive myself, but lying to Ms. Gold was the lesser of two evils. I stood alone, confused, behind the screen door. I felt that by lying, I had protected Mother, that I had done the right thing. I knew Mother was going to get me back and no one could stop her. But then when I thought of how kind Ms. Gold had been throughout everything, I suddenly realized the terrible position I had just put her in. I never meant to hurt anybody, especially Ms. Gold. I became a statue as I stood behind the screen door. I only wished that I could crawl under a rock and hide, forever.

CHAPTER

3

The Trial

*T*wo days later Ms. Gold drove me to the county courthouse. The ride began in total silence. I sat on the far side by the door, staring at the scenery. We drove north on Highway 280 beside the aqueduct, the same water reserve the family used to drive by on our way to Memorial Park years ago. Ms. Gold finally broke the ice, explaining in a soft voice that today the judge would decide whether I was to become "a permanent ward of the court" or be returned to my mother's custody. I didn't understand the "ward of the court" part, but I knew what returning to my mother's custody meant. I shivered at this last part of Ms. Gold's sentence. I looked up at her, wondering whether I would be riding back with Ms. Gold after court or in the back of Mother's station wagon. I asked Ms. Gold whether there was a possibility of Mother taking me back with her today. Ms. Gold reached out, patted my hand and nodded yes. My head slumped forward. I didn't have the energy to resist anymore. I hadn't been able to sleep since our last meeting. The closer Ms. Gold drove to the courthouse, the more I could feel myself slipping from her safety and back into Mother's clutches.

My hands formed into a tight fist. The countdown now began.

I felt a soft caress on my left hand. My arms flew up to protect my face. It took a moment for me to realize that I was only daydreaming. I took a deep breath and nodded to myself, trying to calm myself down. "David," Ms. Gold began, "listen to me very carefully. This is Pam talking, not Ms. Gold, your social worker. Do you understand?"

I let out a deep sigh. I knew we were only a few miles away from the courthouse. "Yes, ma'am, I understand."

"David, what your mother did to you was wrong. Very wrong. No child deserves to be treated like that. She's sick." Pam's voice was soft, and calm. She seemed on the verge of tears. "Remember Monday afternoon when I told you that one day you'd have to make a decision? Well, today is that day. The decision you make today will affect you for the rest of your life. Only *you* can decide your fate. I've done all that I can do. Everyone's done what they can do—your teachers, the school nurse, Aunt Mary, everyone. Now it's up to you.

"David, I see so much in you. You're a very brave young man. Not many children can tell their secret. Someday this whole experience will be behind you." Ms. Gold stopped for a moment. "David, you're a very brave young man."

"Well, I don't feel very brave, Ms. Gold. I feel . . . like . . . like a traitor."

"David," Pam smiled, "you're not a traitor! And don't you forget it."

"If she's sick," I asked, "then what about my other brothers? Are you going to help them, too? What if she goes after one of them?"

"Well, right now my only concern is you. I don't have any information that your mother was or is abusing your brothers. We have to start somewhere. Let's take this one step at a time. All right? And David . . ." Ms. Gold switched off the ignition. We had reached the courthouse.

"Yes, ma'am?"

"I want you to know that I love you."

I looked deep into Ms. Gold's eyes. They were so pure. "I really do," she said, stroking the side of my cheek.

I cried as I nodded my head. Ms. Gold lifted my chin with her fingers. I pressed my head against her hand. I cried because I knew that in a few minutes I would betray Pam's love.

Minutes later we walked into the waiting room of the county courthouse, and Ms. Gold grabbed my hand. Mother and the boys were waiting on one of the benches. Ms. Gold nodded at Mother as the two of us walked by. I stole a glance. Mother was wearing a nice dress and had fixed up her hair.

Ron had a cast on his leg.

No one acknowledged my presence, but I could feel Mother's hate. Ms. Gold and I sat down, waiting our turn. The delay was unbearable.

Burying my head under my right arm, I mumbled to Ms. Gold, asking her for a pen and paper. I proceeded to scribble a small note.

To Mother:
I'm so sorry. I didn't mean for it to come to this. I didn't mean to tell the secret. I didn't mean to hurt the family. Can you ever forgive me?

Your son, David

Ms. Gold read the note and nodded, giving me permission to give the note to Mother. I shuffled over to Mother, becoming a child called *"It"* once again—with my hands stuck to my side and my head cocked down toward the floor. I waited for Mother to say something, to yell at me, snap her fingers, anything. She didn't even acknowledge my presence. I inched my head upward, moving my eyes up her body, and stuck my hand out, holding my note. Mother snatched the paper, read it, then tore it in half. I bowed my head before returning to Ms. Gold, who put her arm around my shoulder.

Minutes later Ms. Gold, Mother, my four brothers and I filed into the courtroom. I sat behind a dark table, gazing in awe at the man above me dressed in a black robe. "Don't be afraid," Ms. Gold whispered. "The judge may ask you a few questions. It's important, very important that you tell him the truth," she said, stressing the last part of her sentence.

Knowing that my final outcome would be decided in the next few minutes, I reached over and nervously tapped Ms. Gold's hand. "I'm sorry for all the trouble I caused you . . ." I wanted to tell her the truth—the real truth—but I didn't have the guts. The lack of sleep had drained all of my inner strength. Ms. Gold smiled at me reassuringly, revealing her pearly white teeth. A subtle yet familiar fragrance filled my head. I closed my eyes, taking in a deep breath . . .

Before I knew it, the clerk began to read off a number and stated my name. At the mention of my name my head snapped up at the judge, who adjusted his glasses and glanced down at me. "Yes, the . . . uhh . . . Pelzer case. Yes. I presume the representative from the county is present?" the judge asked.

Ms. Gold cleared her throat and winked at me. "Here we go. Wish me luck."

The judge nodded at Ms. Gold. "Recommendations?"

"Thank you, Your Honor. As the court is well aware through the extensive briefs from the pediatrician's examinations, interviews with the minor's former teachers, other interviews and my reports, the county recommends that David Pelzer become a permanent ward of the court."

I stared up at Ms. Gold. I could barely make out her voice. I knew it was she who was talking, but her voice cracked. I glanced down at her skirt. Her knees were shaking. I clamped my eyes shut. *Oh my God,* I said to myself. As I opened my eyes, Ms. Gold returned to her seat, covering her trembling hands.

"Mrs. Pelzer? Is there anything you wish to state?" the judge asked.

Every head swung to the right, stopping at Mother. At first I thought Mother did not hear the judge. She simply stared up at his bench with a blank expression. After a few seconds, I realized what Mother was trying to do. She was trying to stare the judge down.

"Uhh . . . Mrs. Pelzer? Do you wish to make a statement in regard to your son, David?"

"I have nothing to say," Mother said in a flat tone.

The judge rubbed his forehead then shook his head. "Fine. Thank you, Mrs. Pelzer. Duly noted."

The judge then turned to Ms. Gold. "This is a very disturbing, very unusual case. I have read thoroughly all of the statements, and I have been troubled with the . . ."

I lost track of time as the judge began to ramble. I felt myself shrinking inside. I knew in a matter of minutes the proceedings would be over and I would be back with Mother. I glanced over to the right to look at her. Mother's face was stone cold. I closed my eyes, visualizing myself back at the bottom of the stairs and sitting on top of my hands, hungry—like a starving animal. I didn't know whether I could go back to that life again. I only wanted to be free of the pain and the indignity.

"David?" Ms. Gold whispered as she poked me. "David, the judge wants you to stand up."

I shook my thoughts clear. I had fallen asleep, again. "What? I don't under . . ."

Ms. Gold grabbed my elbow. "Come on, David. The judge is waiting."

I stared up at the judge, who nodded for me to stand. My throat felt as if an apple were stuck in it. As I pushed my chair behind me, Ms. Gold tapped my left hand. "It's all right. Just tell the judge the truth."

"Well, young man," the judge began. "What it boils down to is this:

If the court so desires and if you believe that your home setting is undesirable . . . you may become a permanent ward of the court, or you may return and reside with your mother at your home residence."

My eyes grew wide. I couldn't believe that this moment had finally come. In unison, every person in the small room turned toward me. A lady with grayish white hair held her fingers just above a strange-looking typewriter. Every time someone spoke, the lady tapped keys that looked like tongue depressors. I swallowed hard and clenched my hands. From the right I could feel Mother's radar of hate turn on.

I tried to look at the judge. I swallowed hard once more before I started to deliver my rehearsed line about how I had lied and that I had indeed caused all the problems at home and that Mother had never abused me. From the corner of my right eye I could see Mother's eyes locked on to me.

Time stood still. I closed my eyes and imagined myself being driven back to The House with The Mother, where she would beat me and I would be forced to live at the bottom of the stairs, dreading the second set of commercials, wishing I could someday escape and become a normal kid who was allowed to be free of fear, to play outside . . .

Without Ms. Gold knowing, I turned to her and inhaled again. Suddenly it hit me—Ms. Gold's perfume. It was the same perfume she wore whenever she gave me a hug or held me as we lay at the end of the couch. I saw myself playing with her hair.

My mind switched to seeing myself outside, laughing with the other children, playing basketball, searching for each other in a game of tag and running at hypersonic speeds through Aunt Mary's home; then at the end of the day being dragged in from outside after hunting for snakes or playing by the creek. I opened my eyes and peeked at my hands. They were no longer red. In fact, my skin had a light tan.

I could feel Mother's radar drill through me. I felt myself leaning to the right, a surge of fear creeping up my back. I took in another whiff of Ms. Gold's perfume.

I held my breath for a fleeting second, then before my courage disappeared I blurted out, "You, sir! I want to live with you! I'm sorry! I'm so sorry! I didn't mean to tell! I didn't mean to cause any trouble!"

Mother's radar of hate intensified. I tried to remain standing, but my knees began to buckle.

"So be it," the judge quickly announced. "It is the recommendation of this court that the minor, David James Pelzer, shall become a ward of the court and remain so until his 18th birthday. This case is closed!" the judge quickly concluded, as he slammed his gavel on a piece of wood.

I felt paralyzed. I wasn't sure what had just happened. Ms. Gold sprang up and hugged me so tightly that I thought she'd crush my ribs. All I could see was a forest of blond strands, and I gagged as I almost swallowed clumps of Ms. Gold's hair. After a few moments, Ms. Gold regained her composure. I wiped my tears and my runny nose. I looked up at the bench. The judge smiled at me. I returned the gesture. Then, for a brief moment, I thought His Honor winked at me.

I felt Mother's radar of hate flicker, then turn off.

Ms. Gold held my shoulders. "David, I'm so proud of you!" Before she could say anything else, I whimpered, "I'm so sorry. I didn't mean to lie to you the other day. I'm sorry I made you cry. Can you ever forgive me? I just wanted to . . ."

Ms. Gold parted my hair from my eyes. "Shh. It's all right. I knew what you were doing. But now, your mother wants to . . ."

"No!" I cried. "She'll take me away!"

"She only wants to say good-bye," Ms. Gold assured me.

As Ms. Gold and I slowly made our way out of the courtroom, I could see ahead of us that Mother was crying, too. Ms. Gold nudged me forward. I hesitated until I felt sure that Ms. Gold would stay nearby. The closer I walked to Mother, the more I cried. Part of me didn't want to leave her. Mother's arms opened wide. I ran into them. Mother hugged me as if I were a baby. Her feelings were sincere.

Mother let go, took my hand and led me to her car. I felt no fear. At the station wagon Mother loaded me up with new clothes and lots of toys. I was astounded. My mouth hung open as Mother continued to fill my arms.

My voice cracked as I said good-bye to my brothers, who shook their heads in response. I felt like a traitor, and I thought they hated me for exposing the family secret.

"I'm going to miss you," Mother cried.

Before I could think, I replied, "I'll miss you, too."

As happy as I was for the judge's decision, I became filled with sadness. I felt torn between my freedom and being separated from Mother and the family. Everything was too good to be true—my freedom, the new clothes, the toys. But the thing I cherished most was the warmth of Mother's hug.

"I'm so sorry about everything," I sobbed. "I really am. I didn't mean to tell."

"It's not your . . ." Mother began. Her eyes changed. "It's all right." Mother's voice became firm. "Now listen to me. You have another chance. This is a new beginning for you. I want you to be a good boy."

"I will," I said, as I wiped away my tears.

"No!" she stated in a cold voice. "I mean it! You have got to be a good boy! A better boy!"

I looked into her swollen eyes. I felt that Mother wanted the best for me. I realized that before Mother went into the courtroom, she had already predicted the outcome.

"I'll be good. I'll try real hard," I said, as I squared my shoulders like I did back in the basement years ago. "I'll make you proud of me. I'll try my best to make you proud."

"That's not important," Mother stated. Before she sent me away, she gave me a final hug. "Have a happy life."

I turned away sniffling. I didn't look back. I thought about what Mother had last said. *Have a happy life.* I felt as if she were giving me away. I almost collapsed when I reached Ms. Gold, who helped me load her car with my prized possessions. We stood together as Mother drove off. I waved to everyone, but only Mother returned my gesture. Her window was rolled up, but I watched Mother's lips as she repeated, "Have a happy life."

"How about an ice cream?" Ms. Gold asked, breaking the tension.

I stood up straight and smiled. "Yes, ma'am!"

Pam gently took my hand, wrapping her long fingers around mine, and led me to the cafeteria. We strolled past the other cars and a few scattered trees. I caught a whiff of the trees' scent. Then I stopped to gaze at the sun. I stood still for a moment, taking in my surroundings. A soft wind blew through my hair. I didn't shiver. The grass was a bright yellow-green. I knew that my world was different now.

Ms. Gold stopped to look at the sun, too. "David, are you going to be all right?"

"Yes!" I smiled. "I just don't want to forget this first day of the rest of my life!"

CHAPTER

4

New
Beginnings

*A*fter the effects of the trial had worn off, my insides became numb.

I fully realized that Mother could not physically harm me. But I still felt an eerie sensation that told me Mother was somewhere out there, coiled like a rattlesnake, waiting to reach out and strike with a vengeance.

But another part of me felt that I would never see Mother or my brothers again. I became confused, sensing that I didn't deserve to live with them, that I was unworthy and that Mother had thrown me away. I tried my best to tell myself that through the wonder of the county's social services and the court system, I had a new lease on my life. I tried my best to isolate my past, to bury my dark experiences deep inside my heart. Like a light switch, I imagined myself flicking off my entire past.

I quickly became accustomed to the routine at Aunt Mary's home, as well as to my new school. Even though I was spontaneous and free at Aunt Mary's, I still became lifeless and shy around my classmates. It seemed difficult for me to make friends. I stood out, especially whenever children asked why I didn't live with my parents. And whenever some of my classmates persisted, I stuttered and turned away. I couldn't look into their eyes.

Other times I'd happily state, "I'm a foster child!" I was proud to be a member of my new family. I began to repeat this saying until one day one of the older foster children pulled me aside at school, warning me not to tell anyone "what" I was because ". . . a lot of folks don't like our kind."

" 'Our kind'? What are you talking about?" I asked. "We didn't do anything wrong."

"Don't worry, little brother. You'll find out soon enough. Just be cool and keep your mouth shut." I obeyed the command, realizing I now lived in another world of prejudice.

During recess, I watched the other kids laugh as they played tag and handball, while I kept to myself and wandered around the school in a daze. No matter how hard I tried, my mind kept flashing back to my other school in Daly City. I thought of Mr. Ziegler and his animated "happy face" suns, which he would draw on my papers, Mrs. Wood-worth's dreaded spelling tests or running to the library, where Ms. Howell played "Octopus's Garden," by the Beatles, on her record player.

In my new school I had completely lost interest. I no longer absorbed my subjects as I had just a few weeks ago. I sat behind the gray steel desk half-dazed, scribbling on my papers, counting down the minutes until the end of the school day. What was once my sanctuary soon became a prison that kept me from my playtime at my foster home. As my attention span drifted, my handwriting, once cursive and graceful, became chicken scratch.

At Aunt Mary's my awkward sense of humor and naïve excitability made me popular with the older foster children. Whenever some of them were granted permission to leave Mary's home for the after-noon, I was allowed to tag along. Sometimes they stole candy bars from the local grocery stores. Wanting total acceptance and having already stolen food for years, I immediately followed their lead. If someone stole two candy bars, I stole four. It seemed so easy to me that after a few afternoon trips, I became a legend within the group. I was fully aware that what I was doing was wrong. I also knew that some of the bigger boys were using me, but I didn't care. After years of isolation, I was finally accepted within a group.

My stealing was done within the foster home as well. Waiting until everyone was outside, I'd sneak into the kitchen and take slices of bread and stash them under my pillow. Then late at night I'd sit up on my bed and nibble on my prize, like a mouse nibbling on a piece of cheese. One Sunday afternoon I grew tired of bread and decided to steal Dolly Madison cupcakes from the freezer. In the early morning hours I awoke to find an army of ants leading to the head of my bed.

As quickly and quietly as I could, I tiptoed to the bathroom and flushed my goodies, along with the ants, down the toilet. The next day, as Aunt Mary prepared our lunches for school, she discovered the missing desserts and blamed Teresa, one of the other foster children.

Even though Teresa was severely scolded and grounded to her room after school that day, I remained silent. I didn't steal from Aunt Mary's home for the thrill of it, but only to have a ready-made storage of food in case I ever became hungry.

It didn't take long for Aunt Mary to discover that I was the one responsible for the missing food. From that moment on, Aunt Mary eyed me carefully around her home and did her best to restrict my afternoon adventures. At first I felt ashamed because I had betrayed her trust and kindness. But on the other hand, I simply didn't care what "Old Maid" Aunt Mary thought of me. My only concern was total acceptance by the older foster children.

My welcome at Aunt Mary's was probably worn out even before the first week of July, when I was placed in my first permanent foster home. Just as before, when the police officer had driven me to Aunt Mary's for the first time, I couldn't wait to see the new home. My new foster mother, Lilian Catanze, greeted Ms. Gold and me at the door. As I followed Mrs. Catanze and Ms. Gold up the wide, open stairs that led into the living room, I tightly clutched a brown grocery bag containing all my worldly possessions. The night before, I made sure to pack my bag and keep it close to my side.

I knew from experience that if I left anything behind, I would never see it again. I was shocked when I first witnessed the foster children who transformed into frenzied piranhas whenever a child left Aunt Mary's home. Within seconds of the child's departure, the others would swarm through the room, checking under the bed, in the closets and through the clothes hamper—everywhere—searching for clothes, toys or other valuables. The ultimate prize was to find a stash of money. I quickly discovered that it didn't matter whether the thieves needed or even desired the items. Possession of an article, any article, meant trading power for other things—household chores, late-night desserts or an exchange for money. As usual, I adapted quickly, and joined in the hunt whenever a child left. I learned that rather than walking a child to the car and wishing him or her good luck, I would instead say my good-byes in Aunt Mary's home . . . and then stay close to the departing child's room so I could have a head start on the other kids. But as a sign of respect, we all knew to never enter a room until the child had left. I also learned that deals were usually made the night before, and as a courtesy the roommate would get first dibs. So I, too, would give away a few shirts and a couple of toys.

As I began to imagine the other foster children ransacking my old room, I heard Mrs. Catanze ask, "Well, David, what do you think?"

Still holding my bag, I shook my head up and down before saying, "It's a very nice house, ma'am."

Mrs. Catanze waved a finger in my face. "Now, we'll have none of that. Everyone here calls me either 'Lilian' or 'Mom.' You may call me 'Mom.'"

I again nodded, but this time at both women. I didn't feel comfortable calling Mrs. Catanze, some lady I just met a few moments ago, Mom.

As the two ladies chatted for several minutes, Lilian leaned close to Ms. Gold, hanging on her every word and shaking her head from side to side. "No contact? None at all?" she asked.

"Correct," Ms. Gold replied. "David is to have no contact with his mother or his brothers, unless Mrs. Pelzer makes the arrangements."

"And the father?" Lilian asked.

"Not a problem. He has your number and should be calling you soon. David's father did not make it to the court proceedings, but I've kept him informed of David's status."

Mrs. Catanze leaned a little closer to Ms. Gold. "Anything special I need to know?"

"Well," Ms. Gold began, "David is still in the adjustment phase. He's a bit hyper and into everything—and I mean everything. He's a bit light fingered, if you know what I mean."

Sitting on the couch, I acted as if I were not paying attention, but I could hear every word.

"David," Mrs. Catanze said, "why don't you wait in the kitchen, and I'll be with you in just a few moments."

As I followed Mrs. Catanze into the kitchen, I still held on to my grocery bag. I sat by the table and drank a glass of water as Lilian closed the sliding door, separating the two rooms. I could hear Mrs. Catanze sit back down, but the two women started whispering. I watched the numbers of a clock radio flip over every time a minute passed. Before I knew it, the sliding door opened.

Ms. Gold smiled at me before giving me a hug. "I really think you're going to like it here," she said. "There's a play park nearby, and you'll have lots of other foster children to play with. I'll check in on you as soon as I can, so be extra good."

I gave Ms. Gold another quick hug, thinking I'd see her in a few days, and waved good-bye to her from the upstairs window. Before Ms. Gold drove down the street, she waved a final good-bye, then blew me a kiss. I stared through the window, not knowing what to do next.

"Well," Mrs. Catanze asked, "would you like to see your room?"

My eyes lit up as she took my hand. "Yes, ma'am."

"Remember what I told you," Lilian warned.

I nodded my head. "I'm sorry. I forget things sometimes."

Mrs. Catanze led me into the first room down the hall. After putting my clothes away I joined her on the twin-sized bed. "I need to explain a few things to you—the home rules. You are responsible for keeping your room clean and helping out with the chores. You do not enter someone else's room without their permission first. There is no lying or stealing in this home. If you want to go somewhere, you first ask me and tell me where and how long you'll be away . . ."

"You mean I get to go anywhere I want to?" I asked, amazed that I suddenly had all of this unexpected freedom.

"Within reason, of course," Lilian responded. "This home is not a prison. As long as you act responsible, you'll be treated as such. Do I make myself clear?"

"Yes, Mrs. Catanze," I said in a soft, slow voice, still feeling awkward calling her Mom.

Mrs. Catanze patted my leg before leaving the room and closing the door. I leaned back on the bed, smelling the fresh-scented pillowcase. I tried to focus on the sounds of cars rushing up and down the steep street, until I finally gave in to sleep. As my mind began to drift off, I began to feel safe and secure in my new setting.

Sometime later I awoke to the sounds of voices, coming from the kitchen. After I cleared my eyes, I walked out of the bedroom and into the kitchen.

"Is this him?" someone with long blond hair chided. "This ain't no kid. He's a runt."

Lilian leaned over and smacked the tall, blond teenager in the arm. "Larry, now watch your mouth! David, please excuse him. This," she said, still staring at Larry, "is Larry Junior. You'll meet Big Larry in a few minutes."

"C'mon Larry, he's small, but kinda cute. Hi, I'm Connie. And I

don't want you going through my things in my room. You got that?"
As Connie leaned over, I nearly choked on her perfume. She had
shiny black hair and long eyelashes, and wore a minidress. I couldn't
help myself as I stared up at her legs. Connie stepped back, and her
face turned red. "Mom, he's a little pervert!"

I turned to Mrs. Catanze. "What's a 'pree-vert'?"

Lilian laughed. "Someone who shouldn't look up young ladies'
dresses!"

I didn't understand. I wanted to know what it meant. I began to ask
the same question when Mrs. Catanze cut me off. "And this is Big
Larry."

I looked as far up as I could, to see a huge man with dark curly hair
and black-framed glasses. He had a kind, gentle face. Big Larry smiled
as he shook my hand. "Mom," he said, "I'm gonna go to the show
tonight. Mind if I take Dave with me?"

Lilian smiled. "I don't mind, but you make sure you take care of
him."

"Yeah," Larry Jr. chimed, "make sure he doesn't get scared or see
anything that's . . . nasty!"

About an hour later Big Larry and I began our journey to the movie
theater. I could tell that he was childlike and shy. I liked him immediately. As we walked up and down the endless streets of Daly City, we
both talked about things of no importance. Somehow we each knew
not to ask why the other was in foster care. It was a sort of code that
was explained to me while I stayed at Aunt Mary's home. The closer
we strolled to the theater, the more Big Larry became my friend.

Larry claimed to have seen the movie *Live and Let Die* a dozen
times, so I couldn't understand why he so badly wanted to see it again.
But after the first 10 minutes of the show, I, too, sat paralyzed. I
became mesmerized by the action scenes and the fast-paced music
that carried the film. After years of living in the dark, craving adventure, I finally saw it on film. While Larry gazed at the girls in bikinis, I
fidgeted in my seat, waiting impatiently for James Bond to make his
next narrow escape from death while at the same time saving the
world from doom. After seeing this movie, the character of James
Bond became etched in my mind, much in the same way as Superman
had years earlier.

The next day was just as special. Rudy, Lilian's husband, loaded
their two cars full of foster children and mountains of food for their
annual Fourth of July family get-together picnic at Junipero Serra

Park—the same park I went to as a small boy when I was considered a member of Mother's Family. When we arrived at the park, I helped carry containers and bags full of goodies, not knowing where to place them. "What do I do with these?" I asked no one in particular.

"David, just place it anywhere," Rudy replied.

"But all of the tables are already full of stuff from other people," I whined.

Lilian stepped beside Rudy. They joined hands. "Yes, David, we know," she said. "These people are our family."

I looked at the scores of adults drinking soda and beer. Kids ran in every direction as they played tag. "Wow, all these people are your kids?"

Suddenly a woman screamed. I nearly recoiled into my protective shell as the woman frantically ran toward me in thick, funny-looking wooden shoes. "Mom! Dad!" the woman howled. She then tried to wrap her arms around both Lilian and Rudy. I stared at her face. She didn't look anything like Mr. or Mrs. Catanze.

Lilian cried as she blew her nose, then gave her handkerchief to the woman and closed her eyes for a brief moment to recompose herself. "David, this is one of our first foster children, Kathy."

Now I understood. I turned my head from side to side, straining my eyes as streams of people flocked over to Rudy and Lilian.

"And Mom, Dad, I got a job. I'm married. I'm going to night school and this . . . is my new baby!" Kathy announced, as a man with a beard handed over a baby wrapped in a yellow blanket into Rudy's open arms. "Oh Mom, Dad, it's so good to see you!" Kathy cried.

A small mob of adults crowded around the Catanzes. Swarms of children jumped up and down, screaming for attention, as babies and hugs were exchanged. After a few minutes, I excused myself from the crowd and made my way to the edge of the hill. I sat down, staring at the planes lifting off from the nearby airport.

"Pretty cool, isn't it?" a familiar voice said.

I turned to look at Big Larry.

"Every year it's the same thing, but more people. I guess you can say they love kids. So what do you think?" Larry asked.

"Wow! There must be hundreds of folks here!" I exclaimed. "Have you ever been here before?"

"Yeah, last year. How about you?"

I stopped for a moment to study a jumbo jet dipping its wing to the west. "When I was a kid . . ." I caught myself, not sure if I really wanted to say anything. I had held back so much for so long. I cleared my throat before continuing. "My parents—my real mom and dad— would always take my two brothers and me to this park when we were just kids." I smiled. "We'd spend the entire day just down the hill, playing on the swing set. . . ." I closed my eyes, seeing Ron, Stan and me as happy, bright-faced kids. I wondered what they were doing now. . . .

"Dave! Hey, David! Earth to Dave, come in!" Larry blared as he cupped his hands together, acting as if they formed into a blowhorn.

"Sorry," I automatically replied. "I think . . . I think I'll take a walk."

After asking permission from Lilian, I strolled down the paved hill. A few minutes later I found myself standing on the same grassy area as I did a lifetime ago. Back then, I was a member of the perfect family. Now I was still a child, searching for my past. I walked toward the swing set and sat on one of the black swings. I kicked the sand, filling the heels of my shoes with some of it. My mind began to drift off again.

"Hey mister? Are you going to play or what?" a small child asked.

I slid off the swing and walked away. My insides felt hollow. In front of me, beneath a shade of trees, a young couple sat on the same table as Mother and Father did years ago. The woman got up and called out to her children with her hands on her hips—just as Mother had done when she had called to her children. For a second our eyes met. The lady smiled at me as she bowed her head. As I heard the sounds of children running from the swing set, I closed my eyes, wishing I had the answers to why everything had gone so wrong with Mother and me.

The two questions that tumbled over and over in my mind were whether Mother ever loved me and why she treated me the way she did.

Later that evening I wanted so badly to talk to Mrs. Catanze, but I couldn't work up the nerve. The next morning I woke up late and shuffled into the kitchen. "She ain't here, runt," Larry Jr. hissed. "You'll have to feed yourself."

I didn't know what to do. I didn't know how to cook, and I didn't know where the cereal bowls were, or even where the cereal was.

"So," Larry Jr. began, "I hear your mother used to kick the crap outta you. Tell me, what's it like? I mean, to have someone use your face for a mop?"

I couldn't believe this creep. Every time I was with Larry Jr., he was always trying to put me down. I bit my lip, trying to think of something to say. I failed to think of anything smooth. A surge of anger began to race through me.

"So tell me, man, what's it like? I mean, I'm curious. Seriously, what's it like to have the crap kicked out of you? Why didn't you fight back? What are you, some sort of wimp?"

I turned away from him and ran to my room. I could hear him laughing behind me as I slammed the door shut. I burrowed into my bed and cried without knowing why. I stayed in the room all day.

"Mrs. Catanze, am I a wimp?" I asked her the next day as she drove me to the shopping mall.

"A wimp? David, where did you hear that?"

I did not want to rat on Larry Jr. But he was a turd, and I didn't like him anyway. I still felt upset about how he and the other big kids thought of me. I swallowed hard before I answered Lilian.

"Pay Larry no mind," Mrs. Catanze said afterward. "He's a very upset young man. David, we have quite an array of . . ."

I gave her a puzzled look.

". . . quite a mixture of young folks who have different . . . special needs. Larry is just at that age when he's rebellious. He wants to fight everything and everyone. Give him a wide berth—lots of room. He's just feeling you out. Give it some time. Okay?"

"Yes, ma'am. I understand, but am I a wimp 'cause I didn't fight back? I mean, is it right to fight your own mother?"

Mrs. Catanze shoved the gear shift into park as she stopped in front of Tanforan Park. She turned to the right as she took off her glasses. "No, David," she stated matter-of-factly. "You are not a wimp for not fighting back. I don't know all that happened, but I do know you're not a wimp. Now come on. I've got a check here for $127 from the county to buy you some clothes. And," Lilian smiled, "I'm not afraid to spend it. Lesson number one: Let's go shopping!"

As Lilian took my hand, I screeched, "Wow, $127! That's a lot of money!"

"Not for a growing boy. And you do plan on growing, don't you? That's all the money they gave us for this year. Wait until you have kids of your own," Lilian stated, as she opened the door into Sears.

A couple of hours and three shopping bags later, Lilian and I returned to her home. I smiled from ear to ear as I closed the door to my room, then laid out all of my clothes as neatly as I could. Next, I arranged the shirts by their colors and folded my underwear briefs and socks just right before putting them away. I sat by the foot of the bed for a few seconds before I ripped open the drawers and rearranged my clothes again. After the fourth time, I slowly opened the drawers. As gently as I could, I removed a dark blue shirt. My hands trembled. I breathed in the smell of cotton. *Yes!* I told myself. *These are* my *clothes!* Clothes that no one had ever touched or worn before. Not rags that Mother had made me wear or clothes she had given me out of pity, that she had stored since last Christmas, or clothes from Aunt Mary that other foster children had worn before.

"Yes!" I squealed out loud. Then without thinking, I flung open the drawers and threw everything back on the bed. It took me forever to repack my clothes. But I didn't care—I was having fun.

A few days later, before lunch, Lilian hung up the phone in the kitchen before calling me away from the television. "So," she asked, "how are you feeling today?"

I shrugged my shoulders. "Fine, I guess." My eyes grew wide. "Did I do something wrong? Am I in trouble?"

"No, no," she said in a calm voice. "Now stop that. Why do you always say that whenever someone asks you a simple question?"

I shook my head. I understood what she said, but I did not know why I always felt on edge whenever someone asked me a question. "I dunno."

Lilian nodded. "Hey, let's say we have some lunch. I'll kick Larry Junior out, and it will just be the two of us, all right?"

My face lit up. "Sure!" I liked it whenever Mrs. Catanze and I were alone. I felt special.

Lilian made a couple of bologna sandwiches as I grabbed a bag of chips. She first warned, then ordered me to slow down my eating and to use better table manners. I obeyed her by not seizing everything in sight or shoving food into my mouth. I smiled at her, proving to her that I could indeed chew with my mouth closed.

Mrs. Catanze seemed to take her time as she delicately ate her sandwich. I almost asked her why she chewed so slow, when I heard a loud banging on the door. Without thinking, I blurted, "I'll get it!" Still chomping on my food, I bolted down the stairs and opened the door. A split second later I nearly coughed up my food. My brain locked up. I couldn't break away from looking at *her.*

"Well, aren't you going to invite us in?" Mother asked in a kind voice.

From behind me, I could hear Lilian rush down the staircase. "Hello . . . I'm Lilian Catanze. We spoke on the phone today. We were just finishing lunch."

"You did say 1:00 P.M., didn't you?" Mother asked in a demanding tone.

"Uhh . . . yes, I did. Please come in," Lilian said.

Mother marched in, followed by the boys. Stan came in last, with a grin on his face as he pushed in my bike, which Grandmother had purchased for me last Christmas. I remembered that day when Mother had allowed me to ride the bike, twice. I had never ridden before, and I fell several times before I got the hang of it. And at the end of the day I ran over a nail, and the front tire went flat. Now as Stan shoved the bike into Lilian's house, I could immediately see that both tires were flat and parts were missing from the bike.

But I didn't care. The yellow and candy-apple-red Murray bicycle with its metallic-red banana seat was my prized possession. I was shocked that Mother decided to give it to me.

Mother and the boys only visited for a few minutes, but Lilian made it a point to stay by my side. Even though Mother's attitude seemed more relaxed—not cold and demeaning, as when she had come to see me at Aunt Mary's—she still wouldn't talk to me. I had so much to tell her. I wanted to show her my room, my new clothes and the artwork that I did in school. Above all, I wanted so badly to prove to Mother that I was indeed worthy of her acceptance.

"Well," Mother said as she got up from the couch, "I just wanted to drop by. Remember, David, I *will* be checking in on you from time to time, so . . . *you be good*," Mother stated in a sly voice.

Lilian raised her hand, stopping me before I could say anything. "Thank you for stopping by, Mrs. Pelzer. And remember, do call *if* you drop by again," Lilian replied, as Mother stepped through the door.

I raced up the stairs. I stopped in front of a tall window and re- mained perched behind the glass as I watched Mother and the boys pile into her faded gray station wagon. As she drove off, I waved frantically, but no one saw me. In my heart I knew my effort was in vain. I wished that just once—just once—someone would smile and wave back.

Lilian let out a deep sigh, then placed her hands on my shoulders. "So, that's your mother? Are you all right?"

I nodded my head yes. I looked up at Lilian. Tears rolled down my face. "She doesn't love me, does she? I mean . . . I just don't understand. Why? Why won't she even talk to me? Am I that bad? Why didn't you tell me she was coming over? Why?

"I'm tired of her treating me like . . . like I'm nothing. I'm tired of her, my brothers, that creep Larry . . ." I pointed my finger at the window. "She didn't even talk to me. She never talks to me. Never!" I spun around to Lilian. "Am I that bad? I try to be nice. I try to be good. I didn't tell her to come over, did I?" I began to rant and rave, throwing my hands into the air as I paced the living room. "Did I tell her to beat me . . . to . . . to not feed me for days or . . . or have me live and sleep in the garage like . . . like . . . *an animal?*

"At night she wouldn't even give me a blanket. Sometimes I got so cold . . . I tried to stay warm. I really did," I cried as I nodded my head.

I wiped my runny nose with my finger and closed my eyes. For a brief moment, I saw myself standing in front of the kitchen sink—back at The House. Beside me I could see a smelly, pink paper napkin. I took a deep breath before I opened my eyes. "I . . . I . . . remember one Saturday afternoon . . . she had me pick up some dog poop . . . and . . . I was in the kitchen; she was in the living room lying down on the couch watching her shows. That's all she does, all day, every day, is watch her shows. Anyway . . . all I had to do was throw the poop in the garbage disposal, and she'd never know. I knew if she found out, it'd be too late. I mean, by the time she heard me turn on the disposal, it would be too late . . . but I ate it 'cause she told me to. As I did, I cried inside, not because of . . . but . . . because I had *let* her do that to me. For all those years I had let her treat me like she did. For years I was so ashamed."

I began to whimper. "I never told. I never told. . . . Maybe Larry's right. Maybe I am a wimp."

"Oh, David! Oh my God!" Lilian cried. "We didn't know . . ."

"Look at this. . . ." I yanked up my shirt. "This . . . this is where she stabbed me. She didn't mean to. It was an accident. But you know why?"

The blood drained from Lilian's face. She closed her eyes before she covered her mouth with her hand. "No, David, I don't know. Why did she?"

"She said she'd kill me if I didn't 'do the damn dishes in 20 minutes.' Ain't that a kick? The funny thing is that ever since the accident, I just wanted to tell her I knew she didn't mean to kill me, that I knew it was an accident. I actually prayed that the accident would bring us together—that somehow she knew she'd gone too far, that she couldn't hide the secret anymore. I wanted her to know that I forgave her.

"But no! I'm the bad guy. She won't even talk to me. Like . . . like I'm the one who's the bad guy!" I could feel my arms tighten up and my hands form into fists. I stared through Mrs. Catanze as I slowly turned my head from side to side. "Damn it! She won't even talk to me! Why? Why? Why?!"

Lilian knelt down in front of me. She was sobbing, too. "David, I don't know. We need to have you talk to someone, someone who can help you. This is something you need to get out of your system. You need someone who's more qualified . . . who knows what to do. Ms. Gold and I will arrange for you to talk to someone who will help you find some answers. All right?"

I felt myself drifting away. I focused on Lilian's mouth moving, but I couldn't make out what she was saying. She took my hand and led me into my room. As I lay in bed, she stroked my hair, whispering, "It's all right. I'm right here. Everything's going to be all right."

Hours later I woke up refreshed and followed Mrs. Catanze as she bounced down the staircase to examine my bike. Moments later I shook my head in disgust. "Stan did this," I said. "Mister Fix-It. It's his way of getting back at me."

"Well, David," Lilian said in a firm tone, "the question is: Are you going to sit here and sulk about it, or are you going to do something about it?" She stopped for a moment as if to ponder an idea. "You know, if you wanted to . . . you could probably earn some extra money and fix up your bike. That is, if you wanted to."

A few minutes later I walked back up the stairs and plopped myself on the couch. I now became consumed with fixing my bike. When Big Larry came home from work, I ran to his room to seek his advice. Throughout the evening, Larry and I schemed on the quickest way to achieve my goal. After 10 o'clock, we came up with the perfect plan, a plan so flawless that Larry guaranteed I would have my bike up and running in 30 days or less. Larry, who claimed to be "a master strategist"—I had no idea what his statement meant—went on to boast that when Mom and Dad saw me coming, they would willingly throw money at me.

"Wow!" I gasped. "This is just too cool!"

Before quitting for the day, Big Larry and I dubbed our plan "Operation: Bug the Parent."

The following morning I stayed glued to Lilian's side, begging her for extra work. An hour later she threw her arms in the air. "All right! I give up! Here, take these rags and clean the bathroom. You do know how to clean a bathroom, don't you?"

I smiled and said to myself, *Like you wouldn't believe!* As I gazed up at her, I cocked my neck to one side. "How much?"

Lilian blinked her eyes. "What?"

"How much to clean the bathroom?" I stated in my most serious voice.

Mrs. Catanze nodded her head. "Oh, I understand. Okay, little big man, I'll tell you what: I'll pay you a quarter . . ."

Before Lilian could complete her sentence, I replied, "No! Not enough."

"Aren't you the greedy one. Okay, how much?"

I could feel myself retreat inside. Big Larry hadn't taught me what to do in this case. "I dunno," I said, as I felt all my confidence shrinking away.

"I'll tell you what," she said, hovering over me. "I'll give you 30 cents. Take it or leave it."

I knew from what Big Larry had instructed me to do that whenever someone said "take it or leave it," it meant I should take the deal and run. I nodded my head triumphantly. "It's a deal. Let's shake on it."

Looking at Lilian, I could tell she wasn't ready for all my high-powered art of deal making. I felt I had tricked her into not only paying me, but giving me more money than she had originally offered.

It took me nearly two hours to clean the bathroom—as Mrs. Catanze put it, "by the employer's standards." I felt that she had somehow taken advantage of me. As I scrubbed the tile floor for the third time, I knew that evening I would need to talk to Big Larry and complain about our foolproof plan.

My mixed feelings suddenly disappeared when Lilian dropped a nickel and a quarter into my eager palm. Forgetting to thank her, I raced into my room, found a jar I had saved and dropped the change into the jar. I stared into the jar every day. In less than a month I had earned over four dollars—more than enough, I figured, to fix my bike. Finally, after the right amount of pestering again, Tony, Lilian's son, drove me in the back of his beat-up orange Chevy pickup truck to the bicycle shop. Tony knew, without my bugging him, all the parts I needed. I didn't seem to notice how when the bill arrived, Tony came up with more cash than I had.

That day, without permission, I borrowed some tools I had found and began to piece my bike together. After dozens of attempts at forcing the inner tubes into both tires I wiped off my bloody knuckles, jumped on my bike and, for the first time in my life, let out a howl of victory as I breezed down the street without a care in the world.

I remember August 21, 1973, as *my* day on *my* bike. That day was the first time I felt that I was a *normal* kid, caught up in the splendor of a never-ending day. For years I had heard the sounds of kids zooming down the street, screaming with joy as they flew by on their bikes. That day I must have ridden up and down the street a thousand times. Mrs. Catanze had to drag me inside. "David Pelzer, it's been dark for over an hour now! Get your little butt in here, now!" she barked, as I sailed past her in defiance.

Even though my legs ached from the strain of pumping my bike up the street, I didn't want my special day to end. As Lilian stood with her hands on her hips, I jumped off my bike and puffed all the way as I walked my bike up to her home. I could tell by the look on her face that she was about to yell at me. But I beat her to the punch by giving her my best smile.

"All right," she said as she threw her arm around me. "Get in here. Don't worry; tomorrow's another day. After you're done with your chores, you can take your bike to the park."

I clenched my fist in victory. "Yes!" I cried.

Early the next morning, as I stepped out of bed, I discovered that I could barely bend my legs. I looked into the mirror and smiled.

"Yes!"

CHAPTER

5

Adrift

After my initial taste of freedom, I spent as much time as I could riding my Murray bicycle. As soon as I rolled out of bed, I'd scramble to the open window (I never slept with the blinds down) and check the weather. Then I'd gulp down breakfast, blitz through my chores, race down the stairs and slam the front door shut, after yelling to Mrs. Catanze that I was leaving.

Mrs. Catanze usually watched my departure through her kitchen window. Never missing an opportunity to show off, I'd wave to her behind my back. At times I'd pedal down the street so fast that I thought I was flying. Minutes later I'd prop my feet on the center bar and coast through the freshly cut grass of the play park. After parking my bike, I'd scramble through the immense tri-layered wooden fort. I'd climb all the ropes, and run and jump on the chained drawbridge. After exhausting myself, I'd lie down to catch my breath. I always stretched out on the highest level so I could feel the warmth of the sun's rays as they inched their way across the park.

Whenever I heard laughter, I'd peek over the ledge of the fort and stare with fascination as other children, mostly younger than I, played with their friends or parents. I wanted to join in, but I always chickened out before I approached them. Somehow I knew I did not fit in.

I always stayed at the park until I could no longer suppress my growling stomach. Then I'd hop on my bike and casually pedal up the street to Lilian's home. As a habit, whenever I'd burst through the front door, I'd suck in my breath and then scream, "I'm back!" Lilian always answered my call, but one day she did not reply. I skipped up the stairs and ran into the kitchen.

I whirled around when I heard someone behind me. "She ain't here, runt." Larry Jr. was in one of his usual moods.

I wanted so badly to tell him off, but I bit my lip and stared down at the floor, acting timid, and nodded my head without looking up, indicating he had won. As I tried to scoot past him so I could go to my room and wait for Lilian, he blocked my path. Without warning he seized my arm.

"Where's Momma's little boy going?" he whined, as he tightened his grip.

I shot a look of hate into his eyes as I tried to squirm out of his grasp. "Hey, man . . . let go!" I exclaimed.

"Yeah, Larr . . . Larry, jus . . . just let . . . ah . . . let the kid . . . go," Chris stuttered. I turned my head upward to Chris, one of my other foster brothers. I was surprised to see him because he usually stayed downstairs in his room.

Larry Jr. maintained his grip on my arm, but I could tell by his snide expression that he was going to turn his attention toward Chris. He gave me a final squeeze before shoving me aside. "Da . . . da . . . what does the retard want? Shouldn't the retard be hiding in his little room?" Larry said mockingly.

Chris was the first person I had known who had cerebral palsy. I could see the pain in his eyes. I knew what it was like to be ridiculed, and I hated it. I also knew Larry's sole pleasure was to hurt Chris's feelings. Chris inched his way toward Larry until he stood toe to toe in front of Larry's face. Larry fluttered his eyebrows as he cocked his right arm up and back. I could almost imagine Larry striking Chris and smashing his teeth. Without thinking I yelled, "No! Stop it! Just stop it!"

Larry Jr. swung his arm toward Chris, but at the last moment he brushed his hand through his hair. "Psych!" Larry sneered. "Hah! It doesn't take much to fool a couple of morons, does it?"

I could feel my body temperature rise. "Go to hell!" I yelled.

Larry's eyes grew wide. "Oh, so Momma's little boy has a mouth. I'm *sooo* scared. I tell you what, runt," Larry snarled, as he pushed me against the kitchen countertop, "Why don't you make me?"

I knew by the size of him that he could snap me like a twig. I didn't care. "Back off, man," I blurted. "I'm tired of you. Just because you're older and bigger . . . that doesn't give you the right to treat us that way, does it? How would you like it if someone picked on you?"

For a moment Larry seemed to be in a daze. Then he shook his head clear. "And who do you think you are—Dr. Spock?" I stopped for a second, thinking of what Larry had just said. *Spock? Did he mean the Vulcan dude from* Star Trek? I asked myself.

"If I were you," Larry continued, "I'd stick to my own business and ride my little bicycle. Otherwise," he added with a wide grin, "I might use your little face to mop the floor."

I lost control. I wanted to climb up his legs and beat his face. I ran up to Larry. "I'm tired of taking crap from guys like you. You . . . you . . . butt head! You think you're so big. You're a creep . . . a bully. You ain't . . . you ain't shit. You're *so* tough, aren't you? Like it really takes a tough guy to pick on someone like Chris. You wanna take a punch? Okay, come on, do it! Show me what you got. Come on tough guy! Well . . . ?"

I could feel my fingers coil. I knew that what I was doing was wrong, but after all the years of being put down by others who *felt* they were so superior, I had had it. And seeing how Larry Jr. treated Chris made my blood boil. I had to do something.

As I felt my breathing become heavier, I could tell I was getting to Larry. His face became tight as I badgered him relentlessly. For once, I was on the giving end. I liked the feeling. Larry's face twisted from side to side until he elbowed me against the kitchen countertop. I felt my head strike something hard, but my anger kept the pain away.

Before Larry stormed out of the kitchen, he raised his fist at Chris. "Hey, man, you better watch yourself, or one of these days you may find yourself getting tripped down the stairs and breaking that retard neck of yours. And know this: it's going to take someone more than this excuse of a wimp to fight your battles!

"And you!" Larry stopped as he looked at me. "You better watch that mouth of yours. If I wanted to . . . I could clean your clock . . . just like that!" he boasted, as he snapped his fingers. "Both of you, stay the hell outta my way. You got me? You pair of freaks!"

I clamped my hands on the countertop until I heard Larry slam the door to his bedroom so hard that the windows upstairs rattled. After a few seconds, I finally released my grip. I closed my eyes as I tried to control my breathing. It seemed to take me forever to breathe normally again.

I opened my eyes and searched for Chris. He had disappeared. As I ran out of the kitchen and into the living room, I heard the door to Chris's room slam shut, too. I raced downstairs and quickly knocked on Chris's door before I burst in. He sat on the foot of his bed, staring at the floor. Tears rolled down his face. I tilted my head to one side. "Did Larry hit you?"

"Na . . . ah . . . no! I ca . . . can take ah . . . care of myself, you know! I don't need a li . . . little runt to . . ." Chris stuttered.

"Man, what are you talking about?" I asked. "Larry is the biggest creep on the planet. I'm tired of him picking on me and you all the time."

Chris's head shot up. "You ah . . . just bet . . . better take care of yourself. Ah . . . you can get into a lot . . . of . . . of trouble. If Mom . . . ah ever heard you ah . . . swear . . . swearing . . . she'd . . ."

I brushed Chris's statement away with my hands as I watched him limp his way to his stereo. He grabbed a thick, red cartridge, then shoved it into a tape machine he called an eight-track player. I had never seen one before. After a couple of clicking sounds, a singing group called Three Dog Night began to wail "Joy to the World." As Chris's worn-out speakers vibrated, I sat next to him on his bed. I realized that what I had done upstairs was wrong. "Hey man," I told Chris, "I'm sorry. I was just ticked off." Chris indicated that he forgave me. I smiled back. "Hey Chris, what does Larry mean when he says he'd 'clean my clock'?"

Chris laughed as drool escaped the side of his mouth. "Ee . . . ah . . . means he'll kick your butt!"

"But why does he pick on you? You never do anything to him. I don't understand."

Chris's eyes shone. "Ah man, you are ah . . . fun . . . funny. Look at me. He don't need a reason. People like Larry pick ons me 'cause I'm . . . I'm ah diff . . . different. You're . . . ah different, too. You's small and gots a big mouth."

I leaned back on Chris's bed as he went on to explain that his real parents had abandoned him as a small child and he had lived in foster care ever since. He told me that he had been in over a dozen foster homes until he moved in with Rudy and Lilian. The Catanzes were the closest thing to a real home for him. I listened carefully as Chris talked. In a way, his stuttering reminded me of myself just a few months ago. But Chris seemed scared. Behind his eyes he looked frightened. Chris informed me that this was his last year in foster care.

"What does that mean?" I asked, as the tape cartridge changed tracks.

Chris swallowed hard, trying his best to concentrate before he answered. "Uhm . . . it . . . ah means that when you turn uh . . . 18, you . . . move out and have to ah . . . to take care of yourself."

"And you're 17?" I asked.

Chris nodded.

"Then who's going to take care of you?"

Chris glanced down at the floor. He rubbed his hands together for several seconds. At first I thought that maybe he had not heard me, but when he looked back up at me, I realized why he was so scared and why he had been crying.

I nodded in return. Now I understood.

After my argument with Larry Jr., I kept to myself and tried to stay as far away from him as I could. But whenever no one was around and I found myself running into him, for no reason I'd blurt out feelings of hatred at him. Sometimes he'd simply swear, while other times he'd chase me around the home. Larry would always catch me and tackle me to the floor. Once, after punching me a few times in the arm, he yelled, "Say 'uncle'!"

I didn't understand. I twisted from side to side, trying to squirm myself out from under Larry as he sat on top of my chest and continued to hit me. "No way!" I yelled back.

After a few minutes I could see the sweat pour from his forehead. "Say uncle! Say it!" Larry panted. "Give up, man!"

Even though I was exhausted from struggling to get away, I felt that I was wearing Larry down. "No way! You ain't my uncle. Now get off!"

Larry let out a laugh as he rolled off me. Without thinking, I laughed, too. He patted me on the back. "You okay, kid?" I nodded. "I'll say one thing for you, runt: you got a lot of nerve. You never give up," he said, still panting. "But you are the most craziest son of a . . ."

Suddenly I sprang up and shoved Larry on the floor with all my might. I pointed my finger at him, and he seemed dazed by my actions. "I'm not crazy! And don't you ever, *ever,* say that to me again!" I screamed, as I burst into tears.

From below I could hear Mrs. Catanze close the front door. I fixed my eyes on Larry as long as I dared, before hiding in my bedroom.

"What's going on now?" Lilian asked with a huff. "Are you two fighting again? I tell you, I've about had it with the both of you."

"Mrs. C., it ain't me, but the runt," Larry said in a low voice. "He ain't right. I mean, he's loony toons, man. I was just playing with him, and he went off on me."

I turned away from the door and cried.

I didn't know why I was so stupid. I had tried so hard to understand what the other foster kids were saying so I could learn—so I could be accepted within the group of the older kids. I wanted so badly to be liked. But I still couldn't comprehend. *Maybe,* I told myself, *I am a moron. Maybe I* am *crazy.*

I turned when I heard a faint tapping on the door. I quickly wiped my nose with the sleeve of my shirt before opening the door. "Can I come in?" Mrs. Catanze said with a bright smile. I nodded my head yes.

"So, you and Larry were at it again?" she asked.

I nodded my head again, but more slowly.

"Well, what do you think we ought to do?"

I closed my eyes as tears rolled down my face. "I just don't know why I feel so bad," I cried.

Mrs. Catanze wrapped her arms around my shoulders. "Not to worry. This is something we'll just have to work through."

A few days later Rudy and Lilian drove me to a doctor's office. Rudy stayed in the blue Chrysler as Lilian walked me to the office. She and I waited for several minutes until an elderly woman directed Lilian into another room. After a few minutes Lilian returned. She knelt down and told me I was going to see a special doctor who was going to make me feel better "up here," Lilian said, as she pointed to my head.

Moments later, I followed the same lady who had escorted Lilian. She opened a wide door and waved her hand as if telling me to enter. As carefully as I could, I walked into the room. The lady closed the door behind me. I stood alone in a dark room. I searched for an open window, but I could tell that the shades were drawn. The room had an eerie feeling. I remained standing in the middle of the room for several seconds until a man, whom I hadn't seen when I came in, told me to sit down. I jumped when I heard the stranger's voice. The man flicked on the light on his desk. "Come on now, sit; sit down." I obeyed, finding an oversized chair. I sat and stared at the man. I waited for him to say something, anything. *Am I in the right room, the right office? Is he the doctor? Surely he can't be a psychiatrist!*

Seconds turned into minutes. Though I tried, I could barely make out the outline of the man's face. He rubbed his two hands together as he appeared to study me. My eyes darted from side to side. I could see there was a long couch against the wall behind me. The other walls of the room were covered with shelves filled with books.

As the man continued to stare at me from behind the desk, I began to fumble with my hands. I couldn't take it any longer. "Excuse me, sir, are you the psychiatrist? Do you want me to lay down on the couch, or is it okay to sit here?" I asked in a broken voice.

I could feel my words trailing off as I waited for some sort of response from him. He folded his hands. "Why did you ask that question?" the man asked in a flat voice.

I bent my head down so I could hear better. "Sir?" I asked.

The man cleared his throat. "I said, why did you ask that question?" he said, emphasizing every word.

I felt about 10 inches tall. I didn't know what to say. It seemed to take forever before I replied, "I dunno."

In a flash, the man picked up a pencil and began to scribble on a piece of paper. A moment later the pencil disappeared. He smiled. I smiled back. I knew my last statement was a dumb one, so I tried to think of something clever to say. I wanted the man to like me. I didn't want him to think I was a complete idiot. I nodded my head with confidence. "Kinda dark in here, huh?"

"Really?" the doctor immediately began to write again, at a frantic pace. I then realized that whenever I said anything, the man—the doctor, I assumed—would record everything.

"And why did you ask that question?" the doctor asked.

I thought very carefully before I answered. " 'Cause . . . it's dark," I said, searching for approval.

"And you are afraid of the dark—yes?" the doctor said, as if finding his own answer.

Crazy, I said to myself. *He thinks I'm crazy.* I squirmed in my seat, not knowing how to reply. I began to rub my hands. I wished Mrs. Catanze would burst through the door and take me away.

A long stretch of silence followed. I felt I'd be better off not digging my grave any deeper. I looked down at my moving fingers. The doctor cleared his throat. "So, your name is Daniel?"

"David, sir. My name is David," I proudly stated, as my head snapped forward. At least I knew my name.

"And you are in foster care, is that correct?"

"Yes . . . sir," I answered slowly, as I began to think about where his questions were leading.

"Tell me, why is that?" the doctor asked, as he folded his hands behind his head and looked up at the ceiling.

I was not sure of the question. "Sir?" I asked, sounding hollow.

The doctor tilted his head toward mine. "Tell me, young David, why is it that you are in foster care?" he asked with irritation in his voice.

The doctor's question was like a punch in the face. I felt creepy all over. I did not mean to make him mad, but I just did not understand his questioning. "I . . . uh . . . I dunno, sir."

He picked up his pencil and began to tap the eraser on top of his desk. "Are you telling me that you have no idea why you are in foster care? Is that what you are telling me?" he asked as he made more notes.

I closed my eyes, trying to think of an answer. I could not think of the right response, so I leaned close to the doctor's desk instead. "Whatcha writing, sir?"

The doctor flung his arm on his desk, covering his notes. I could tell I had upset him. I sat rigid in the back of the seat. He fixed his eyes on mine. "Perhaps I should set the ground rules. *I* ask the questions. *I* am the psychiatrist. And *you*," he said, pointing his pencil at me, "are the patient. *Now*, do *we* understand each other?" He nodded his head as if telling me I should agree and smiled when I returned his nod. "So," he said in a kinder voice, "tell me about your mother."

As I cleared my thoughts, my mouth seemed to hang open. I felt so frustrated. Maybe I wasn't so smart, but I didn't think that I deserved to be treated like an idiot. The doctor studied my every expression as he took more notes. "Well," I began, as I fumbled for words, "my mother . . . I really don't think . . . she was . . ."

He cut me off with a wave of his hand. "No! In here *I* perform the analyses, *you* answer the questions. Now tell me, why did your mother abuse *you?*"

I let out a deep sigh. My eyes scanned behind his desk. I tried to imagine what was behind the window blinds. I could hear the sounds of cars rushing past the building. I imagined Rudy, sitting in his Queen Mary-sized car, listening to the radio station that played oldies. . . .

"Young man? Daniel! Are you with me today?" the doctor asked in a bellowing voice.

I lurched deeper into the back of the chair, ashamed that I was caught daydreaming in the presence of a doctor. I felt ashamed for acting like a little kid.

"I asked you, *why* did your mother abuse *you?*"

Without thinking, I snapped back. "How do I know? *You're* the doctor. You figure it out. I don't understand you . . . your questions . . . and every time I try to answer them, *you* cut me off. Why should I tell you about me when you don't even know *my name?*"

I stopped to catch my breath, when I heard a buzzing sound. The doctor pushed a button, picked up the phone, nodded, then put the phone back down. He waved his hand in front of me as he jotted down another note before saying, "Would you hold that thought for me? That's all the time we have for this week, and I'll . . . let me see . . . I'll pencil you in for next week. How's that sound? I think we have a real good start here, Daniel, okay? So I'll see you next week. Good-bye now," he said, with his head bent over his desk.

I gazed at him in total disbelief. My mind was so jumbled that I didn't know how to react. *Is this the way a session normally goes with a psychiatrist?* I asked myself. Something was wrong, and I felt that that something was me. I sat motionless for a few moments, then slid out of the chair and walked to the door. As I opened it, the doctor muttered for me to have a nice day. I turned around and smiled. "Thank you, sir," I said in a cheerful voice.

"Well," Mrs. Catanze said, "how did it go in there?"

"I dunno. I don't think I did too well. I think he thinks I'm dumb," I said, as Lilian led me back to the car. "He wants to see me next week."

"Well then, you must have made a good impression. Relax; you worry too much. Come on now, let's go home."

I slid into the backseat of Rudy's car. I became lost as the streets signs streaked by. I felt more upset than I had before. I wanted to tell Lilian how I felt, but I knew if I did, my words would come out wrong and I would make a fool of myself in front of her and Rudy.

Lilian broke my concentration. "So, how do you feel?"

I crossed my arms tightly across my chest. "Confused," I announced in a firm tone.

"Well," she said, as she tried to find the right words to make me feel better, "these things take time."

My next session was just as bizarre.

"Today, let's begin our session by telling me . . . Daniel, how did you feel when your mother abused you? I understand that at one time she . . ." The doctor flipped through an open file that I had figured was on me. He began to mumble to himself until he closed the folder. "Yes," he stated to himself. "You were eight years old when your mother . . ."—he put on his glasses as he began to read a paper from the file—". . . held your arm, your right arm . . . ," he nodded again, but at me, ". . . over a gas stove. Is that correct?"

A bomb exploded inside my stomach. My hands began to twitch. Suddenly my entire body felt like rubber.

I stared at his facial movements as he casually replaced the sheet of paper on his desk—a paper that contained the most horrible parts of my life. *Scribbled on that sheet is my life—my life, which the great doctor holds in his hands—and he still doesn't even know my name! My God!* I yelled to myself. *This is nuts!*

"Daniel, why do you think your mother burned you that day? You do remember that incident, don't you . . . Daniel?" he paused for a moment.

I stroked my right forearm as I felt myself hovering in time.

"Tell me," he added, "how do you feel toward your mother?"

"David," I said in an ice-cold voice. "My name is *David!*" I shouted. "I think she's sick and so are you!"

He didn't even blink an eye. "You hate your mother, don't you? That's perfectly understandable. Express yourself. Go on, tell me. We have to begin somewhere so we can work through these things, problems, in order to . . ."

I lost track of the doctor's voice. My right arm began to itch. I scratched it before I glanced down. When I did, I saw that my right forearm was engulfed in flames. I nearly jumped out of my seat as I shook my arm, trying to put out the fire. I clenched my fist as I blew on the flames. *Oh my God, no! I* screamed to myself. *This can't be happening! Please help me! Please!* I tried to cry out to the psychiatrist. My lips parted, but nothing came out. I could feel the sides of my face flooding with tears as flames of orange and blue danced on my arm. . . .

"Yes! That's it!" the doctor yelled. "Good! Let it out! That's fine, Daniel. Now, Daniel, tell me, how do you feel right now? Are you . . . upset? Do you feel violent? Do you want to take out your aggressions on someone or something?"

I looked at my arm. The fire was gone. As much as I tried, I could not control myself from shaking. I cupped my arm and gently blew on it as if to make myself feel better. I leaned forward to get up, still clutching my right arm. I wiped my face as best I could before I opened the door to leave.

The doctor sprang up from behind his desk. "All right, you can leave early. We've made progress today. Don't let this upset you. I'll pencil you in for next . . ."

Slam! I closed the door with all my might.

In the outer office, the elderly receptionist jumped from her seat. I stopped by her desk for a moment. The woman seemed as if she were about to scold me, until she took a long look at my face. She stopped mid-sentence and turned away as she seized the phone. The next patient turned his head, too, as I marched out of the office.

By accident I slammed the door to Lilian's car. She flung her paperback book into the air. "David! What . . . ? You're early. Is everything all right?"

I clenched my two hands together. "No! No! No!" I yelled. "That man," I pointed my finger at the building across the street, "is sick! He asked me the weirdest questions. Today he asked me how I felt when . . ."

"Well, David," she said in a firm voice, "that's his job. He's the doctor. I'm sure he's only trying to help. . . ."

"No!" I blurted, as I shook my head. "He doesn't ask questions like you or Ms. Gold, but sick ones. Like, *what did it feel like to be burned on a gas stove?* And that *it was all right to hate my mother*," I said, imitating the doctor's tone of voice. "I don't know what to say or do around him. He's weird. He's the one who needs help, not me. He's the sick one."

"Is that the reason why you were so upset last week? Did he treat you like that last time?" Lilian asked.

I nodded. "I just don't know. I feel so dumb, so small. I mean, I know what happened with Mother, and I was wrong and I'm really trying to forget all about it. I mean, maybe my mom's sick. I know it's the booze, but I have to know: Am I sick, too? Am I going to end up like her? I just want to know. I just want to know why it all happened the way it did. We were the perfect family. What happened?"

After I blew off my steam, I stretched out in the passenger seat. Lilian leaned over. "All better now?"

"Yes, ma'am," I answered. She started the car. I could feel myself drifting off to sleep. I held my right arm just above my wrist. I strained myself to stay awake a little bit longer. "Mrs. C., I don't ever want to go back there—ever," I said. And then my world went black.

I stayed by myself in my room for the next few days. Then Big Larry asked if I wanted to watch him bowl. I happily accepted, and once again my big foster brother and I set out for another adventure. I found out our destination as we rode our bikes through nearby Daly City. Larry and I rode down the small street that led into the parking lot of Thomas Edison Elementary School. Slowing my bike, I watched as the children played on the swing sets. I skidded to a stop, breathing in the smell of fresh tanbark. It seemed like a lifetime ago that I was a child who happily played in the same play yard during recess.

A heavy fog seemed to hover over the school before it lowered itself. The outline of the children became lost as the gray mist seemed to swallow them, too. After a few minutes, only their sounds of laughter told me that the children were even there.

I shook off the thoughts of my past as I pumped my bike up another hill and away from my old school. About 10 minutes later, Larry and I stopped at the Sky Line grocery store—the same store I had stolen from when I ran from the school during my lunch recess. I stayed close to Larry's side. I thought for sure someone would recognize me. "Are you okay?" Larry asked as we strolled down the aisles.

"Yeah," I answered in a low voice. My eyes darted around every corner. I walked in slow motion and grabbed Larry's belt to tell him to slow down. I was on Mother's turf now.

"Hey man, what's your problem?" he asked after my last tug.

"Shh. I used to live here," I whispered.

"Really? Cool," Larry said, as he chomped on a fruit pie as we were walking outside the store. "Is that why you acted funny at that school?"

"I . . . I guess so," I answered.

After Big Larry finished two more cream pies, a few candy bars and two sodas, we set off to the bowling alley. The ride up Eastgate Avenue became too much for me. I hopped off my bike and stared down the street as I walked past. "Stop!" I barked without warning.

From behind me Larry was panting like a dog. "What's up?"

"Do me a favor," I said. "Let's take a break and ride down this street."

A cloud of mist escaped his mouth. "Yeah, okay. What gives?" he asked.

"You promise not to tell?"

"Yeah man, what's up?"

"Don't tell . . . but I used to live on this street."

Larry's head swiveled to the street sign. "Cool! Which house?"

"The dark green one. On the left side, in the middle of the block," I said, as I pointed down the street.

"Hey, man, I don't know about this," he said, shaking his head. "Mom would definitely say no. So, no it's not a good idea! What if your mother or your brothers are outside?"

I parked my bike behind a clump of bushes, staying close as I peered down the street. I could hear Larry stumbling behind me. My heart raced. I knew that what I was doing was wrong and dangerous. "If you decide to accept this mission . . ." Larry whispered, as if we were both working on an assignment from *Mission: Impossible*.

"Come on. The coast is clear," I said, giving Larry the high sign.

Larry shook his head. "I don't know about this."

"Come on," I begged. "I've never asked you for anything. Mrs. C. will never find out. Besides, I'll . . . I'll do your chores for a whole week. Okay? Please?"

"Okay, kid. It's your neck."

I jumped back on my bike and kept the pressure on my brake as I slowly rode. No one seemed to be outside. I could see that the garage door to Mother's house was closed. As we approached the green and black house, I let out a shriek of joy. *This is so cool,* I told myself. Suddenly a pair of heads popped up from my brothers' bedroom window. "Shit!" I muttered.

"What's wrong?" Larry asked.

"Just go!" I snapped.

"What?"

"I said, let's go!"

"Hey man, what's the problem?"

"Not now!" I yelled. "Come on! Go! Go! Go!"

I leaned forward on my handle bars and pedaled so hard that I thought my chain would fly off. I skidded to a stop at the bottom of the street. My heart seemed as if it were stuck in my throat. I waited for the garage door to swing open, followed by Mother racing out in her station wagon or my brothers flying on their bikes and chasing after me down the street. I had already calculated several escape routes.

"Did you see that?" I asked.

"See what? Man, what's wrong with you?" Larry asked.

"The window!" I said, still panting as I pointed up the street. "My brothers . . . they saw me!" My eyes stayed fixed on every sound, every movement, from The House.

Nothing happened.

"Man," Big Larry whined, "you got too much of that James Bond stuff in your head. I didn't see nothing. You're just seeing things. Come on, let's go. And remember," Larry said, as he pedaled off, "a deal's a deal."

"Just as long as Mrs. C. don't find out!" I replied, as I tried to catch up.

Hours later I felt a cold chill as Larry and I returned to Lilian's home. "What's up?" I whispered to Larry. He gave me one of his "I dunno" looks.

"Hey," he said, "I'll go upstairs, get a bite to eat and check things out for you, okay?"

I eagerly agreed as I watched Larry from the bottom of the stairs. Suddenly Mrs. Catanze came into view. By instinct I hid in the shadows. "Larry!" she barked. "Get that overstuffed face up here this moment! And you," she pointed her finger down at me, "I can see you! You can wait for me in your room. Now move it! The both of you."

My eyes became the size of silver dollars. I smiled wide, showing my teeth as I pointed at my chest. "Me?" I asked. She returned my smile. I could see that her hands were on her hips. That was the moment I knew I was in serious trouble. I waited in my room and wondered what I may have done. I hadn't stolen any candy from the local stores in the last several days. And Larry Jr. and I were staying out of each other's way. I had no idea what I did wrong.

I didn't have to strain my ears to listen. ". . . you're supposed to be responsible when David's with you. He's just a baby. You've seen what he's like."

"Come on now, Mom. He's 12 years old. He does okay for himself. Besides, we didn't do nothin'," Larry shot back. I still had no idea what Larry and I did wrong.

"No? Then why has David's mother, the Mother Superior, been on the phone with me all afternoon?"

Uh oh, I said to myself as I swallowed hard. From outside I heard the sound of a car door slam shut. I jumped to the window to see Rudy wave at me. I slumped back on my bed, waiting my turn.

"*Mister* Pelzer . . . get your little butt in here, now!" Lilian yelled.

In an instant I sprang up and ran into the kitchen. I knew I was in an interesting position. Even though I was in trouble, it wasn't as though Mrs. Catanze was going to beat me. As I entered the kitchen, I became anxious to see what exactly Lilian had in store for me. This was the first time that I was in what Big Larry had called "The Dog House."

"Tell me," Lilian began, with her hands glued on her hips, "tell me that you didn't convince this walking paramecium over here to drive by your mother's house."

I swallowed hard and again attempted to turn on my charm, flashing Mrs. C. my best smile. "Para . . . ?"

"An insect with no brains! And that's what you're going to be if I don't get any answers!" Lilian spouted.

"What in the Sam Hill is going on here?" Rudy shouted as he entered the kitchen.

"Freeze! Don't either one of you move!" Lilian warned, as she turned to her husband.

Without her knowing, I cupped my hand to my mouth and let out a giggle. I thought her remark about Big Larry was hilarious. I could imagine him with big bug eyes and oversized wings, flying around, trying to find something to eat. I had never seen Lilian get that upset before. And I knew that all I had to do was ride out the storm. *What's the big deal?* I said to myself.

On the other hand, Big Larry looked as if he had just weathered some pretty rough seas.

Lilian marched right up to Rudy, whose eyes darted between Larry and me. "The moron twins—Doofus and Wonder Boy here—took a little ride by his mother's house."

"Jesus!" Rudy exhaled.

I stood in front of the three of them, not understanding the consequences of my actions. *What's the big deal?* I asked myself again.

"I'm sorry," I blurted. "It's all my fault. I asked Larry to do it. All we did was ride down the street. What's the problem?" I asked innocently.

"Well, your mother has been on the phone all afternoon, ranting and raving about you," Lilian said, pointing a finger at me, "terrorizing the streets."

"No!" I shook my head. "She's lying! All we did was ride down the street. We didn't do anything, honest," I said, doing my best to sound calm.

"David," Lilian said as she let out a deep breath, "don't you understand? *You* are not *allowed* to go anywhere near her house, her boys or her."

My hands shot up in the air. "Wait! Slow down. What do you mean,

I'm not allowed?" I shouted, as I tried to get Lilian's attention. But I couldn't stop her; she was on a roll.

"That's only the half of it. Your mother, the sainted Mother Teresa, tells me that if *I* cannot *manage The Boy, she'll* find someone who can!"

My mind fought to sort out the words *allowed* and *manage.*

Lilian bent down. "Don't you ever, ever do that again! You're grounded!"

"Grounded?"

"That's right, you're grounded until . . . until I decide to unground you!" Lilian finished with a huff before I could ask her what she meant.

Larry stood in disbelief. "Man, I told you that was a bad idea."

"So . . . ? That's it?" I asked. I knew Lilian was mad, but I expected . . . well, I didn't know what to expect. *This I can handle,* I told myself.

As Big Larry wiped his forehead, Lilian marched back in the kitchen. "Wipe that smirk off your face, Wonder Boy," she said as she looked at me. "I forgot—your father's coming over tomorrow morning at 7:00, so you'll have to get up early. You can *manage* that, can't you?" Lilian asked with a sly smile.

"Yes, ma'am. I can *manage,"* I replied in a sheepish tone.

"And you!" she yelled as she turned her attention to Larry. "Go to your room!"

Larry shrugged his shoulders. "Oh, Mom, do I have to?"

"Move it!" Lilian barked.

Once Larry left the kitchen, Lilian wiped her eyes. "Come here and sit down. Now listen very carefully. Your mother . . ." She stopped to clear her throat. "David, I've been taking care of kids since I don't know when. I have never, ever met anyone as cold as your mother."

"You're telling me!" I interrupted.

"David, this is not the time to act funny. You have to understand something: You're a foster child. *A foster child.* And because of that, you've got two strikes against you. You have to be careful of everything you say and everything you do. If you get into trouble, we . . . we could lose you."

I knew by the seriousness of her tone that what she was telling me was important. But I simply could not understand the message.

Lilian nodded, indicating she was again talking over my head. "David, if you get into trouble, you could end up in the hall—juvenile hall. That's where they send foster children who end up in trouble. It's a place you never want to end up. I don't know what your mother's up to, but *you*, young man, better learn how to *manage* yourself a little better. Otherwise you'll be grounded—for a year." Lilian patted my knees and then walked out of the kitchen.

I knew that she was using Mother to scare me. I also knew that Mother could never get to me, now that I was in foster care . . . *could she?*

"Hey, Mrs. C.," I shouted, "what's *grounded*?"

"Oh, don't you worry. You'll soon find out," Lilian laughed, as she strolled down the hall and into her bedroom. *"You'll manage!"*

That evening I thought long and hard about what Lilian had told me. After Rudy and Lilian left for dinner, I had an overwhelming urge to call Mother. Strangely, I just wanted to talk to her, to hear her voice. I picked up the phone several times, but I couldn't bring myself to dial her number.

I wiped away my tears as Connie bounced into the kitchen. "Hey, what's up?"

I broke down and told her what I was trying to do. Without a word, Connie took the phone and dialed my mother's number. Moments later I nearly choked as I heard the recording that Mother's number was ". . . no longer in service." Connie persisted and called the operator, who confirmed the number was now unlisted.

I stood in front of Connie not knowing what to say or do. I didn't know how I should feel. I knew that Mother had changed her telephone number as a form of another "game"—I was not *allowed* the privilege of *her* number.

After Connie's date came to pick her up, I sat down and stared at the television. I had never been alone in the house before. I counted the hours until Father would pick me up the next morning. I drifted off to sleep as I watched the black-and-white snowflakes dance across the TV screen.

The next morning I stumbled out of bed as I rubbed my eyes, then made my way over to the bedroom window. I turned and looked behind me. I didn't remember how I got to bed. After I put on my best clothes and washed my face, twice, I ran to the living room window. I stood tall as I waited for Father.

After a few minutes my shoulders became sore, but I remained rigid as the clock in the living room struck 7:00. At 7:35 I heard the distinctive sounds of Father's borrowed VW. I allowed myself a smile after making sure my hair was just right. I could see an off-brown VW struggle as it made its way up the street. But the car continued to drive by. *Well, maybe he doesn't have the right address,* I told myself. *He'll be back in a few seconds.*

At 7:55 I heard the sound of another VW Bug go past Lilian's home.

I then convinced myself that I had heard the wrong time—that Father would pick me up at 8:00, not 7:00; that I had made another mistake. *Whoops, stupid me!* I said to myself.

Eight o'clock came and went, as did more than a dozen cars that cruised by. As every car drove up the street, I knew in my heart that the next car had to be the one with Father in it.

Around nine o'clock Lilian yawned as she stumbled into the kitchen. "David, are you still here?" I merely nodded. "Well, let me check the calendar. I know your father said 7:00 A.M. sharp. For goodness sake, I wrote it down."

"I know, Mrs. C.," I said, trying not to show my feelings. "He'll be here any . . ." My head spun to the window when I heard the rumblings of another VW lurch its way up the steep street. "See? Here he is!" I cried out, as I pointed at the window. I grabbed Lilian's hand. I wanted to show her off as Dad pulled into the driveway. "Yes!" I shouted.

The car slowed for a moment, but only to shift into a lower gear before chugging its way past. My hand fell from Lilian's grip. She looked at me as if she wanted to say something to make me feel better.

My insides felt tight. A solid lump was caught in my throat. "Don't say it!" I yelled. "He'll be here! I know he will! You'll see! My dad will be pulling up here any second! You watch! My father loves me! And one of these days we're going to live together and . . . and we'll be happy for the rest of our lives. I know *she* doesn't love me, but my dad does. *She's* the one who needs a psychiatrist, not me. *She's* the sick one. . . ."

My chest seemed to shrink as I continued to ramble on. I felt a firm grip on my shoulder. I clenched my right fist, spun around and swung wildly. As my eyes focused on my target, I tried to stop. But I couldn't. A moment later I struck Rudy, square in the forearm.

I looked up with tears in my eyes. Rudy had never seen me act like that before. In an instant I wanted to apologize, but I couldn't. I was tired of being sorry for everything—for not understanding words or phrases; for feeling so humiliated by Larry Jr. and the crazy psychiatrist; for riding my bike down a street; or for just trying to hear my mother's voice. And then I was telling myself that *I* was the one who got the time wrong for when Father would drop by!

I had known all along that Father wasn't coming; that he was probably lost in some bar. He never made it for a visit. But I had always told myself that this time was going to be different, that today Father was going to make it and we would have such a good time.

I just could not accept the realities of my life. *How in God's name did I let it come to this?* I asked myself. I knew, as I stood staring out the living room window, that I would spend another day hiding in the only place I felt safe and warm—the covers of my bed.

I looked up at Rudy and then at Lilian. I wanted to tell them both how sorry I was, how bad I felt inside. I opened my mouth. Before I could say the words, I turned away. As I marched into my room, I could hear Rudy whisper to Lilian, "I think we have a serious problem."

CHAPTER
6

The Defiant One

A few weeks before I started the sixth grade, I began to turn off my feelings. By then I was completely drained of emotion. I had become fed up with the teeter-totter effect of my new life. On the up side, I was elated to play in the bright rays of the summer sun. On the down side, I dreaded being teased by other children or having to wait like a trained dog for the remote possibility of a visit from Father. I was fully aware that a cold change was taking place inside of me. I did not care. I told myself that in order to survive, *I* had to become so hard so that *I* would never allow anyone to hurt *me* again.

At times, instead of riding to the park, I would journey to the local grocery store and stuff my pockets full of candy that I would steal. I didn't even want the sweets; I knew I could never eat all those candy bars. I stole to discover if I could get away with it. I felt a gut-wrenching thrill of calculating my next move, followed by the spine-tingling sensation of strolling out of the store uncaught. Sometimes I'd steal from the same store two or three times a day. Whatever I did not smuggle into Mrs. Catanze's home, I'd give away to kids in the park, or I would leave the candy in small piles just outside the store's entrance.

When swiping candy became too boring, I raised the stakes by stealing larger objects—toy models. I became so arrogant that several times I would simply strut into the store, snatch an oversized model and stroll right out—all in less than a minute. Some of the kids from the neighborhood who had heard of my candy giveaways would follow me to the stores and watch me. I loved the attention. It got to the point where the kids would dare me to steal things for them. My only concern was for acceptance. It was almost like the days when I would play with the younger foster children at Aunt Mary's home. I felt so good inside whenever the kids would call my name or greet me as I rode into the play park. Now I was receiving the same kind of attention again.

Whenever I decided to steal a serious item, I became extremely focused inside. Before making my move I would imagine every aisle and the entire layout of the toy shelves. I plotted my primary and alternate routes of escape. In the event that I was caught, plan number one called for an "off-the-cuff" lie, while plan number two meant that I would simply run like hell.

One time, as a group of kids waited outside the store, I turned myself off, once again becoming a cyborg—half human, half machine. My mission: grab and go. Johnny Jones wanted a B-17 Flying Fortress model airplane. I accepted the challenge, taking three deep breaths before grabbing the glass door and pulling it toward my chest. I could hear the boys cheering me on, but I shut them out as the door closed behind me. I knew that somewhere in the store Johnny was watching. He wanted to see my bravery in person. I didn't care. I had an objective to accomplish.

In order not to be noticed by the string of checkout clerks, I walked down the first aisle leading to the back of the store. I then swiveled right and slowed my pace. By then my ears had become like radar, distinguishing between the sounds of the shoppers and the store employees. I slowed my pace before I turned right again and bent my head down to see if anyone was behind me. The coast was clear. My heart was racing as my objective came into view on the top shelf of aisle 4. I knew this job was going to be a challenge. For a split second something didn't feel right. I thought of aborting. *Negative,* I told myself a second later. As I reached up with both hands, I could hear, then feel someone walking up the aisle. I shook the thought clear as I strained my legs to reach a little higher. A moment later I plucked my prize from the shelf. I showed no emotion as I marched down the aisle, passing Johnny, who was grinning from ear to ear.

My chest was beating like a drum. *Now the hard part.* Just in front of me was the door to victory. Ever so slightly, I dipped my head and listened for anyone behind me or someone shouting for me to stop. The delicate moment had arrived. My face became tight as I reached out to push the door open, just enough to allow me to slide out so in case someone had followed me, that person would have to spend the extra time and effort of pushing the door open-providing me an additional chance of sprinting away. I smiled to myself, knowing that I had thought of everything.

Behind the glass door, I could hear the group of boys clapping and shouting for me. Johnny was already outside, his eyes as big as pancakes. I broke my concentration for a moment—but only for a moment—thinking what my latest risk would do for my acceptance among the group. At times in the past, the boys had teased me and played tricks on me in the park. I knew all along that they were taunting me, but I went along with the gags anyway. Any attention was better than none.

I held my head high, smiling as I slid out the door. By then the boys were laughing, and they began to attract attention. I thought I heard the sound of the door swish open from behind me. I started to reach over with my right hand and toss my prize to Johnny, when screams of laughter erupted. Johnny laughed so hard that he had tears in his eyes. I snapped out of my concentration and laughed, too. "David," Johnny howled, "I'd like you . . . oh man, this is just too much!" he giggled. "I'd like you to meet my dad." In an instant my feet transformed into solid blocks of ice. I turned to see a man in a red Walgreens vest with a name tag that read "Mr. Jones—Store Manager."

Mr. Jones snatched the model, then grabbed my shirt. I walked in front of him as he opened the door to the store. As the glass door closed behind me, I turned my head. The group of boys leaned on their bikes and yelled, "Busted!" at the top of their lungs.

"We've had our eye on you for a quite a while. My son told me all about you . . . David."

I closed my eyes, thinking what a complete fool I was. I wasn't sorry for stealing. I knew that what I was doing was wrong and I had accepted that fact. I even knew that my luck would eventually run out. But to be set up by the kid's father! I knew that Johnny himself was swiping candy at the store next to Walgreens. *I should have known better,* I told myself. *I knew they couldn't have liked me for just being another kid.*

About an hour later I returned to Lilian's home. I opened the door and could hear her run from the couch. As I dragged myself up the stairs, she stood with her hands glued to her hips. Her face was cherry red.

I slid into the kitchen chair before Lilian began her fury of questions, statements and past observations on my past behavior. I simply stared through her, nodding when I felt a response was necessary. I tried to convince her that I was indeed sorry. As the words spilled out, they seemed too easy. I knew my heart wasn't in it. Afterward, I plodded off to my room where I lay on my bed, staring at the ceiling. I was grounded for a week. *Big deal,* I told myself.

A few moments after Rudy came home, I stood in front of him. I silently let out a sigh. *Round 2,* I told myself.

"I don't know what it is with you," Rudy began to rave, "but I'll tell you this. I'm not putting up with a thief! I know I've let some things slide by, and I know that Lil's a bit easy on you. I can accept that. I also know you've had some hard times . . . but I'm not going to stand for this anymore—that potty mouth of yours, the fighting, the hitting, the yelling, calls from your mother, slamming my doors around this home. Do you now how much doors cost? Well, do you?"

I shook my head no.

"Well, it's more than you'll ever make. I work hard, and I love you kids. But I don't need your crap. You hear me?" Rudy yelled.

I nodded again, knowing that Rudy knew I didn't care.

"Are you the one who's been stealing my cigarettes?"

My head swung upward. "No, sir!"

"And you expect me to believe you!" Rudy shot back. "If I hear you've caused any more problems . . . I'll send your little butt to The Hill."

My face lit up. *"The Hill?"*

"Oh! Now I have your attention. Ask around." Rudy twirled around. "Ask Larry Junior here. I've driven him to The Hill a time or two, haven't I, Larry?"

Larry Jr., who had been chuckling behind Rudy's back, now put on a serious, frightened face. "Right, Dad," he said in a fearful tone, as he bowed his head.

"I don't want to—you're a bit young—but I'll load that butt of yours in the car and haul you myself. If there's one thing I will not tolerate, it's a liar and a thief!" Rudy huffed, as Lilian approached his side. "And Lil can cry her eyes out, but that's the way it's going to be in this house. Am I clear, young man?"

I nodded.

"Are you too big in the britches that you can't say yes or no?" Rudy barked.

"Yes, sir," I said in a defiant tone. "I understand."

"Then go to your room. You're grounded."

I sat in my room and stewed. *Yeah,* I said to myself, *grounded. Big deal.* I wasn't mad at Rudy or Lilian for yelling at me, or even for being set up by Johnny and the other kids. I was furious for allowing myself to let down my guard. *David!* I yelled at myself. *How could you have been so stupid?* I then jumped off the bed and began pacing the floor, becoming more upset at everything in my life.

That Saturday I put little effort into my chores. I carelessly vacuumed the home and barely removed the dust from the furniture. When the chores were completed, Rudy took Lilian shopping for groceries. All alone, I rocked on Rudy's recliner chair and flipped through the TV channels. I soon lost interest when I realized that the morning cartoons had already been on.

I rolled out of the chair and strolled over to the living room window, staring outside. I thought that maybe Dad would visit me tomorrow. After a few seconds I chuckled to myself, knowing how foolish I was being. Suddenly the blur of a kid whizzing down the street on his bike caught my eye.

Without thinking I ran into my bedroom, emptied my money jar into my hand and grabbed my jacket before trotting down the stairs. I proudly wheeled out my bike and made it a point to slam the door extra hard. I had decided that I was going to run away.

I felt a rush of excitement as the howling wind struck my face, and I pedaled up and down the slopes leading into Daly City and the Serramonte-6 movie theater. Once there I parked my bike and watched James Bond three times in a row before sneaking into the other shows. Later that evening the theater attendant kicked me out so he could close for the day. The reality of my decision began to sink in. As I unlocked my bike, I shivered from the chilling fog that seeped through my clothes. After my stomach growled, I dug into my pocket to count my savings—$2.30. I pocketed the change and turned my hunger off, focusing on shelter instead. To help stay warm I pedaled my bike. Only after I rode past the darkened homes in the neighborhoods did I realize that it was after 11:30 P.M.

Sometime later I rode down the street leading to my old elementary school. I coasted past the play yard, listening to the sounds of the swings sway from the breeze. Afterward, I walked my bike up the seemingly endless hill of Eastgate Avenue. When I reached the top of

Crestline Avenue, just as I had a few weeks before, I hid beside a clump of bushes as I peered down the foggy street.

I couldn't resist riding down the street. I stopped a few houses above Mother's house. A soft yellow light shone through her draped bedroom windows. I wondered whether Mother ever thought about me as I did her. I began to think of how my brothers spent their time at Mother's house. A howling wind blew through my hair. I rolled up the collar of my shirt. I realized that the house I was spying on was not the same home that had entertained an army of children when Mother was a Cub Scout leader, or the same home that had been the most popular home on the block during Christmas season, so many years ago. After Mother turned off her bedroom light, I said a prayer before I coasted down the street to return to the area by the movie theater. That night I fell asleep curled up, shivering underneath an air-conditioning unit.

The next day I spent the entire day in the movie theater and fell asleep to Bruce Lee's *Enter the Dragon.* That evening after the theater closed, I rode up to the local Denny's restaurant, where I salivated as plates of food whizzed by the counter. The manager, who had eyed me for two days now, sat down and talked to me. After a few minutes of prodding, I gave him the Catanzes' phone number. I gulped down a burger before Rudy picked me up in his blue Chrysler.

"David," Rudy began, "I'm not going to badger you. All I can say is, you can't keep acting like this. This is no way to live—for you or for us. You've got to shape up."

Once we arrived at their home, I took a quick bath, then drifted off to sleep as Rudy and Lilian discussed how to handle me.

The next day Ms. Gold made a rare appearance. She didn't seem to be her bouncy self, and I noticed she forgot to give me a hug. "David, what seems to be the problem here?" she asked in a firm voice.

I played with my hands as I tried to avoid looking at Ms. Gold. "How come you never come to visit?"

"David? Now, you know there are lots of other children who, like you, need my help. You understand that, don't you?"

"Yes, ma'am," I said in agreement. I felt guilty taking Ms. Gold's time away from the other children, but I missed seeing her as much as I had before the trial.

"David, Mrs. Catanze tells me that you're having a very hard time adjusting here. Is it that you don't like the home? What's going on inside of you? Where's that cute little boy I knew a few weeks ago, huh?"

I stared at my hands. I was too embarrassed to answer.

After a minute of silence she said, "Don't worry, I know all about the psychiatrist. It's not your fault. We'll find you one who's used to relating with kids. . . ."

"I'm not a kid. I'm 12 years old, and I'm tired of being picked on!" I stated in a cold tone. I had to catch myself before I revealed another side of my personality that, until recently, had never existed.

"David, why are you so upset?"

"I dunno, Ms. G. Sometimes I just . . ."

Ms. Gold scooted closer to me from the other side of the couch. She lifted my chin with her fingers as I sniffled and wiped my nose. "Are you getting enough sleep? You don't look so good. Do you not like it here?"

"Yes, ma'am," I nodded. "I like it here a lot. Mrs. Catanze is real nice. It's just that sometimes . . . I get scared. I try to tell her, but I can't. There's just so much I don't understand, and I wanna know why."

"David, I know this may be hard for you to swallow, but what you're feeling right now, right this moment, is perfectly normal. If you weren't a little confused or worried, then I'd be concerned. You're perfectly fine.

"*But* what I *am* concerned about right now is your behavior. I know you're a better boy than you've been acting here recently. Am I right? And Mr. Catanze is not very happy with you right at this moment, is he?"

"So I'm okay?"

Ms. Gold smiled. "Yeah, for the most part, I'd say so. We've still got to iron out a few wrinkles, but if I could only get you to modify your behavior, you'd be fine. Now, do you have any questions for me?"

"Yes, ma'am. . . . Have you heard anything from my dad?"

Ms. Gold raised her eyebrows. "Hasn't he been by to visit? He was supposed to have seen you weeks ago," she said, as she flipped through her notebook.

I shook my head no. "I've wrote him some letters, but I don't think I have the right address. I don't get any letters back . . . and I don't have his phone number. Do you know if my dad's okay?"

She swallowed hard. "Well . . . I . . . do know your father's moved into another apartment . . . and he's been transferred to a different fire station."

Tears dribbled down my face. "Can I call him? I just want to hear his voice."

"Honey, I don't have his number. But I promise I'll try to call your father as soon as I can. I'll try to call him today. Is that why you drove by your mother's house and tried to call her a few weeks ago?"

"I dunno," I answered. I didn't dare tell Ms. Gold about cruising by Mother's house the other Saturday night. "How come I'm not allowed to call her?"

"David, what is it you're expecting? What are you looking for?" she asked in a soft tone, as she, too, seemed to search for answers.

"I don't understand why I'm not allowed to see or talk to her or the boys. What did I do? I just want to know . . . why things happened like they did. I don't want to turn into the kind of person she is now. The psychiatrist says I should hate my mom. You tell me what I'm supposed to do."

"Well, I don't believe you should hate your mother, or anyone else for that matter. How could I put this . . . ?" Ms. Gold put a finger to her mouth and gazed at the ceiling. "David, your mother's a wounded animal. I have no logical answer why she changed her telephone number or why she acts the way she does." She drew me to her side. "David, you're a little boy—excuse me, a 12-year-young man—who's a little confused, thinks too much about some things and not enough about other things. I know you must have had to think ahead a great deal in order to survive, but you need to turn that off. You may never find your answers, and I don't want your past to tear you up. *I* don't even know why these things happen to children, and *I* may never know. But I do know that you need to be very careful of what you're doing right now, today, rather than trying to find the answers to your past. I'll help you as much as I can, but you have to really make a better effort to maintain yourself."

Ms. Gold held me for a long time. I heard her sniffle and felt her body shudder. I turned to look up at her—my loving social worker. "Why are you crying?" I asked.

"Honey, I just don't want to lose you," she said, smiling.

I smiled back. "I won't run away again."

"Honey, I can only tell you one more time. You need to be very, very good. I don't want to lose you."

"I'll be good, I promise," I said, trying to reassure my angel.

After Ms. Gold's visit, I returned to my usual joyful self. I felt good inside again. I didn't think about the nutty psychiatrist, I made an extra effort to get along with Larry Jr. and I performed my chores with pride. I did not even mind being grounded. I simply snuck downstairs, borrowed some old car wax and polished my bike from end to end. I kept my room spotless, and waited impatiently for a change of pace and for the start of the school year.

Once school started I kept to myself, as I watched other kids from my class show off their fancy clothes and their colored markers. During recess I strolled out to the grass and watched some of the boys play football. I turned my head for a moment and a second later a football struck the side of my face. As I rubbed the sting on my right cheek, I could hear laughter. "Hey, man," the biggest kid shouted, "throw us the ball." I became nervous as I bent down to pick up the ball. I had never thrown a football before. I knew I couldn't throw a smooth spiral. I tried to imitate the other boys as I sucked in my breath, then flung the ball. The football wobbled end over end before it dived a few feet in front of me.

"What's the matter, man?" a kid said as he picked up the ball. "Haven't you ever thrown a football before?"

Before I could reply, a boy from my class strolled over. "Yeah . . . he's the one I was telling you guys about. Check out the clothes and the shoes, too. He looks like his mother dresses him or something. The kid's a walking dork!"

Without thinking, I spread my arms and examined my outfit. I felt proud of my blue shirt. My pants had a patch on each knee and my Keds sneakers were a little scuffed, but they were still new as far as I was concerned. After inspecting myself I studied the other boys, who all seemed to have better clothes and fancier shoes. Some of them were wearing thick, black turtleneck sweaters. I stared at myself again, feeling ashamed. But I wasn't sure why.

In class I became a nervous wreck whenever I was called on by the teacher. Sometimes I'd stutter in front of everyone. Afterward, the football boys would imitate me as I slid down into my seat, trying to hide from their remarks. During English I'd always write a story about how my brothers and I had become separated and struggled to find each other. I always drew pictures of my brothers and me being separated by either a body of dark water or black jagged cliffs. In every drawing I'd borrow my teacher's crayons and draw big smiles on every face, and a giant happy-face sun that shone above my four brothers and me.

Once while walking home from school, a couple of the football boys teased me about using crayons. I wanted so badly to tell them off, but I knew I'd probably screw that up, too. I ran off, my feelings hurt. Soon I met up with another kid from my class named John. Like me, John stuck out. He had scraggly, long black hair and thin, worn-out clothes. John had a very distinctive walk, and I suddenly realized that no one seemed to pick on him. As I ran up to John, I noticed a cigarette in his hand.

"Hey," John said, "you that new kid in school?"

"Yeah," I replied, feeling proud as we began to stroll along.

"Don't worry about those guys," John said, pointing behind him. "I know what it's like to be picked on. My dad used to beat up on my mother and me. He don't live with us anymore." I quickly zeroed in on his rough attitude. John went on to explain that his parents had just divorced and his mother had to work full-time in order to feed his other brothers and him. I felt bad. At the end of the corner we said good-bye. As I made my way up to Lilian's home, a cold feeling reminded me of how much I had dreaded returning home from school.

I met John the next day in the schoolyard during recess. He seemed extremely upset because our teacher had scolded him in front of the class about not turning in his homework. John boasted to his two other friends and me that he was going to get even with the teacher. He seemed to guard his words as I leaned in closer to hear his plan.

"Hey, man, you're not going to fink on me, are you?"

"No way!" I assured him.

"All right. You see, you have to be a member of my gang to hang around me. I tell you what. You meet us at the parking lot after school. I'll tell you the plan then."

I accepted John's challenge, knowing I was getting into trouble. In class he would always act tough; even the rich football boys stayed away from him. As I daydreamed in class that day, I thought a thousand times about chickening out. I told myself that when the bell rang at the end of the day, I'd stay behind and be the last person to leave. Then I'd sneak around the parking lot, missing the boys. The next day I'd simply tell John that I had forgotten.

When the bell rang that afternoon I flung the lid to my desk open as if I were frantically searching for something. I heard the kids' feet shuffle as they flocked out of the class. When I felt I was safe, I slowly closed the lid to my desk . . . and saw John standing in front of me. I let out a sigh, accepting the fact that I had to go with him. John flipped up the collar of his black vinyl jacket. At the parking lot, John's two friends fidgeted as they, too, tried to look cool.

"This is it," John bragged. "I've decided the new kid here is good enough to join our gang. He's going to flatten the tires of Mr. Smith's new car. And I mean *tires,* as in two or more," he stated as he stared into my eyes. "That way Smith won't be able to use his spare tire. Pretty smart, eh?" John laughed.

I turned away from him. I knew that when I stole candy and toys from the stores, I was wrong. But I had never hurt anyone's personal property before, and I didn't want to now. I could feel the stares around me. I swallowed hard. "Gosh, John . . . I really don't think we oughta . . ."

As John's face turned red, he punched me in the arm. "Hey, man, you said you wanted to be *my* friend and join *my* gang, didn't you?"

Some of them began to close in around me. The two other boys nodded in approval.

"Yeah, man, all right. I'll do it. *But,* after that, I'm in the gang, and I don't have to do anything like this again, *right?*" I said in a broken voice, as fear overtook my weak efforts to sound tough.

John slapped the back of my shoulder. "See, I told ya! The kid's all right!"

I narrowed my eyes and tightened my face. I became cold inside. "Let's do it!" I said in my new macho voice.

John led me to a brand new, light yellow sedan. He nodded at me as he eased himself away from the scene of the crime. The two other boys giggled as they followed their leader.

I let out a deep breath and knelt down, not believing what I was about to do. I could feel my heart race. I wanted to stand up and run away, but I shook it off. *Come on!* I yelled at myself. *Just do it! Come on!*

I scanned the area before I tried to unscrew the cap to the tire stem. After a few seconds my fingers began to tremble, and I still had not removed the rubber cap. I felt as if every eye were on me, as the sounds of other people slamming their car doors echoed above my head.

Finally, the black cap fell onto the ground. Immediately I snatched a pencil from my back pocket. I turned behind me and met John's eyes. His face was tight, and he raised his eyebrows telling me how disappointed he was with my performance. John then mouthed, "Come on, move it!"

I took a quick breath before I jammed the end of the pencil into the stem of the tire. The air seemed to explode as it howled out of the tiny opening. I knew that everyone could hear what I was doing. I hesitated for a second as I searched for John, who nodded for me to continue. A blanket of fear seemed to cover me. *No!* I yelled at myself. *This is totally wrong!* On purpose I snapped the end of my pencil, stood up and walked past John, who dared me to finish the job. I brushed past him as I made my way out of the parking lot. John and the *gang* taunted me all the way down the street, until they turned the corner to John's house.

The next day, John's razzing continued. In the schoolyard, without warning, he shoved me to the ground. As I got up, a small circle formed. "Fight! Fight!" they chanted. I kept my head down as I tried to break through the crowd. A round of insults flew above me.

Within minutes, the entire school seemed to know that I had betrayed John and his gang. I felt a coldness that was worse than the one at Thomas Edison Elementary School.

The next morning, I made a string of excuses to Lilian about how I felt too sick to go to school. I never told her about John or my social problems at school. If I did, I knew Rudy and Ms. Gold would be furious.

After a few weeks of the cold shoulder, I apologized to John *and* his gang. As a way of showing my friendship, I presented John with a carton of Marlboro cigarettes I had stolen the day before. "All right, kid," John smiled. "The boys and I forgive your weakness, *but* you still have to be initiated into our group."

I nodded to myself as my mind replayed all the stories I had heard about John punching and kicking the two other boys of his gang until they fell to the ground. I saw myself with a bloody face, broken glasses and smashed-in teeth. I stared into his eyes, giving him my tough-guy look. "Okay man, I can handle it!" I said smoothly.

"No man," John said as he showed off his unlit cigarette. "I've got something special for you. Listen carefully. I'm tired of Mr. Smith. He thinks he's so tough 'cause he's the teacher. He wrote a letter to my mother, and because of him she's on my ass. So . . . I say . . . let's burn down his class!"

My mouth fell open. "Nah, man, you, ah . . . can't be serious?"

"Hey, I'm not saying you got to do it. I'm just saying I need you to be the lookout for me, that's all. I can't count on those two wusses. They're wimps. But you . . . you've got guts." Suddenly John's voice changed. "And if you ever fink on me, I will stomp all over you." A split second later he changed his tone back again. "Hey man, don't sweat it. I'm not talking about doing it today. Just be there when I need ya. All right?"

"Yeah, man," I nodded. "I'll help you out. I'm cool." I walked away, telling myself that he was just acting tough. *Nobody ever burns down a school,* I assured myself. *But what if he's serious? What should I do?* I couldn't tell Mrs. Catanze and especially not the teachers. But no matter what, I would never turn John in. Not because I wanted to be nice, but because of the fear of being brutalized and living through the humiliation afterward.

I dreaded running into John over the next few days, as he continually renewed his vow that one day soon, *he* was going to teach the teacher a lesson. As the weeks dragged by, I began to think that he was simply showing off to receive attention from anyone who'd listen. At times, whenever a large crowd gathered, I'd brag, too, stating that John and *I* had developed "The Plan" that would show everyone in the school just how tough we were. The more I boasted, the larger the crowds grew. I was amazed at how the kids who had ridiculed me before were now hanging on my every word. After a few days of spinning tales, John's involvement disappeared, as I found myself stating that *I* would be the person who would do the deed.

Weeks passed, and soon I had forgotten about "The Plan"—until one day after school, John had a deep, cold look in his eyes as he ordered me to be back at the school in an hour. I felt a lump creep up my throat. "Okay man, I'll be back," I said, before I could think of an excuse. About an hour later, as I walked back on the school grounds, I prayed that he had chickened out.

The smell of papers burning filled the hallway. I broke into a run as I followed the smoke and made my way to the classroom module. Seconds later I found John bent over a small hole, as black smoke poured out of a kicked-in air vent. I stood in total disbelief. I never thought he'd actually do it.

"John!" I yelled.

John's head shot up. "Jesus, man. Where ya been? Come on . . . help me!" I stood behind him, still unsure of myself. "Come on, man, help me! Help me put out the fire!" he cried.

My brain locked up until I shook my head clear, as smoke continued to escape the open vent. John's face was seized with terror. After a few seconds, he fell backward. "No way, man! It's out of control! I'm outta here! Come on, let's go!" Before I could reply, I saw his shadow disappear down the hall.

I bent down in front of the vent and turned my head, coughing from the dark smoke. A small, red orange fire began to take form. In a flash I grabbed the can of lighter fluid that John had left and pulled it out from the vent. As I withdrew the can, I squeezed it so hard that a stream of fluid ignited, racing from the can and toward my hand, soaking it with the clear fluid. For a moment I thought the tin can would explode—and my right hand with it.

I hurled the can behind me and searched for help. Time seemed to stand still until I finally heard the sound of small shoes skipping across the hallway. A little girl stopped a few feet beside me then gawked. "Get help!" I yelled. "Pull the alarm! Pull the alarm!" The girl threw both hands on her tiny mouth. "Come on!" I ordered. "Move your ass!"

The girl blinked her eyes. "Oh . . . I'm telling," the girl cooed before she broke into a run. A few moments later I heard the clanging sound of the alarm. Using both hands, I scooped up pebbles of gravel and tossed them into the flames. Knowing that fire needed oxygen to grow stronger, I intended to shovel enough gravel to snuff it out.

When I saw that the mountain-sized pile of gravel smothered the flames, I fell backward to watch the wisps of gray smoke that rose. I wiped the sweat from my face with my blackened hands. My head snapped to the right when I heard someone scream, "Over here! The fire's over here!" A feeling of fear crept up my spine. A moment later I sprinted down the street as the screeching sounds of fire trucks pierced my ears and a small fleet of trucks raced by. Out of habit, I waved. A fireman strapped to the end of one of the trucks smiled as he waved back.

The next morning I met John on the corner by his house. We both agreed to deny any involvement in yesterday's fire, and he again stressed his threat to me. "Besides," John said with a wide smile, "you're a member of the gang now. You're vice president."

I felt on top of the world, until I strolled into the classroom. Every head turned my way as my sixth-grade teacher, Mr. Smith, sprang up from his desk, grabbed my arm and led me into the principal's office. "How could you have done it?" my teacher asked. "I would have never expected something like that from you."

Later I sat in front of the principal, who informed me he was going to call the police, the fire chief and my foster parents. I shuddered at the last part of his statement. All I could think of was Rudy's face. "Before you say anything," the principal stated, "you've already been identified as starting the fire . . . ."

"No!" I blurted. "I didn't do it! Honest, sir."

"Really?" the principal smiled. "Fine. I believe you. Show me your hands."

I stuck out my two arms, unsure of the principal's intentions. He leaned over and grabbed my hands. Then he rubbed the stubbles from my burned hairs. "I think I've seen enough," he said as he flung my arms back at me.

"But I didn't do it!" I began to cry.

"Look at yourself. I can still smell the smoke on you. I have statements from teachers claiming that you were the child who's been bragging about this same thing. For goodness sake, your father's a fireman. You don't need to say another thing. The police will be here soon, and you can tell your story to them. You're excused to wait in the other room. *I* have phone calls to make," the principal said, with a wave of his hand.

I closed the door behind me and began to sit down. I could feel the resentment from the elderly secretary. I nodded at her as I took my seat. She gave me an evil glance before she huffed in my direction and turned away. "Foster child! We don't need *your kind!*"

I gripped the arms of the chair and leaped out of the seat. "I know what you think of me! All of you! But know this. *I* didn't do it!" I yelled, as I slammed the door behind me. A moment later I could see the principal fly out of his office, waving his fist at me. Without thinking I ran from the school and didn't stop until I reached the bottom of the hill by John's house. I hopped the fence, hid in his play fort and and waited for him.

"Man, this is too cool! You escaped!" John panted, when he discovered me knocking on his back door hours later.

"What?" I exclaimed.

"Man, the kids in school think the police came to arrest you and you beat 'em up and ran off. Man, this is just too much!" he said, unable to control himself. "Everyone thinks you're so cool!"

"Wait a minute, man! Stop it! Wait up!" I yelled, cutting him off. "The principal thinks I did it. He thinks I started the fire and that I've already been identified. You gotta help me, man. You gotta tell them the truth!"

"Hey man, no way," John said, backing away from me with his hands in the air. "You're on your own."

I shook my head from side to side. Tears were starting to swell in my eyes, but I held them back. "Man, this is serious. You gotta help me. What am I going to do?"

"Yeah man, all right. You can't go home. . . . Tell you what. I'll hide you here until we figure out what to do."

"Okay," I said, trying to relax my heaving chest. "But you gotta tell them what really happened at school." John's mouth quivered. He began to mutter something. In a flash I grabbed his shirt. "Shut up and listen! *You* did it! I didn't! I saved your ass! I put out the fire! You tell 'em the truth! I mean it!" I yelled.

John's tough-guy act melted away. "Yeah . . . all right. Tomorrow, man, okay? Just relax."

That night I shivered on a makeshift wooden bed in John's clubhouse outside. Earlier I had picked up the phone to call Lilian, but I slammed it down when I heard Rudy's stern voice on the other end. "David!" he had said after a long pause, "I know it's you! If you know what's good for you, you'll . . . ."

The next day the hours seemed to drag on as I waited for John's return. When he finally came home, he flung the sliding door open. I ran inside to warm myself. "Okay?" I asked, rubbing my hands. "Everything's all right. You told 'em, right? You told them the truth?" I asked, feeling relieved that the incident was over and I could go back to the Catanzes.

John slumped his shoulders and stared at the floor. I knew even before he spoke that I was doomed. "Man, you promised!" I whimpered.

"Well . . . the principal pulled me from class," he said in a soft voice, as he continued to stare at the floor. He stopped for a moment. I thought he was about to give me another excuse when he looked up and into my eyes and smiled. "I told him . . . you did it. That it was your idea."

My hands began to shake. "You *what? What* did you do?"

John grinned. "What did *I* do? *I* didn't do a thing. Man, you gotta go. You can't stay here," he said in a dry voice.

I was dumbstruck. "Where do I go? What do I do?"

"You should have thought about that before *you* burned the room, man."

My mind tumbled in confusion. "I thought you were my friend," I pleaded, as John turned away.

Moments later I quietly closed the door to his house, then made my way to the local shopping center in hopes of finding food to steal. I jumped in a clump of bushes whenever I heard a car coming. *This is stupid,* I yelled at myself. *I can't live like this.* I turned around and made my way to Rudy and Lilian's home. Taking a deep breath, I opened the door and crept up the stairs, hearing the television set blare above me. As I shuffled into the living room, I was greeted by Larry Jr.'s alligator smile. "He's . . . here!"

Lilian dropped the blanket she was crocheting. "My God, David, where have you been? Are you all right?"

Before I could reply, I could feel the floor vibrate from Rudy storming down the hallway. "Where is he?" he bellowed.

I swallowed hard before I gave my prepared speech, that everything was a simple misunderstanding. That I, in fact, was the one who *put out* the fire, and not the person who started it. I knew Rudy would yell at me for a few minutes and he'd probably ground me for another week for not coming home, but I knew once they understood the truth, everything would go back to normal. I smiled at Rudy, who breathed above me like a dragon. "You're not going to believe this, but . . ."

"You're damn right I'm not!" Rudy roared. "I don't believe anything anymore. In the last two days I've had calls from the school, the police, juvenile probation, your father and that mother of yours. Ever since he stepped foot in this house . . ." Rudy pointed at Lilian before focusing again on me. "I told you to keep your nose clean, and now you go off and do something like this! What in the hell were you thinking about? I can't believe it! Stealing isn't good enough for you? No, you've got to prove yourself, is that it? You say you feel lost, that you don't fit in—well, I know who you are. You're an arsonist! That's what you are! Were you the one who's been setting all those grass fires around here . . . ?"

"My God, Rudy, settle down," Lilian broke in. "He wasn't even here back then."

"Well, I've seen enough. I've heard enough. That's it—he's out of here!" Rudy yelled. Then he shook his head and let out a deep sigh, indicating he was finished.

A long silence followed. He breathed over me while Lilian stayed glued by his side. Up until a few moments ago, I felt I could have cleared up the confusion with a few words, but I suddenly realized it was my past actions that had led Rudy to his conclusion. To him I was guilty, and I knew that nothing I could say would change his mind. I gazed up at Rudy with tears in my eyes. I wanted so much for him to believe in me.

"Those crocodile tears might work on Lil, but they won't do a bit of good with me," he stated.

I cleared my throat before whimpering, "My dad called?"

Lilian indicated yes by nodding her head before tugging on Rudy's sleeve. "Let's put it to bed for now, hmm?"

Rudy turned his frustration on Lilian. "Wake up Lil. For God's sake, we're not talking about snatching another candy bar. He burned a school. . . ."

"No!" Lilian said, cutting him off. "The principal believes there was another boy involved!"

Rudy seemed tired. I could see the dark circles under his eyes. "Come on, Lil, does it matter? He's a foster child. He's been picked up for shoplifting, and his mother's filed bogus police reports against him. Who do you think they're going to believe? That's the bottom line."

Lilian broke out in tears. "Rudy. I know. *I know* he's not a bad child. He's just . . ."

I wanted to hug her and take away all the pain I had caused her.

"Well," Rudy replied in a calmer voice, "Lil, I know he's not half bad . . . but he's got one foot in the grave and the other on a banana peel. He's dug himself a deep grave this time and . . . well . . . ," he said, rubbing his forehead.

"David," Rudy said in a reassuring voice as he held my shoulders, "I know I bark at you quite a bit, and you may think I'm an ogre. But I do care about you; otherwise I would have shipped you out of here a long time ago. You're in some mighty hot water, and there's not a thing I can do. That's why I'm so upset. But no matter what happens, I want you to know that we care for you." He stopped for a moment to rub his eye. He stared down at me and massaged the tops of my shoulders. "I'm sorry, son, but it's out of my hands. Tomorrow I have to take you to Hillcrest." Tears began to trickle down Rudy's face.

CHAPTER 7

Mother's Love

CHAPTER

7

Mother's Love

*A*s Rudy Catanze drove me to San Mateo County Juvenile Hall, I nearly blacked out from hyperventilation. The upper part of my chest felt as if a giant rubber band were tied around it. Even as Rudy gave me his last-minute advice, I couldn't concentrate because I was so terrified of what would happen to me next. The night before, Larry Jr. had been very descriptive about what the bigger, older boys did to the young, soft, puny kids—the "fresh meat." I felt so degraded as I stripped in front of the counselor during my in-processing, spread my butt cheeks before I showered, then put on the stale-smelling "county clothes."

I shuddered when the thick oak door to my cell slammed shut behind me. It took me less than a minute to examine my new environment. The walls were composed of dirty white cinder blocks. The cell had a faded, waxed cement floor. I stuffed my wet towel, change of underwear and socks in the tiny shelf. I sat on the foot of the wall-mounted bed and felt an urgent need to go to the bathroom—when I noticed there was no toilet in the cell. After I covered my head with the black wool blanket, the invisible bands around my chest began to loosen. Moments later I drifted off to sleep.

The first time the door to my cell opened for afternoon recreation time, I walked down the hall as if I were walking on eggshells. The other kids seemed more like giant, walking tree stumps than they did teenagers. In my first few days I developed a plan for survival. I would fade into the background so as not to draw attention and, for once, keep my alligator-sized mouth clamped shut. During my initial week at Hillcrest, six frenzied fights broke out in front of me, three of them over whose turn it was to play pool. I bumped into a few walls as I spent a lot of time with my head bent down for fear of making eye contact, and I stayed the farthest away from the pool table.

I breathed a little easier when I was transferred from the new-detainee section, the A-Wing, to the upstairs C-Wing section that housed the smaller, more hyperactive kids. I learned that the new wing's set of directives were less strict. I didn't feel the need to scurry to my cell, the way I had whenever the staff from the A-Wing turned their backs as the kids were sent to their rooms. The counselors in C-Wing seemed more open, more outgoing when dealing with the kids. I felt safe.

One afternoon I was unexpectedly called from the recreation room. Moments later I discovered I had a visitor. As the counselor instructed me on the visiting procedures, my stomach tightened from excitement. Up until that moment, I did not know I could be seen by anyone, so I wondered who had come all the way to Hillcrest to visit me.

As I burst through the small door, visions of Ms. Gold and Lilian filled my head. A second later my body became limp. Behind the tiny desk, Father sat with his chair against the wall. Besides Mother, Father was the last person I wanted to see while I stayed at juvenile hall.

My hands trembled as I reached for a chair.

"So, David," Father said in an emotionless tone. "How are you?"

"Fine, sir," I replied, as I tried to avoid Father's gaze.

"Well . . . you've grown some. How long has it been?"

"About a year, sir."

My eyes inched up Father's body. I tried to remember the last time I truly looked at him. *Was it when I lived at The House?* I asked myself. Leaning on the small table in front of me, Father seemed so thin. His face and neck were dark red and leathered. His once finely combed hair was now an oily gray. He coughed every few seconds. His hand disappeared into his jacket pocket and fumbled for a pack of cigarettes. He pulled one out and tapped it on the table before lighting it. After a few drags, his hands quit shaking.

I felt too ashamed to look into his eyes. "Uhm . . . Dad, before you say anything . . . I just want you to know . . ."

"Shut up!" Father's voice suddenly cracked like thunder. "Don't even begin to tell me your lies!" He inhaled deeply before smashing his cigarette and lighting another. "For Christ's sake, if they ever find

out about this at the station . . . do you know what this could do to
me? It's not like I don't have enough problems to deal with there!"

I bowed my head, wanting to disappear.

"Well?" Father's voice rumbled. "And if that weren't enough,
you've given that crazy mother of yours all the ammunition she's ever
needed!" He stopped to take another drag. "Jesus H. Christ! You had
it made! Then, out of nowhere, I get call after call from that social
worker lady . . ."

"Ms. Gold?" I muttered.

"I finally make time to give her a call, and she tells me you've run
away and have been stealing and landing yourself into all kinds
of . . ."

"But Dad, I really didn't . . ."

"You had better shut that mouth of yours before I shut it for you!"
Father roared. He stopped for a moment and blew out a cloud of
smoke. "You couldn't let it go, could you? It wasn't enough for you to
involve the police and have them take you away from school, then
drag your mother and brothers into court. Jesus! You're really a work
of art, aren't you? You had everything. A new life, a new start. All you
had to do was keep your nose clean. And you couldn't do that, could
you?

"Do you have any idea what your mother wants to do with you? Do
you?" Father demanded, raising his voice. "She wants me to sign some
papers. She's been after me to sign them for . . . how long . . . do
you know?" he asked, more to himself than to me. "Do you have any
idea how fuckin' long she's been after me to sign those papers?"

I shook my head no, tears rolling down my face.

"Years! Ever since she threw you out that one day. Hell, maybe she
was right all along. Maybe you do need . . . You think it's easy on
me? How do you think it makes me feel to have a son of mine at a
place like that . . . or a place like this?" Father's eyes seemed so cold
as they pierced through me. "Arson. They're charging you with arson!
Do you know how many firemen die because of arsonists? Hell, maybe
she's right. Maybe you are incorrigible."

I watched the orange ring of the cigarette creep its way toward
Father's fingers.

"Well," he said, after several minutes of silence, "I've got to get the
car back. I'll, ah, see . . ." Father stopped mid-sentence as he pushed
himself away from the table.

My eyes scanned his body. His eyes looked so tired and empty. "Thanks . . . for coming to see me," I said, trying to sound cheerful.

"For Christ's sake, boy, keep your nose clean!" Father snapped back. He began to push the door open when he stopped and looked deep into my eyes. "I've given up a lot for you. I've tried; God knows I've tried. I'm sorry for a lot of things in my life. I can forgive you for a lot of things—for all the trouble you've caused, for what you did to the family—but I can never, *never* forgive you for this." The door shut behind him, and he was gone.

"I love you, Dad," I said, looking across the empty table.

That evening at dinner, while a sea of hands fought for any portion of every container of food, I nibbled away at my salad. I felt so sick and hollow inside. I knew I was the reason why my parents were so unhappy, why they had separated, why they both drank so much and why my father—a man who had fought to save so many people's lives—now lived in a crummy apartment. *I* had knowingly, willingly, exposed the family secret. I suddenly realized that Father was right. Father had been right all along.

After dinner, as I performed my work assignment, mopping the dining-room floor, one of the counselors peeked around the corner. "Pelzer. Visitor at the front desk." Minutes later I sucked in a deep breath and closed my eyes before I again opened the door to the visitor's room. I prayed deep inside that Mother had not come.

It took several blinks of my eyes for me to comprehend that it was Lilian's face, and not Mother's, that I was gawking at.

Lilian leaped up and hugged me from the other side of the desk. "So, how are you?" she asked.

"Fine! I'm great now!" I exclaimed, "Wow, I can't tell you how . . . it's so good to see *you!*"

Lilian sandwiched my hands between hers. "Sit down now and listen. We have a lot to talk about, so pay attention. David, has your father come to see you yet?"

"Yes, ma'am," I replied.

"If you don't mind my asking, what did you two talk about?"

I leaned back in my seat, trying to visualize the entire scene so that I could repeat word for word my visit with Father.

"Did your father mention anything about a paper . . . ? Anything at all?" Lilian gently prodded.

"Uhm . . . no. No, ma'am, not that I remember," I said, scratching my head.

Lilian tightened her grip on my hands until it was so hard they hurt. "David, please," she begged, "this is important."

In a flash I recalled Father's frustration about a set of papers Mother wanted him to sign. I carefully attempted to reconstruct Father's words. "He said something about Mother being right and that he was thinking of signing papers saying that I was . . . *in-carriageable?*"

"But he didn't sign them?!" Lilian burst.

"I don't . . . I don't know. . . ." I stuttered.

"Damn it!" she barked. I lowered my head, thinking I did something wrong—again. Lilian looked away from the gray table, then at me. "No! No! It's not you, David. It's just . . . have you heard from your mother? Has she come to see you?"

"No, ma'am!" I stated, shaking my head.

"Listen carefully, David. You do not have to receive a visit from anybody you do not want to see. Do you understand? This is important. When you're told you have a visitor, ask who that person is." Lilian stopped to collect herself. She seemed on the verge of tears. "Honey, I'm not supposed to tell you this, but . . . don't accept a visit from your mother. She's fighting the county to have you put away."

"You mean like to stay here? An institution, right? Oh, I know all about that. It's okay!"

Lilian's face turned snow white. "Where did you hear that?"

"A lady from mental health. She says she works with all the young kids who come here to The Hill. She kept asking me about consent. . . . Yes!" I shrieked. "That's it! The lady said it would be a lot easier for me if I gave my consent for the institution." I knew by Lilian's expression that something was horribly wrong. "Doesn't it mean that by me signing the paper, that I promise, I *consent*, to be on my best behavior while I'm here? Does it, Mrs. C.?"

"David, it's a trap! She's trying to trick you!" Lilian said with panic in her voice. "Listen to me! I'm going to spell it out for you: Your mother is claiming that your past behavior at her house *warranted* her to *discipline* you because you were so incorrigible. She's trying to have you put away in a mental institution!" Lilian exhaled.

I leaned back in my steel chair and stared at her. "You . . . ah . . . mean . . . a crazy home . . . don't you?" I stuttered as my breathing accelerated.

Lilian plucked a tissue from her purse. "I could lose my license as a foster parent, but I don't give . . . I don't care anymore. You can never, ever, repeat this to anyone. I've spoken with Ms. Gold, and we think your mother has somehow cooked up this plan—this institution thing—to somehow validate everything she's ever done to you. Do you understand?"

I nodded yes.

"David, your mother has contacted this lady from mental health and has told her all sorts of things. David, I'm going to ask you a question and I need the absolute truth, okay? Did you ever start a fire at your mother's house, *in the garage of her house?*" Lilian carefully asked.

"No!" I exclaimed. I then curled my fingers into the palms of my hands. "Once . . ."

Lilian gritted her teeth as I continued.

". . . once, when I was four or five, I set the napkins by the candles before dinner . . . and they caught on fire! I swear, cross my heart, I didn't mean to, Mrs. Catanze! It was an accident!"

"Okay, all right," Lilian said, as she waved her hands. "I believe you. But David, she knows. Your mother knows everything. From Walgreens, to running away—even the problem you had with the psychiatrist. Ms. Gold thinks she may have slipped up and told your mother more than she needed to know, but Ms. Gold is required to keep your mother informed about you. Damn it all! I've never seen anyone fight so hard to have their own flesh and blood . . ."

My body temperature shot up. "What do you mean, the problem with the doctor? I didn't do anything!"

"Now, I'm getting this secondhand from Ms. Gold. . . ."

"How come I'm not allowed to see Ms. Gold anymore?" I interrupted.

"Because you have a probation officer now: Gordon Hutchenson," Lilian replied, as she shook her head, trying to remain on track. "Now please, listen. I'm not even supposed to know this, but from what I understand, the psychiatrist wrote a report claiming that you have violent behavior tendencies. He's claiming something about you jumping from your seat, waving your arms and nearly attacking him?" she said, looking more confused than her question sounded.

My head swiveled from side to side. "No, ma'am! He told me I should hate my mother, remember?" I cried as I flung my head backward, hitting the wall. "What's happening? I don't understand? I didn't do it! I didn't do anything!"

"Listen! Listen to me!" Lilian cried. "Ms. Gold thinks your mother's been waiting for you to screw up—and now she has you."

"How can she? I live with you!" I said pleadingly, as I fought to understand how my world could suddenly crumble.

"David," Lilian said with a huff, "Rudy and I are just your legal guardians, that's all. A piece of paper states that we maintain your well-being. We foster you. Legally, your mother has quite a bit of latitude. This is her way of striking back. Your mother has probably been fighting to put you away ever since you were placed in foster care, and this school incident makes her case."

"So now what?" I whimpered.

"Understand this. You're in for the fight of your life. If your mother can convince the county that it's in their best interest, she'll have them put you in a mental institution. If that ever happens . . ." Lilian's face suddenly erupted in a fury of tears. "I want you to know this. I don't care what anybody, *anybody,* tells you. Rudy and I are fighting for you, and we'll do whatever it takes. If we have to hire a lawyer, we'll do it. If we have to go to hell and back, we're prepared to do that, too. We're here to fight for you. *That's why we're foster parents!*"

Lilian stopped for a moment to collect her thoughts. She then began in a low, calm voice. "David, I don't know why it is, but for some reason a great deal of individuals look down on foster care. And these people believe that you children are all bad, otherwise you wouldn't be in foster care. And if they can keep *you* out of *their* society, well, the better for them. You understand, don't you?"

I shook my head no.

Lilian raised a finger to her lips while rethinking her statement. "You know what the word *prejudice* means, don't you?"

"Yes, ma'am."

"It's the same thing. You see, if these same people acknowledge—admit—a need for foster care, that means they are admitting to a bigger problem of what got you kids into foster care in the first place. And that means admitting to things like alcoholism, child abuse, children who run away or get into drugs. . . . You get it? We've made a lot of changes in the last few years, but we still live in a closed society. A lot of folks were raised to keep things to themselves, hoping no one ever finds out about their *family secret.* Some of them are prejudiced, and that's why whenever a foster child gets in trouble . . ."

Her statement hit me like a ton of bricks. Now I understood. The bands around my chest seemed to come alive as I began to wheeze.

"Uhm . . . before . . . when I first came to your house . . . and I got into trouble . . . ?"

"Yes?" Lilian whispered.

"I heard what you said back then . . . but I just didn't listen."

Lilian cupped my hands in hers. "Well, all that's in the past. I know that being here at The Hill isn't easy, especially for you, but you have to be on your absolute best behavior. I mean that," she emphasized. "The counselors write behavior reports on you that are turned in to your probation officer. You've met Gordon Hutchenson, haven't you?"

"Yes, ma'am," I replied.

"Those reports will have a strong impact against your mother trying to place you in an institution. All she has right now is a pack of lies she's been feeding everyone. Your mother has made you out to be some crazed child—which you are, of course!" Lilian joked. "So if we can prove to the court that you did not set the fire and that you've been a model child, this blows your mother out of the water—once and for all."

"So what do I do?" I asked.

Lilian smiled. "David, just be yourself. That's all you have to do. Don't ever try to be someone you're not. The staff here will see through that in a heartbeat. Just be the boy who first came into my house—before you landed in all this hot water. But," she warned, "no mistakes. Don't you fly off the handle when you get upset. You put a lid on that potty mouth of yours. You got me?"

I nodded again.

"David, you've got your head in a noose. Lord knows, one more incident, and you're hung for sure. You've overcome more in 12 years than most folks will ever accomplish in a lifetime. If you can do that . . . you can do this too. But you have to fight a good fight! You do whatever Mr. Hutchenson or the staff here tells you. I don't care how off-the-wall it sounds. I've known Gordon for years, and he's the best. You just think long and hard before you do something you're gonna regret. All right?"

As Mrs. Catanze held my hands, I wanted to explain how sorry I was for all the trouble I had caused her and her family. But I knew I had told her that so many times in the past—when I really didn't care. So, I asked myself, *why would she believe me now?* I peered into her gentle eyes, knowing that I was the cause of her sleepless nights and hours of frustration.

Lilian did her best to give me a wide smile. "Oh, before I forget, I have something for you," she said, as her hand disappeared inside her purse. A second later she pulled out a small, chocolate-coated-cherries box. Her face lit up as she pushed the box over to me.

"Candy?" I asked.

"Just open it," Lilian said, beaming.

I carefully opened the tiny lid and let out a shriek as I gazed at my tiny redear turtle, twisting its neck up at me. Gently I plucked my pet from the box and placed him on my hand. The reptile quickly retreated into his shell. "Is he okay? Is he eating?"

"Yes, yes," Lilian replied in her motherly voice. "I'm taking care of him. I'm changing his water. . . ."

"Every other day?" I said, with concern for my pet.

"Every other day, yes. I know, I know. Of all things, I never thought I'd ever be taking care of an ol' turtle."

"He's not an old turtle. He's just a baby . . . see?" I cooed. "I thinks he likes you." Lilian gave me a stern look as I thrust my turtle toward her face.

"David," she said lovingly, as she leaned over to stroke my hair, "looking at you with that turtle . . . If only they saw you the way I do."

I carefully replaced my turtle in the candy box. Then I reached out to Lilian's hands. "I know I've been bad and that I deserved to be punished for what I did, but I promise—cross my heart and hope to die—I'll be good. Real good. I promise . . . Mom."

That evening, while I stared out of the window of my cell, a warm feeling from deep inside my soul began to take form. *I'm going to do it!* I vowed. *I'm going to prove to Mrs. C., Mr. Hutchenson and to* Mother *that I* am *a good kid!* I knew that my court date was only a few weeks away. *So,* I told myself, *I'll have to work a little harder.* I fell asleep, no longer feeling afraid.

Within days, my daily behavior scores nearly doubled. I had thought I was doing rather well before, but when Carl Miguel, the C-Wing superintendent, told me in front of everyone what a great week I was having, I wanted to prove myself even more. By the end of that week, I had achieved the highest status that the wing held: gold. Mr. Hutchenson informed me that it normally took a pretty good kid three to four weeks to make gold. I smiled inside, knowing that I had made it in under two weeks. During that visit, Gordon informed me that my court date had been moved up a few days. "So, when do we go to court?" I asked.

"The day after tomorrow," he answered. "You gonna be okay?"

"Yes, sir," I said, trying to sound sure of myself, when inside I was terrified.

"David, I'm not going to confuse you on what can or cannot happen when we get in the courtroom. I've seen enough to know that some cases can go either way, and you have one of those cases. I can only tell you to keep your cool, and if you believe in God, I recommend you pray."

Alone in my cell, I could feel myself become lightheaded. I closed my eyes, turned off my anxiety, and prayed.

Two endless days later, I sat perfectly upright as I strained to remember everything Lilian and Gordon had fed me. I nodded to Lilian, who sat behind me, and I smiled to her. As I turned away from her, I saw Mother sitting to the right of me in one of the front-row seats. I closed my eyes for a moment to make sure they weren't playing tricks on me. But when I opened them, I could see Mother cradling Kevin in her arms.

My feelings of confidence evaporated. "She's here!" I whispered to Gordon.

"Yeah, and remember, keep your cool," he warned.

Moments later my case number was announced. I squirmed in my seat before stealing a glance at Mother. My lawyer, whom I had met only a few minutes earlier in the outer chamber, stood up, rattling off dates and other official-sounding numbers and statements so fast that I wasn't sure whether everything he stated was about my case or someone else's.

The judge acknowledged my lawyer after he returned to his seat. From my right, another man in a dark suit cleared his throat before he spoke. Gordon leaned over and tapped me on the knee. "No matter what he says, keep your cool. Don't smile, don't move and don't show any emotion."

"Your Honor, on or about the week of January 10, the minor, David Pelzer, after extensive premeditation, did knowingly commit arson and attempted to burn a classroom at the Monte Cristo Elementary School. . . ."

A slow panic began to consume my body.

"The minor, Your Honor, has an extensive history of extreme rebellious behavior. You have the brief from the minor's psychiatrist, as well as statements from the minor's teacher and staff members of Monte Cristo Elementary. I have statements from the minor's former social worker, who also claims that 'while David's naïveté can be rather enchanting, he does, at times, require close supervision. While residing under the most liberal foster conditions, David has displayed *aggressive behavior toward others* and *has,* on occasion, *been argumentative and disruptive* while in foster care.' "

I sank into my seat. The same building that had granted me freedom would now be my doom. After an eternity the other lawyer thanked the judge before taking his seat, then nodded to Mother.

"Did you see that?" I asked, nudging Gordon.

"Shh," he warned, "don't blow it!"

"Rebuttal?" the judge, sounding bored, asked in my direction.

"Your Honor," my lawyer chuckled as he stood up, "Ms. Gold's statement is taken totally out of context. I submit that his Honor take the time to read the entire text. As for the charge of arson, the case has been founded on purely circumstantial evidence. While David was initially the suspect for the charge, I have in my possession statements attesting to the fact that David *stopped the spread of the fire set by another minor.* As for behavior reports while under detention, David has been, and I quote, 'exceptional.' As for David's foster placement, the Catanzes eagerly await David's return. Thank you, Your Honor."

The judge scribbled down some notes before nodding at the other lawyer, who sprang from his seat. "Your Honor, while no direct corroboration has *yet* been made, the minor *has* an established pattern of *extreme* dysfunctional behavior. In addition, I have a signed affidavit, from the minor's biological mother, Mrs. Pelzer, stating that the minor *has* set several fires in the basement of his former residence. Mrs. Pelzer regrettably confesses that she could not control the minor under any normal conditions, and that the minor is extremely manipulative and harbors violent tendencies. Please review the order transferring custody, dated last March."

"Your Honor, it has become dramatically apparent, for whatever reason, that the minor cannot be managed in his former home setting or in foster care. The county believes that the minor is an extreme burden to society. The county hereby recommends the minor to be immediately admitted to psychiatric evaluation for possible admission into a facility that can best support his needs."

"What does all that mean?" I asked Gordon, after the lawyer was through. Before Gordon could even hush me, the judge rubbed his temples and asked, "Juvenile probation?"

Mr. Hutchenson buttoned his coat as he stood. "Probation recommends continued monitoring and consultation from a different psychiatrist. I have seen nothing to make me believe that David is a threat to himself or to others. I recommend replacement with David's foster guardians."

"Gluttons for punishment, are they?" the judge chuckled before continuing. "Prior convictions?" he asked, as he turned to my lawyer.

"None, Your Honor," the lawyer stated, as he leaned forward.

The judge leaned back into his chair. As his eyes looked down on me, I could feel the hairs on the back of my neck begin to rise. I moved my left hand to scratch my right arm. I held my breath, waiting for the judge's answer. The judge fingered his mustache. With a sudden nod of his head he turned to the court reporter. "Pending no further verification on the charge of arson . . . the court recommends sentencing of . . . 100 days in juvenile detention, honoring time already served.

"And off the record," the judge stated, "young man, the charge of arson is a most serious one. The only reason I am not sentencing you for that is I have no direct proof. While it appears you *may not* have committed this crime, you have in fact been skating on thin ice for quite some time. You appear to have some good qualities and ample guidance," the judge said, nodding to Mrs. Catanze, "but . . . be wise enough to employ them both."

Immediately after the judge struck his gavel, Gordon whispered, "You'll be out in 30, 34 days."

"But I didn't do it!" I whined.

"Doesn't matter," Gordon stated matter-of-factly. "That's rarely the issue. Believe me, kid," he said, pointing to the judge, "that guy's a Santa Claus. If the prosecution had any hard evidence, I'd be fitting you for a straitjacket for the funny farm right about now. Besides, the ol' man has a soft spot for scrawny little wimps like you. Come on, back to your cell, you animal," Gordon joked, as we stood up.

Without warning, Mother stepped in front of Gordon and me. "You're wrong! You're all wrong! You'll see! I warned that social worker broad, and now I'm warning you!" Mother screeched, as she thrust her finger at Mr. Hutchenson. "He's bad! He's evil! You'll see! And next time he'll hurt somebody! The sooner *that boy* is dealt with, the sooner you'll see that I was right and I didn't do a damn thing wrong! You're fooling yourself if you think this is the end of it! You watch! There's only one place for *that boy*. You'll see!" Then she stormed out of the room, yanking Kevin behind her.

I inched my way to Gordon, whose face was chalk white. "Where does your mother live?"

"At home," I replied.

"Oh?" Gordon asked, as he raised his eyebrows. "The home you *burned?* I mean, if you burned the basement . . . you must have gutted the house, too."

"Yeah!" I laughed, after I realized he was only joking.

Thirty-four days later, I cried as I stuffed my collection of arts-and-crafts projects and the folders of schoolwork I had acquired into a small cardboard box. In an awkward sense, I didn't want to leave. In "the outs"—the outside world—it was too easy for me to get into trouble. While at Hillcrest, I had grown used to my surroundings. I knew exactly what was expected of me. I felt safe and secure. As Carl Miguel escorted me to the front desk, he explained that the outside world would indeed be the real test of my survival. "Pelz," Carl said, as he took my hand, "hope I never see you again."

I returned Carl's handshake before I gleamed at Mrs. Catanze, who seemed shocked at the sight of my pants, which I had grown out of. "Well?" she asked.

"How's my turtle?" I inquired.

"Right about now, I'd say he's soup."

"Mom!" I whined, knowing Lilian was only teasing me. "Come on," I said, as I spread my fingers, "let's go home!"

Lilian's face lit up like a Christmas tree when she realized that this was the first time I had called her house my home. She took my open hand. "Home it is!"

CHAPTER
8

Estranged

Estranged

*T*hings were never the same after I was released from juvenile hall and returned to the Catanzes. The other foster kids seemed to eye me with suspicion. Whenever I walked into a room, they would suddenly quit talking and flash me fake smiles. Whenever I'd try to join in on a conversation, I'd find myself standing in front of everyone with my hands buried in my pant pockets. Then after an eternity of silence I'd leave the living room, feeling stares on the back of my neck. Even Big Larry, whom I once considered my "big brother," brushed me off before he moved out. After a few days of the cold shoulder, I found myself spending all of my time fiddling in my room. I didn't even care that my Murray bike began to rust.

One Friday afternoon, in July 1974, Gordon Hutchenson dropped by. I felt a surge of excitement as he marched up the stairs and to my room. I couldn't wait for someone to talk to. But I knew by his grim look that something was horribly wrong. "What is it?" I asked in a low voice.

Gordon placed a hand on my shoulder. "You need to pack a bag," he said with pity.

I brushed his hand away. Visions of Hillcrest filled my head. "Why?" I exclaimed. "What'd I do?"

Gordon gently explained that I was not in any trouble and that he knew about the struggle I was having at the Catanzes' home since I had moved back. He also stated that he had been trying to move me into another foster home with fewer kids. "Besides," he confessed,

"I'm in a jam. I got a bigger kid being released next Monday from The Hill and, well, he's been assigned to live here. So come on now, move it."

I wanted to cry, but instead I ran to my room. My heart raced from a combination of excitement and fear of not knowing what was going to happen to me next. With the speed of lightning I flung drawers open, yanked clothes from hangers and stuffed everything I could into a large brown grocery bag. Minutes later, I stole a moment of time to take a final look at the room I had slept, cried, played and spent so much time thinking in for just over a year. Even when I had thought that my world was crumbling around me, I always felt safe and secure in *my* room. As I gently closed the door, I closed my eyes and yelled at myself for again being so stupid. The first two ultimate rules of being a foster child that I had learned while at Aunt Mary's were never to become too attached to anyone and never to take someone's home for granted. And I had foolishly broken both rules. I had been so naïve as to convince myself that I would live with Rudy and Lilian for the rest of my life. I closed my eyes as I fought back the tears.

After Gordon placed a phone call to another foster home, he had to separate Lilian and me as we sobbed in each other's arms. I looked into Lilian's eyes, promising her that I would be a good boy and that I'd stay in touch. Outside, Gordon swung open the door to his brown Chevy Nova, then hurled my belongings in the backseat before allowing me to slide into his car. As he backed out of the driveway, I could clearly see the streaks of black mascara run down Lilian's face. She stood in front of the same living room window where I had spent so many endless hours—waiting for the remote possibility of a visit from my father. As I waved good-bye to Lilian for the last time, I suddenly realized that she and Rudy had cared for me and treated me better than my own parents.

Neither Gordon nor I spoke a single word for several minutes. He finally cleared his throat. "Hey, Dave, I know this is all coming at you pretty fast, but, ah . . ."

"But why?" I whined.

Gordon's face tightened with frustration. "Listen!" he barked. "It's rare, damn rare, that a kid stays in a home for as long as you did. You know that, don't you? And you were there for how long? Over a year? Hell, that's a record."

I sank in the seat, knowing that everything he was saying was true. I had taken so much for granted for so long. I turned my head to the window, watching familiar parts of the city zoom past.

Gordon broke my concentration. "Hey, David, I'm sorry. I shouldn't have dumped on you like that. It's just that sometimes I forget what it's like to be a kid in your position. You see, I had assigned you to another home yesterday, but I got stuck in court before I could pick you up. And, well, now that home has another kid and . . . hell, I don't know what to do with you."

"You could take me back to the Catanzes," I suggested in a soft voice.

"Can't do that. Like I already said, I had signed you out of the Catanzes' yesterday, which means they are no longer your legal guardians. It's, well, very complicated to explain. The bottom line is, I've got to find you a home."

As Gordon stumbled for words, my heart seized with fear. I suddenly realized that I had forgotten my bike and, more important, my pet turtle. Gordon laughed when I told him, so I playfully tugged his arm. He knew how much my things meant to me, but we both knew finding me a place to stay was far more important.

Gordon stopped off at his home. Soon the phone became glued to his ear as he pleaded, then begged, foster parents on the other end of the line to take me in, if only for a few days. After several hours, he slammed down the phone in frustration. "Damn it!" he said. "There are never enough homes! And all the homes we have are full!" I watched him as he again attacked the phone. Seconds later his tone changed. Even though he turned his back to me, I could still hear him quietly ask, "What's the count on A-Wing? Yeah? Okay, put a bed on hold for Pelzer. No, no, he's clean; no charges. I'm just trying to *place* him, and I'm running out of homes. Okay, thanks. I'll give you a call before we come in."

As Gordon spun around to look at me, he realized I knew what was about to happen. "Sorry, David, I just don't know what else to do."

I was so mentally exhausted, I no longer cared. In a strange way I actually looked forward to the routine at The Hill and seeing counselors like Carl Miguel again. Before I could tell Gordon to drive me to The Hill, he snapped his fingers and grabbed his jacket, streaking out the front door and ordering me to follow him to the car. Inside the Chevy Nova he gave me a sly smile. "I should have thought of this earlier. It's impossible for some of these parents to say no, once they've had a good look at you kids. I know it's a raw deal, but desperate times call for desperate measures."

I squinted my eyes as I tried to understand what Gordon's words meant. Before I could ask, my chest jerked forward as he jammed the gear shift into park. "Well," he proudly announced, "this is it. Put on your best face." Gordon surged with pride as he rapped his knuckles on the screen door, a split second before he marched in.

I felt like a burglar as I tiptoed into someone else's home without permission. A pair of heads popped out from a nearby kitchen. "Just be cool and have a seat." Gordon gestured to a couch before giving me a wink. He spun on his heels and opened his arms. "Harold! Alice! Good to see ya! How have you been?" He strolled into the kitchen.

I shook my head and chuckled to myself at Gordon's chameleon-like personality. I knew if he wanted to, he could charm anyone into anything. He reminded me of those crazy guys on TV who desperately tried to con people into buying cars.

Before Gordon pulled up a chair at the kitchen table, I knew we were in trouble. The man, Harold, who was wearing a straw hat, shook his head. "Nope, can't take any more. Gots no room," he grumbled as he took a drag from a thin cigarette.

I clutched my already crumpled bag and was about to stand up to leave when the lady, Alice, said, "Now, Leo, settle down. He looks like a good kid." Alice leaned over and gave me a smile. I raised my eyebrows and smiled back.

"We're not licensed for boys. You know that," Harold stated.

Gordon butted in. "It'd only be for a few days, just until I can find him another home. I should have a place for him by, let's say, Monday . . . Wednesday by the latest. You'd really be doing me, and David, a big favor."

"And the papers?" Alice asked.

Gordon raised a finger. "Uhm . . . I don't have them with me, but . . . I'll bring them by next week and . . . we'll just . . . we'll just backlog the dates. . . . Hey, look at the time! I gotta run! Thanks again. I'll see you next week," he said, and fled from the house before Harold and Alice could change their minds.

I sat glued to the couch, hugging my bag to my chest. I kept my head bent down while Alice and Harold eyed me with caution and crept into the living room. "Well, where's he going to sleep?" Harold asked in a stern tone. After a small squabble, Alice decided I would share a room with Michelle, a 17-year-old foster child who worked at night. Harold continued to protest, claiming that sharing a room with a young lady was not proper. Trying to make a good first impression, I marched up to him, looked him straight in the eye and shrieked, "Oh, it's okay! I don't mind!"

As the words spilled out, I knew I was in trouble. For the next four nights, I curled up beneath a set of old wool blankets on the living-room couch. I didn't know why I had made Harold so upset, but at least I had a place to stay. For that, I was thankful.

The next week, after taking a quick survey of my contents in my grocery bag and waving good-bye to Alice—Mrs. Turnbough—I climbed into Gordon's car as we set out for another foster home. He assured me that he had discovered the perfect home, even though my new foster parents had never had any foster children before and only received their license yesterday. My head began to swim with emotions. The more Gordon tried to convince me about my new foster parents, the more I knew how desperate he was to place me.

A half mile later, Gordon parked his car in front of a small brown house. Stepping out of the car, I exhaled and gave the woman who stood on the porch a false smile. Before Gordon could introduce us, the woman flew down the stairs and smothered me against her chest. My arms hung from my side as the woman's sandpaper-like hands scoured my face. I wasn't sure what to do. I thought the woman mistook me for another child. After an eternity of cheek pinching and another round of bone-crushing hugs, the lady held me at arm's length. "Oh, just look at you!" the woman cooed, as she shook my shoulders so fast that my head bounced up and down. "Oh, I could just eat you alive! Gordon, he's *sooo* cute! David," the woman shrieked, as she jerked me up the stairs and into the house, "I've waited so long for a boy like you!"

I stumbled into a small living room, fighting hard not to lose my balance. The moment my head cleared, the crazy woman shoved me onto her couch. Gordon tried his best to calm the woman down by forcing her to read endless stacks of papers before assuming custody of me. Finally, he sat her down and explained everything he could about my character, over and over again, emphasizing the fact that if she had any questions, to give him a call. "Oh, not to worry," the lady said, as she smiled at me and seized my hand. "A little boy like this should be no problem at all."

Gordon and I blinked at each other at the same moment. "Well then," he chuckled, "I'll be on my way and let you two get to know each other."

I walked Gordon to the door. Without the lady knowing, he bent down and whispered, "Now be a good *little* boy." I cringed, as he knew I would.

After Gordon drove away, the woman flopped onto the couch. She batted her eyes and shook her head from side to side for several minutes. I thought she was going to cry. "Well . . . just look at you!"

I returned her smile, and without thinking, I stuck out my hand. "I'm David Pelzer."

The woman covered her mouth with her hand. "Oh, how silly of me. I'm Joanne Nulls, and you may call me Mrs. Nulls. How's that sound?"

I nodded my head, knowing full well that Joanne thought of me as a kid rather than the 13-year-old teenager that I wanted to be recognized as. "That's very kind of you . . . Mrs. Nulls," I replied.

In a flash, Mrs. Nulls sprang up from the couch and proudly showed me a framed picture of her husband. "This is Michael," she cooed. "*Mr. Nulls.* He works at the post office," she stated, as she cradled the photograph to her chest and patted it as if she were holding a child. But I felt better after finally meeting Mr. Nulls, who insisted that I openly address him as *"Michael."* I knew by the look on Joanne's face that she didn't like Michael's easygoing nature or having her rules challenged.

She would always seem to bite her lip in front of Michael, but the moment he left for work, she would return to treating me as if I were a toy doll. Joanne insisted on washing my hair, prohibited me to ride my bike past the corner of the block and instead of the $2.50 allowance I had received from the Catanzes, she proudly dropped two quarters into the palm of my hand. "Now, don't spend this all in one place," she warned.

"Oh, don't worry. I won't," I assured her, wondering what to do with two measly quarters.

Because of Joanne's restrictions, I spent most of my time wandering through her home. The living room was smothered with every item from the Avon catalog. I'd spend hours gazing at the thousands of articles. By early afternoon I became so bored that I'd plop down in front of the television and watch Speed Racer cartoons. When I could not stand another animated episode, I'd drag myself to my room and kill time by coloring in a coloring book she had given me.

Just as when I lived with Mother, I seemed to know when something was wrong. Even with my bedroom door closed, I could hear
hushed disagreements turn into raging battles. Several times I heard
Michael yelling about my presence in *his* home. I knew that having me
as a foster child had been Joanne's idea because, as she had told me,
she was lonely and could not have any children. Whenever Joanne and
Michael fought, thoughts of Mother and Father raced through my
head. I fully realized I was not in any physical danger, but I stayed
huddled against the far corner of my room with a blanket over my
head. Once, a few days before school started, their yelling became so
extreme that the windows to my bedroom would shake.

The next morning I tried to talk to Joanne, who seemed to be on
the verge of a collapse. I stayed by the side of the couch the entire day,
watching her clutch her wedding picture to her chest as she slowly
rocked back and forth in the chair. As quietly as I could, I tiptoed to
my room and packed my clothes into my weathered brown paper bag.
At that moment I knew it was only a matter of time before I would be
moving on.

My problems with the Nullses evaporated my first day at Parkside
Junior High School. I sat tall and proud at the big round table in my
homeroom class. I smiled at the other boys who openly joked with me.
One of them, Stephen, nudged me, claiming that a girl from the other
table kept looking at me. "So?" I asked. "What's the big deal?"

"If you like a girl, you call 'em a *horror*," Stephen explained.

I tilted my head to one side. While I thought about the word Stephen wanted me to say, the other boys nodded with approval. After
extensive coaching from my new friends, I tried to be cool as I bent
over to the girl and whispered, "You're the best-looking *horror* I've
ever seen."

The entire room, which had been rumbling with noise, suddenly
became quiet as a church. Every head swung toward me. The girls at
the table clamped their hands to their mouths. I swallowed hard,
knowing I had screwed up—again.

When class ended, the entire room full of kids fought for the door.
The moment I stepped outside, the sun seemed to disappear. I gazed
straight up and stared into the face of the most gigantic eighth-grader
I had ever seen. "What'd you call my sister?" he sneered.

I swallowed hard again. I tried to think of something clever to say.
Instead I told him the truth. "A *horror*," I whimpered. A second later

warm blood gushed from my nose. The eighth-grader's fist was so fast that I didn't see it coming.

"*What* did you call her?" he repeated.

I closed my eyes before giving him the same answer.

Smash.

After six blows to my face, I realized I shouldn't say the word *horror* because it meant something very bad. I apologized to the gorilla-sized kid, who struck me again and bellowed, "Don't you ever, ever, call my sister a *whore* again!"

That afternoon at Joanne's home, I stayed in my room as I tried to fix the frames of my bent glasses. I didn't seem to notice that Joanne stayed inside her room as well. As the days passed, I so desperately wanted to ask her and Michael what a "whore" was, but I knew by the way they acted toward each other that I'd be better off keeping my problems to myself.

A couple of weeks later, returning from school, I found Joanne with her head buried in her hands. I rushed up to her. She whimpered that she and Michael were getting a divorce. My head began to throb. I sat by her feet as she informed me that Michael had been having an *affair* with another woman. I nodded as Joanne wept, but I didn't know what she really meant. I knew better than to ask.

I held her until she cried herself to sleep. I felt proud. For the first time in my life, *I* had been there for someone. I turned off the living-room lamp and covered Joanne with a blanket before I checked my belongings in my grocery bag one last time. I lay on my bed, knowing deep in my heart that I had somehow been one of the reasons for the Nullses' divorce. Two days later I turned my head away from Joanne, who wept from her porch as Gordon eased his Chevy Nova down the street.

I dug into my pant pocket and pulled out a crumbled piece of paper containing the addresses and phone numbers of all my former foster homes. Borrowing one of Gordon's pens, I drew a line through Joanne and Michael Nulls. I didn't feel any remorse. I knew that if I thought about my feelings toward Joanne Nulls, Alice Turnbough or Lilian Catanze, I would break down and cry. I felt I was beyond that. Carefully I folded my address sheet and stuffed the paper back into my pocket.

I cleared my head of any feelings I had about the Nullses—or anyone else—as I glanced out the car window. My eyes blinked. For a moment I thought Gordon was driving me to Daly City. "Are you going in the right direction?" I asked in a squeaky voice.

Gordon let out a breath. "David, ah . . . we've run out of foster homes. The only one left is a home by your mother's."

I felt a lump creep up my throat. "How close?" I whimpered.

"Less than a mile," Gordon replied in a dry voice.

I nodded my head as Thomas Edison Elementary School came into view. I calculated the distance from my old school to Mother's house to be under a mile. I could feel my chest begin to tighten. The thought of living so close to Mother made my heart skip a beat. But something seemed out of place. I nearly pressed my face to the side of the window. The school looked radically different. "What happened?" I asked, shaking my head from side to side.

"Oh it's a junior high school now. That's where you'll be going."

I let out a sigh. *Doesn't anything stay the same anymore?* I asked myself in a sarcastic voice. A flicker of excitement over seeing my teachers that had rescued me soon vanished. Only when Gordon wheeled his car away from the school, in the opposite direction of Mother's street, did I breathe a little easier. I felt as if I had stepped into a time warp as the Chevy Nova chugged up streets that were lined with houses of the same style as Mother's on Crestline Avenue. I couldn't believe how small they seemed. Strangely, though, I felt secure. I let out a smile as I marveled at the tall palm trees in the front yards of the single-story homes that seemed so tiny now. I couldn't believe it had been nearly two years since my rescue. I rolled down the window, closed my eyes and breathed in the moist, chilly air.

Gordon parked his car at the top of a steep hill. I followed him up a set of red-colored stairs to a house that looked identical to Mother's. When the front door opened, my eyes nearly popped out of my head. Gordon leaned over to my side. "You going to be all right? You're not prejudiced, are you?"

I shook my head as my mouth hung open. "Prejudiced?" I asked. I had never had black foster parents before. A tall lady shook my hand and introduced herself as Vera. I automatically took my position on the living-room couch as Gordon and Vera talked in the kitchen. My eyes darted in every direction, searching every corner, every beam of Vera's home. The entire floor plan seemed the same. I remembered that the walls of Mother's house usually reeked from the thick, choking smell of cigarette smoke and the heavy stench of animal urine. But

Vera's home had an open, clean feeling to it. The more I gazed at Vera's home, the more I smiled.

Minutes later Gordon sat down by me on the couch. With his hand on my knee, he warned me that Mother's house was off limits, with a radius of one mile. I nodded my head, understanding the meaning of Gordon's order. But I was frightened of Mother finding me. "Are you going to tell her where I'm at?"

"Well," Gordon began, as he fought to say the right words, "by law I am only required to inform your mother that you are residing in the city limits. Other than that, I really don't see a need to tell her anything else. As you can tell, I'm not a big fan of hers." Then his facial expression changed. "And for God's sake, you make damn sure you stay the hell away from her! Am I clear on this?"

"Like crystal," I replied, giving him a salute.

Gordon playfully slapped my knee as he got up from the couch. I walked him to the door and shook his hand. Having Gordon leave me in a strange home was the hardest, but most familiar, part of our relationship. I always felt a little scared. He seemed to always sense it. "You'll be fine. The Joneses are good people. I'll check in on you in a few weeks."

Vera gently closed the door behind Gordon, then led me down a narrow hallway. "I'm sorry, but we weren't expecting you," she explained in a kind voice, as she opened the bedroom door at the end of the hallway. I stepped into a vacant, white-walled room containing a twin-sized mattress on one side of the wall and a box-spring on the other. Vera reluctantly explained that I would be sharing the room with her younger son. I gave Vera a false smile as she left me alone in the room. Very slowly I plucked my rumpled clothes from my grocery bag and stacked them in neat little piles by the head of my box-spring bed. I killed time by rearranging my clothes as if they were in a dresser drawer. Suddenly I closed my eyes and cried inside at the thought of never being with the Catanzes again.

Later that afternoon I was introduced to the seven other foster teenagers who lived in a makeshift room in the garage. Mattresses were crammed into every corner and any other open space available. A pair of old lamps gave the room a soft glow, and makeshift bookcases were used to store whatever belongings the teenagers possessed. I shrugged off whatever anxiety I had after meeting Jody, Vera's husband, who chuckled like Santa Claus as he hoisted me so high that my head almost struck the ceiling. I quickly learned that no matter what was going on, whenever Jody came home, everything and everyone came to a halt and competed for his attention. As cramped as things were, there was a genuine family bond. I only hoped I would stay long enough to memorize their phone number.

My first day at Fernando Riviera Junior High was a huge improvement over the one at Parkside Junior High in San Bruno. I kept my mouth shut and my head down. At recess I desperately tried to find out what happened to my former teachers, only to discover that they had been transferred to other schools across the district. I felt empty and sorry for myself, until one day I made friends with Carlos, a shy Hispanic boy. We shared most of the same classes, and at recess we'd stroll throughout the school. We seemed to have a lot in common, but unlike my "friend" John at Monte Cristo Elementary, Carlos didn't have a mean bone in his body. Because Carlos could not speak English very well, we did not feel a need to talk to each other that much. In an odd sense Carlos and I had a way of knowing what the other was thinking, just by our expressions. We soon became inseparable. At the end of the school day, we always met by our adjoining lockers so we could walk home together.

One day, out of boredom I convinced Carlos to walk across the street to the new Thomas Edison Elementary School. As Carlos and I strolled down the corridors, I couldn't believe how puny the other kids looked. Loads of children bubbled with laughter as they raced to the play yard or for their rides home. With my head bent to the side, I turned a corner and bumped into a big kid. I muttered an instant apology before I realized the kid was my brother Russell. His head reeled back for a second. My eyes examined his every feature. I knew in a flash that Russell would let out a blood-curdling scream, but I couldn't break away from staring at him. His eyes flickered. I felt my body tense the way it always did the moment before I sprinted away. My head leaned forward when Russell's lips began to quiver. I sucked in a deep breath and told myself, *Okay, David, here it comes.*

"Holy cow! Oh my God! David! Where did you . . . how the hell are you?" Russell asked with a choking voice.

My mind raced with all my options. Was Russell for real? Would he strike out and hit me or run and tell Mother that he saw me? I turned to Carlos, who raised his shoulders. I wanted so badly to hug Russell. My mouth suddenly went dry. "I'm, ah . . . I'm fine," I stuttered, shaking my head. "You okay? I mean . . . how are you? How's things at home? How's Mom?"

Russell's head dipped to his worn-out sneakers. I realized how withdrawn he looked. His shirt was paper-thin and his arms were spotted with small, dark purple marks. My head snapped up to his face. I knew. I shook my head, not knowing what to say. I felt so sorry for him. For years I had been the sole target of Mother's rage. Now in front of me stood my replacement.

"Do you have any idea of what she'd do if she ever found out I talked to you?" Russell said, his voice trailing off. "Things are bad. I mean *real* bad. All she does is rant and rave. She drinks more than ever. She does *everything* more than ever," Russell said, again looking at his shoes.

"I can help!" I stated with sincerity. "Really, I can!"

"I . . . ah, I gotta go." Russell spun away, then stopped and turned around. "Meet me here tomorrow after school." Then he flashed me a wide smile. "Hey man . . . it's really good to see you."

I walked forward. I felt an overwhelming urge to be close to him. I stuck out my hand. "Thanks, man. I'll see ya."

Afterward I smiled at Carlos. "That's my brother."

Carlos nodded. *"Si, hermano! Si!"*

I thought about Russell the rest of the afternoon. I couldn't wait to see him the next day. *But what can I do?* I asked myself. Would Russell come to Jody and Vera's home with me so Jody could call the police and maybe rescue him as I had been? Or did I imagine the marks on Russell's arms to be abuse rather than battle wounds from playing hard? Maybe, I thought, Russell was trying to set me up like he did years ago when he planted candy bars in my rag box, then ran off to inform Mother that he had caught me stealing. He then had the privilege of watching me receive my punishment for my *crime*. Mother had trained Russell to be her spy, but then again, he was only a small child back then.

That night I tossed and turned in my bed, wondering what to do. Some time in the early morning hours I finally drifted off to sleep. In my dream, I found myself waiting for *her*. My head tilted to one side when I heard Mother's forced breathing. Our eyes locked for a moment. I saw myself walking toward her. I wanted to talk to her, to ask her—to plead with her—why me, why Russell? My mouth moved, but the words didn't come. In a flash Mother's face turned cherry red. *No!* I yelled at myself. *You can't keep doing this! It's over!* The shiny razor-edged knife suddenly appeared above Mother's head. I tried to twist my body and run away, but my feet failed to respond. I tried to yell her away. My eyes followed the knife as it flew out of her hands. I knew I was dead. I screamed for my life, but I couldn't hear my terror.

My head bounced off the floor. I found myself scrabbling to stand up. I stood alone in a dark room, unsure whether I was awake or still in my dream. I strained my eyes, searching through the darkness. My heart seemed stuck in my throat. *My God!* I said to myself. *What if I'm still there with her?* I emptied my lungs when I recognized the sound of Jody's son snoring in his bed. Grabbing a piece of my clothing, I held it to my chest as I waited for the sun to come up.

The next day after school, I physically dragged Carlos to Thomas Edison Elementary. "This no good idea," Carlos stated. "Your *mamasita,* she *loca!*" he said, twirling a finger to the side of his head. I nodded in agreement. I had decided after my nightmare that nothing would keep me from seeing Russell. Carlos and I stopped in the same hallway as the day before. A group of children screamed and yelled as they seemed to run through our legs. As the kids grew bigger in size, I twisted my neck in search of Russell. My eyes found him at the far end of the hall with his head bent down. "Russell!" I shouted. "Over here!" Russell's head bobbed, but he didn't make eye contact as he had the day before.

I felt something tug on my arm. I smirked at Carlos, whose eyes darted in every direction. "This no good. Your mama, she *loca!*" he warned.

"Not now!" I said, still keeping my eyes fixed on the top of Russell's head. "My brother . . . ah, *si hermano! Si?* He needs help, like me, remember?" I said, pointing toward Russell, who slowed his pace.

I leaned forward when Carlos grabbed my arm. "No!" Carlos shouted. "You wait here!"

I brushed Carlos's hand away. Fighting my way against the tide of children, I made my way to Russell. Still walking, I extended my hand. Russell saw me, but for some reason he kept his head down. I stopped mid-stride.

My legs buckled. My arm seemed to just hang in front of me. Even before Carlos yelled, I knew something was horribly wrong. "Run, David!" Carlos shrieked. "Run!"

I looked just above Russell's hair and saw Mother walking behind him with her head bent down. Mother's ice-cold, evil eyes locked onto mine as her face came into full view. Kids seemed to dance around her as they scattered in every direction. Inches in front of me Russell stopped, then turned toward Mother, who smiled. Her hand disappeared into her purse as she came closer still. For a split second Mother's face seemed to hesitate, as she withdrew a shiny piece of metal. . . .

I lost my balance when my arm jerked backward. I fell on my back, my eyes still fixated on Mother. Above me Carlos began to drag me backward. I knew this had to be a dream, but Carlos's badgering made everything real. I struggled to stand up, feeling Carlos's hands lift me to my feet.

I blinked my eyes and saw Mother's bony fingers stretch out toward my neck. She was so close I caught a whiff of her putrid body odor. In a flash Carlos and I weaved our way through the mass of smaller children. As we fled, I looked behind me. Mother seized Russell's arm as she quickened her pace. Carlos grabbed my hand, leading me to the parking lot. My chest heaved from absolute terror and lack of oxygen. My arms swung wildly. I ran into the parking lot and again searched behind me. My eyes sought out any sign of Mother and Russell. Without warning, I tripped off the curb. As my body flew through the air, I tried to swing my head forward in an effort to regain my balance. A second later my chest collided against the hood of a moving car. Behind the windshield, a woman's eyes grew wide. I felt myself rolling off the hood as I tried to grab anything that would keep me from falling. My hands slapped the far end of the hood, fingers flailing, as I tried to latch onto the wiper blades. I closed my eyes and felt my body sink in front of the car. My ears burned from the sound of my own scream.

A moment later my head struck the pavement. I heard a screeching sound. I tried to cover my head with my hands. Somewhere in the crowd I heard someone else scream. I closed my eyes and emptied my lungs. Seconds later I uncovered my face and peeked through my fingers. Inches in front of my nose were the grooves of a front left tire.

Carlos plucked me from the pavement. I drooped an arm across his shoulder as he led me to the sidewalk. I looked back at the car. A young woman flung open the car door, and stood and shook.

Without skipping a beat, Mother marched at full speed to her station wagon.

Without my saying a word, Carlos understood my fear. My legs felt rubbery, and he had to practically drag me up the same small hill that I had, years ago, raced from into Mother's waiting arms before we left for the river. Now that same hill seemed to be my doom. My legs became tangled, my knee scraped the sidewalk and my teeth were clenched from the jolt of pain.

From the top of the hill Carlos and I could see small clusters of children and adults pointing in our direction. My eyes scanned the stream of cars as they emptied from the parking lot. I would not know in which direction to flee until I spotted Mother. After a few sweeps I shook my head. "She's gone! She's not there!"

Carlos jabbed my sore arm. "There!" he pointed. Mother's station wagon had climbed the hill in no time flat. I could see the rage on her face as she pounded wildly on her horn. Because of the traffic, she could not make her left turn. Carlos and I nodded to each other before running across the street and up another hill to his house. My energy seemed to come from nowhere, and my ears picked up the distinctive rumbling sounds of the worn-out muffler on Mother's ancient station wagon.

Carlos and I bolted up the stairs to his house. He dug into his pockets and fumbled with the keys to the door. "Come on!" I pleaded. Carlos's twitching fingers dropped the keys. Even though I could hear the sound of Mother's car chugging up the hill, I stood and watched the shiny reflection from the keys that tumbled down the stairs. *Keys!* I yelled at myself. *Mother wasn't taking a knife out of her purse! It was a set of keys!*

Carlos's shouting woke me from my spell. I raced down the stairs and tossed the keys to Carlos, who jammed a key in the lock before flinging the door open. On my hands and knees, I scrambled up the stairs, rolled into Carlos's house and slammed the door shut. No one was home. Creeping to the front window, we stayed glued to the floor and peeled back the drapes as much as we dared, just as Mother's station wagon rocketed up the street. Carlos and I began to let out a laugh—until I heard the familiar sound of Mother's car creep down the street, as she tapped the brakes every few feet, her eyes piercing into every house. "She's searching for us," I whispered.

"*Si,*" Carlos replied. "Your mama, she *loca!*"

After hiding behind the living room curtain for over an hour, Carlos and I walked to the halfway mark to Jody's home. We grinned at each other. His brown eyes smiled. "Just like, eh, James Bondo!"

"Yeah," I laughed. "James Bondo!" I shook his hand and nodded to him that I'd see him tomorrow. I watched Carlos stroll down the street, then disappear as he rounded the corner. I never saw him again.

I jogged up the set of hills and didn't stop until I slammed the front door to Jody's home. I huffed behind the door for several seconds until I realized that Vera and Jody were screaming at each other in the kitchen. I cursed to myself, knowing that Mother must have just called. I sailed past the kitchen and into my room, knowing that Jody would soon yell for me. As I sat on my box-spring bed, I knew I had broken one of the most important rules Gordon Hutchenson had pounded into me—stay the heck away from Mother. Thoughts of Gordon driving me to juvenile hall filled my head.

After a few minutes I leaned against the bedroom door to better hear what the commotion was all about. I discovered that Jody and Vera were not yelling about me, but about some girl. I opened the door and sneaked down the stairs to the older boys' room. All at once every head snapped up in my direction. Their faces were long and withdrawn. They all seemed busy, their bodies bent over as they stuffed their clothes and other belongings into brown bags and pillowcases. I knew, but I had to ask. "What's wrong? What's going on?"

The oldest kid, Bobby, stated, "They're shutting down the house. You better pack whatever you got 'cause tomorrow we're outta here."

My mouth hung open. "Why? What's wrong?"

No one answered. I ran to the bottom of the stairs and tugged on Bobby's shirt. As he looked down at me, I could tell by his eyes that he had been crying. I didn't know that older kids did that. Bobby shook his head. "Jody's been accused of statutory rape."

"Statue . . . what?" I asked.

"Hey little dude, the word is that the Joneses took in this girl a few months back, and this chick now says she was raped, even though Jody was never alone in the house with her. If you ask me, I know it's all a lie. That chick was crazy," Bobby said. "Just go pack your stuff and don't forget to check the laundry basket. Now scram!"

It only took me a minute to repack my things. As I stuffed my grocery bag, I turned off any feelings of sorrow I had for the Joneses. They were nice people, and I felt sorry for Jody and Vera, but my worldly possessions came first. To me it was a matter of survival.

The next morning a fleet of cars arrived, and one by one the other foster children and I said our good-byes. I kissed Vera on the cheek and hugged Jody's jolly tummy. As the social worker drove me down the hills, then past my school, I took out my sheet of addresses and scratched the Joneses from my list. I had stayed at their home for just over two months—my third foster home in half a year.

The social worker informed me that some of the other foster kids I had lived with would end up in juvenile hall because there were no homes available. He went on to explain that Gordon couldn't pick me up because he had called in sick. But, the social worker smiled, Gordon had given him a lead to a foster home that might take me in for a few days.

I slumped in my seat and nodded my head. *Yeah, yeah,* I said to myself. *How many times have I heard that before?*

A couple of hours later I burst from the county car and into Alice Turnbough's living room. I hugged Alice with all my heart. Moments later the social worker knocked on the screen door before entering. "You two know each other?" he asked in a weary tone. My head rattled up and down like a puppy dog. "Mrs. Turnbough, I, ah . . . I know it's kind of short notice, but we had a situation. . . . Can we place David here . . . for a while?" he pleaded.

"Well, I really don't have the room, and I can't have him sharing a room with the girls. Is there any other . . . ?"

My heart ached. I wanted to stay with Alice so badly. My eyes began to water as I looked up at the social worker, who hesitated for a moment. I then turned to Alice, who seemed to act the same.

Alice shook her head. "I don't think it's right, for David, I mean. . . ."

A long stretch of silence followed. I let go of Alice and gazed at the carpet. "Well," Alice said in a defeated tone, "can you at least tell me how long you expect him to stay? I guess I can put him back on the couch. That is, if you don't mind too much, David."

I clamped my eyes shut for the longest time. My head swam with a stream of endless thoughts. I didn't care. I didn't care whether I slept on a couch or a bed of nails. I just wanted to stay at a place that I could call *home.*

CHAPTER

9

Coming
Around

*M*y stay with the Turnboughs was day by day. The days turned into weeks, with still no word of where I would end up. Out of frustration, Alice re-enrolled me into Parkside Junior High. As happy as I was to return to school to see my teachers again, I still felt a dark cloud over me. I dreaded walking to Alice's home after school. I'd peck around the corner looking for a county car, knowing I'd soon be driven off. Every day, out of fear, I'd bug Alice in my desperate effort to find out any news from Gordon Hutchenson. I just wanted to know.

As the weeks turned into months, I found myself still sleeping on the couch and living out of a grocery bag. My clothes became weathered and moldy because I only washed them on Saturday afternoon after 3:00 P.M. or on Sunday—I knew that those were the only times I was safe from being moved. After forgetting my pet turtle at the Catanzes, I didn't want to take the chance of losing anything else again. Every night after everyone had gone to bed, I would pray on the couch that tomorrow Gordon would decide my fate.

One day, when I returned to Alice's home after school, she sat me down. I swallowed hard as I braced myself for the bad news. But no word had come. Alice informed me of something else: I would be seeing a psychiatrist tomorrow. I shook my head no. Alice went on to explain that she understood the problems about my former doctor. I was surprised that she knew so much about my past, when I hadn't told her anything. "So, you've been talking to my probation officer, and he still hasn't seen me?" I asked, feeling exposed and ashamed.

Alice explained that she was working on a plan to have me placed with her, but it would take time to receive a license to have boys in her home. "But not to worry," she stated. "Harold and I have decided that we'd like you to stay with us for a while."

Without hesitating I gave Alice a kiss. Then I thought about her last statement and gave her a frown. "You mean Harold wants me to stay, too?"

Alice laughed. "Just because Harold doesn't talk that much to you doesn't mean he doesn't like you. He just has a hard time understanding you. Frankly, I'm sure a lot of people would. But take my word, if Harold didn't want you, you wouldn't be here." Her big hands wrapped around my skinny fingers. "Ol' Leo likes you more than you know."

Alice's explanation of Harold meant the world to me. Ever since I had blurted out to him about sharing a room with a girl, I felt Harold thought of me as a weird kid. He never seemed to talk to me. Whenever he did utter a few words in my direction, he'd try to get me to read rather than watch television. Every night after dinner, like clockwork, Harold would always pull out an old Western paperback and smoke his Camel cigarettes before going to bed precisely at 9:00 P.M.

I respected Harold so much, although he never knew. As a carpenter, he had a passion for his craft. I hoped I could stay with the Turnboughs long enough for Harold to teach me a few things. Ever since I was a small child I had fantasized about building a log cabin at the Russian River, so at times I'd imagine Harold and me working on a project together, in hopes of bringing us closer. Maybe, I thought, by then I could prove myself to him.

The next day, after much prodding from Alice, I hopped on a bus and went to meet my new psychiatrist, Dr. Robertson, who turned out to be the complete opposite of "The Great Doctor" I had before. He greeted me with a handshake and told me to call him by his first name, Donald. His entire office was bathed in bright warm sunlight, but the thing that meant the most to me was that Dr. Robertson treated me like a person.

On my weekly visits to Dr. Robertson, I never felt forced to talk about anything, but soon found myself initiating the conversation about my past. *I* questioned *Dr. Robertson* about everything, including whether I was doomed to follow in my mother's footsteps. Dr. Robertson always tried to steer me in another direction, but I fought to maintain my lifelong course of finding my answers. I learned to trust him as he gently led me through the maze of the sensitive parts of my past.

Because of my persistence, Dr. Robertson suggested some books for me to study on basic psychology. Soon afterward, Harold and I seemed to bicker about who was hogging the lamp by the end of the couch, as I tried to read books on self-esteem by Norman Vincent Peale or others on the stranger side, such as *Your Erroneous Zones*. I found myself intrigued with the basic theories of survival traits, as written by Dr. Abraham Maslow. At times I'd become frustrated with the big words, but I hung tough and soon discovered it had taken a lot just for me to make it as far as I had. Although on the inside, parts of me still felt awkward and hollow, I realized *I* was stronger than most of the kids at school who seemed to live in a "normal" world.

At Alice's home I found myself opening up to her about everything, all the time. Sometimes she and I would gab far into the early morning hours. I never worried about how I talked or what I said. Whenever I became nervous and began to stutter, Alice would teach me how to slow down my train of thought, and have me picture myself saying the words before I spoke them. Within a few weeks my speech problem disappeared.

Every Saturday afternoon, after Alice danced her usual jig to *American Bandstand*, she and I would venture past the railroad tracks on our way to the same mall where Mrs. Catanze had taken me shopping for my clothes. We always saw a movie, and that was the only way Alice could get me to sit still for any length of time. As I sat quietly beside her, I'd wring my hands as I scrutinized every scene. My mind raced to stay one step ahead of the sometimes mindless plot. I became fascinated by complicated screenplays and how the director pieced everything together. After every show, Alice and I went back and forth with our own critiques.

Other times, for no special reason, she would buy me toys "just because." At first I felt awkward and unworthy, partly because I was not used to receiving presents, and also because I knew how hard Harold worked and how he saved every penny. In time I learned to accept presents. For me that was a very hard lesson to swallow.

The most important gift the Turnboughs gave me was my one last chance at being a kid, while preparing me for my life as an adult. In an effort to show Alice and Harold how much they meant to me, one afternoon at the kitchen table—the famed "Table of Talk"—I plucked a soiled piece of torn paper from my pant pocket and ripped it into tiny fragments. "Now, what's that all about?" Harold scowled, as tears rolled down Alice's cheeks.

"I don't need it anymore," I boasted. "And I know your phone number, too. Wanna hear?" Alice nodded her head yes. "It's 555-2647," I proudly stated, as I looked straight into Harold's blue eyes.

"Well, maybe now's the time to get that unlisted phone number," he grumbled, before winking at me.

Whenever Alice and I talked for any great length of time, the subject of my future always came up. Even the simple question "What do you want to do when you grow up, David?" caused me to become scared from the bottom of my soul. I always seemed to picture Chris, the foster kid from the Catanzes' home, and how frightened he was to turn 18. I had never thought that far ahead. In order to survive against Mother's torture, I only had to plan hour by hour, or day by day at the most. Being alone in the wide open world was the most frightening thing I could ever possibly imagine. I'd become so scared and tense that I'd begin to stutter again. Alice always seemed to calm me down, but at night, when I finally had a room of my own to sleep in, I'd shiver with fear at the thought of how I was going to buy food or where I would live. I would think so hard that I'd fall asleep with an enormous headache. For me, at age 15, the countdown began.

Soon after the initial shock wore off, I decided to find ways to make money. I started out by shining shoes, and my first day out I earned $21.00 polishing dozens of shoes in just under six hours. I felt so proud as I juggled my shoe-shine kit and a box of doughnuts in one hand, and a bouquet of flowers for Alice and a couple of paperback books for Harold in the other. I soon added a job at a watch repair shop, where I worked about 20 hours a week for $10.25 take-home pay. The amount of money wasn't important to me. At the end of the work week, I'd fall asleep feeling I had accomplished something—and that was what was important. While other kids played street ball or hung around the mall, I was becoming self-sufficient.

It was very difficult for me to find anything I had in common with the other kids at school. Most of them fought to impress others by acting cool. I knew that on the outside I didn't fit in, so I simply gave up trying. At times I played the role of class clown, but for the most part I didn't care what my classmates thought of me. Whenever they bragged about their weekend ski trips, I'd think about how I could squeeze in an extra hour of work.

One Friday, a few weeks before I graduated from Parkside Junior

High, a group of rich kids were bragging about their upcoming graduation and plans of going to Disneyland or traveling to Hawaii first-class. Instead of feeling sorry for myself, I ran from the bus stop that afternoon and nearly knocked down the screen door to Alice's home. "What is it?" she shrieked.

I gulped down a glass of water before answering. I was pushing 16 and did not know how to cook for myself. Alice assured me that she would teach me when the time came. I persisted. I wanted to learn how to cook *now*. I gave her one of my serious looks, the kind I had learned from Mrs. Catanze, who always placed her hands on her hips. It worked. Even though Alice had just cleaned her home for their bridge party, which would be held in just a couple of hours, she decided to teach me how to make pancakes.

Alice's decision was her undoing. In a matter of minutes I went through two boxes of Bisquick pancake mix, four dozen eggs and two gallons of milk. Every square inch of the gas stove was covered with the thick, white, gooey mix, and the ceiling was splattered with a few well-intended tossed pancakes. The floor looked as if a blizzard had blown through, and every time Alice or I shuffled across it, we nearly suffocated from the clouds of white powder. The strain on her face was quite visible, but she laughed with me—and I didn't quit until I made the perfect pancake.

Every day seemed to hold a new adventure. Sometimes after school, I'd play on the living-room floor with my Legos or my Erector set, while other times I was the little big man, returning to Alice's home after school just long enough to change clothes before zipping off to work at one of my jobs. For the first time, I had a real life.

By July of 1976 my life took another turn. I grew tired of riding my bike to work every morning, while everyone else was still fast asleep. Then one afternoon, after a frustrating day on the job, I returned from work to find that not one, but two older foster boys had moved in. I took an instant dislike to one of the boys, Bruce, partly because I had to share a room with him and partly because I knew he got away with conning Alice blind. Even though both boys were 17, they didn't seem too concerned about supporting themselves. I began to resent them both. Whenever I pedaled off to work, they spent the day at the mall with Alice. In an odd sense I felt threatened and violated by their presence. I knew my childlike times with Alice were over, but I just wanted to hang on a little bit longer before I had to grow up.

After a few weeks, I discovered that my stash of money and some of the things I had bought through my earnings were missing. At first I thought I had misplaced my items, but one day, for no special reason, I had had enough. I marched up to Alice and demanded that either they leave or I would. I knew I sounded like a spoiled brat, but I could no longer tolerate trying to hide my things all the time, wondering at work how to make up for the stolen money. Everything I had worked so hard for slowly disappeared. I hoped Alice would give in, but I soon found myself packing. I felt like a complete fool leaving the Turnboughs. To me it was a matter of honor—if I said something, I had to be responsible for my word.

I stayed at juvenile hall for a few weeks until my new probation officer, Mrs. O'Ryan, placed me with John and Linda Walsh, a young couple in their 20s who had three kids. John had long black hair and played piano in a rock-and-roll band, while Linda was a beauty consultant at the local Walgreens drugstore. They were both very nice, and I was extremely surprised by their carefree attitude. They pretty much allowed me to do as I pleased. When I wanted to buy a minibike, John said yes. One day when I timidly asked John if he could drive me to the local sport shop so I could buy a BB gun, he replied, "Let's go." I was stunned. I would have never even thought of asking Mr. or Mrs. Turnbough, but John didn't even blink. His only condition was that he had to teach me gun safety, and I could only shoot against paper targets under his supervision. I soon forgot about looking for another job and developed the Walshes' laid-back attitude.

A few weeks into my freshman year in high school, John and Linda told me that they were moving. Without thinking, I huffed into the room I shared with their two-year-old boy and crammed everything I owned into a pillowcase. I was livid. It seemed that every time, *every time*, I adjusted to a new environment, something happened. I realized that John and Linda seemed to fight all the time, but I got used to that as well as having to babysit their bratty kids. With my belongings slung over my shoulder, I marched back into the living room. "All right," I demanded, "let's go! Take me to The Hill!"

John and Linda both looked at each other and laughed. "No, man," John said, as he waved his hand in front of his face. "I said we're moving, and *you're coming with us;* that is, if you don't have a problem with that?"

I became so upset at myself. So I stood in front of them and stewed for several minutes, until I smiled and said, "I don't know what you two are laughing at, but I'm already packed! What about you?"

Linda jabbed John in the gut. "Smart kid."

The next day I stood in the back of an oversized U-Haul while John drove to the edge of the county. When he finally stopped, I leaped from the trailer. I couldn't believe what I saw. It was as if the Walshes and I had moved into the *Leave It to Beaver* neighborhood. I stepped around the U-Haul and gawked at the entire block. Every lawn was perfectly manicured. The immaculate houses looked more like miniature mansions than ordinary homes, and every car in its driveway had a blinding shine, as if it had just been waxed. As I strolled down the middle of Duinsmoore Drive, I breathed in the sweet smell of flowers, and I could hear the sound of the wind fluttering through a giant weeping willow.

I shook my head and smiled inside. "Yes!" I shouted. "I could live here!"

In no time at all I made friends with Paul Brazell and Dave Howard, two neighborhood teenagers who seemed fascinated by my dark, rusty-red minibike and my Daisy BB gun. Their eyes seemed hungry for adventure. I was more than happy to feed them. I discovered Paul had a minibike, too, and soon the three of us held drag races in the middle of the lifeless street. Paul always won, for three reasons: his minibike had more horsepower than mine, he weighed less than I did, and he had brakes—allowing him to slow down long after I did.

Out of the hundreds of races, I won only one. That day my throttle became stuck. I wasn't worried since I had a cutoff switch—which I immediately discovered would not shut off the engine. Since I didn't have any brakes, I tried to slow down by dragging my feet. As I did, my shoes slipped and the bottom of my shirt became caught in the rear sprocket. For a moment I had one hand on the throttle while the rest of my body flailed, before being dragged down the middle of the street. I was too scared to let go. I finally released my grip, and a split second later my minibike jumped the sidewalk, flying up and over a bush.

Just in front of me, Dave hit the ground, rolling with laughter. Seconds later Paul pulled up. His eyes were as big as silver dollars. "Man, that was too cool! Can you do that again?" As I struggled to stand up, I could see some of the adults from the neighborhood staring in our direction. They seemed more concerned over the damage to the bush than my medical condition. Trying to forget the unfriendly looks, I blocked out the pain and gave Paul my widest smile. From that moment on I was dubbed "The Stuntmaster of Duinsmoore."

That evening the three of us plotted our next adventure. Paul's parents had a 16mm camera, so Paul decided to make a James Bond-style movie, casting me as the lead actor. The climax of the film was to have Dr. Strange, played by Dave, drag Bond up and down the street while Paul filmed from all angles. I told Paul I wasn't so sure about the stunt, while Dave panted like a dog, claiming he wouldn't mind watching my knees turn into hamburger. Dave doubled as my stunt coordinator, which entailed keeping the street clear of all traffic under the age of 10 and having a set of Band-Aids at the ready whenever my gag was completed. I was thankful the next day when Paul's camera ran out of film—before my death-defying climax.

One day Paul helped me prepare to meet a girl from around the block. I had never talked to a girl before, but Paul loaned me his best shirt and coached me on what to say. At that time in my life I was barely looking at myself in the mirror, let alone having the confidence to talk to a girl. After combing my hair, hearing more coaching and having no more excuses, I let Paul kick me out of his house, and I strolled down Duinsmoore. As I turned the corner, I felt like a normal person. I lived in a perfect neighborhood, my foster parents let me do as I wished, I didn't have to work and most important, my life was centered around the best friends in the entire world.

Minutes later I rapped on the front door and waited. My hands shook, and I felt lightheaded, as sweat seemed to escape from every pore of my body. I was actually excited to be a little frightened. This was a good scare. I began to rub my hands when the door opened. I thought my mouth would fall to the floor. I felt tingly all over as I stared into the face of the prettiest girl I had ever seen. Without the girl knowing, I regained my composure as she began to talk. The more she spoke, the better I felt about myself. I couldn't believe how easy it was to make the girl laugh. I was enjoying myself—right up until the moment when the girl's mother pushed her aside.

It took a moment for my eyes to adjust. When they did, I looked up at a woman who looked more like the lady from *The Brady Bunch* than someone's mother. The woman quickly jabbed a finger in front of my face. "You're that little . . . that little *F-child*, aren't you?" she sneered, with a tight smirk on her face.

I was too stunned to speak.

"Have you no respect for elders? Answer me, boy!"

"Ma'am?" I said, shaking my head.

"Listen to me," the woman raved, "I know all about you and . . .

those motorcycles, making all that reverberating noise and the willful destruction of private property. How did *the association* ever approve of . . . *your kind* of people residing in *our* neighborhood. I know all about *your kind*. You're a filthy little hooligan! Just look at your attire—you reek of street trash. I don't know what you children do to become . . . *fostered children,*" she said, covering her mouth as if she had just spoken a swear word, "but I'm sure *you* did something hideous, didn't you?" The woman's face turned so red that I thought she was going to explode. "Don't you dare approach *my household* or converse with *my children*, ever!"

I stood mesmerized by the woman's perfectly manicured red fingernail in my face.

"And just a piece of advice," the woman went on. "Don't waste your time trying. *You* don't have what it takes to make it. *I* know! Believe me, *I'm* actually doing you a favor!" She smiled as she tossed her hair to the other side of her face. "You'll see! *I'm* a very open-minded person who knows a thing or two. So the sooner you learn that you're only an *F-child*, the better off you'll be! So stick with your own kind!"

Before I could respond, the front door slammed shut with such a fury that I felt a rush of air hit my face. I stood by the door dumbstruck. I didn't know what to do. I felt as if I were an inch tall. I gazed at the sleeves of Paul's red-and-black flannel shirt. They were a little short, but I thought the shirt looked nice. I ran my hand through my oily hair. *I guess I could use a bath*, I muttered to myself. I knew that on the outside I was a walking geek, but on the inside I felt better about myself than ever before. I tried so hard to do things that normal kids took for granted. I just wanted to fit in. I wanted to be like a normal kid.

Minutes later, with my head hung low, I passed Paul, who danced around me as he pestered me with questions about meeting the girl. I waved off my best friend and hid in my room for the rest of the day.

The next afternoon, while I was tinkering with my minibike, a tall man walked up to me with a beer can in one hand and a baby stroller in the other. "So, you're the neighborhood threat?" he said with a sly grin. I kept my head down as I felt my body temperature begin to rise. Before I could mouth off, the man breezed on by.

About half an hour later, the man reappeared in the opposite direction. I waited for another put-down, but this time I was ready to fire off an insult. He gave me a wide smile before saying, "Good on you, boy! Get some!"

I shook my head, thinking my ears were clogged. *Good on me? Get some? Get some what?* I asked myself.

I stood up, wiped a spot of black oil onto my dirty white tank top and watched the man as he bobbed past me to the driveway next door. He gave me another nod before disappearing into the garage. I was so stunned that I sat down on the grass and thought about what the crazy man meant. As demented as he seemed, he did have a way with words.

The next afternoon, at the same time, the man reappeared in the same outfit: a pair of white shorts that showed off his ash-white, bony knees, an undersized T-shirt that read "Fudpuckers—We've Been Flying Since the World's Been Square," a baseball cap with silver-winged feathers pinned in the middle and a cigarette that seemed to dangle from his bottom lip. Again, with a beer in one hand and a baby stroller in the other, he stopped in front of me and winked. "Airborne material you're not, but don't worry, Slim; every dog has his day." And he pushed on.

I repeated his message over and over again as I tried to find a meaning to the phrase "every dog has his day." Just like clockwork, the man returned 30 minutes later. I jumped up and waited for his eloquent words of wisdom. "Know this," the man said with a bow, "there's always profit in mass confusion."

"Hey, mister . . ." I said before I could think.

The man's head spun around like a top. "You inquired?"

My mouth hung open. I didn't know how to respond. I could feel myself choke up. He bowed his head. "If you can wash your hands and change your attire, you may join me at my humble abode."

In a flash, I raced through the Walshes' house, scrubbed my arms and hands, dirtying their bathroom sink, and changed my shirt before bursting through the man's front door. Before I could yell my presence, a giant hand slapped me in the center of my chest. I lost my breath and thought my chest would cave in. The man looked down and smiled. "Let's try that again, shall we?" he said, as he led me out the front door and closed it in my face.

I frowned to myself. "How rude!" I said out loud. For a moment I thought I was being put down the way *The Brady Bunch* lady had done. I was about to leave when I heard a muffled voice from behind the door state, "Knock on the door."

I rolled my eyes as my knuckles rapped on the front door. A moment later, the door flung open, and the man bowed at the waist as he waved his arm, permitting me to enter. He smiled as he introduced himself. "Michael Marsh: keeper of the faith, soldier of fortune and the Doc Savage of Duinsmoore Drive."

And so began my first of many visits to "Marsh Manor." Days later I met Mr. Marsh's wife, Sandra, who was quiet and shy compared with her peculiar husband. I was instantly taken with their two boys, William and Eric. Watching their toddler, Eric, dribble as he crawled around the house reminded me of my brother Kevin when he was that age.

The Marshes treated me like a real person. While the Walshes argued more than ever, the Marshes' home became my safe haven. Whenever I was not promoting chaos with Paul and Dave, I spent hundreds of hours sitting in a corner of Michael's famed "Hall of Knowledge," reading books about movies, race cars and airplanes. Ever since I was a prisoner in Mother's house, I developed a fascination for aircraft. The many times I would sit on top of my hands in the bottom of the cold garage, I'd escape by fantasizing I was Superman. I always wanted to fly.

Although I was never allowed to take any of Mr. Marsh's books to the Walshes' home, I'd sometimes sneak off with a book and stay up all night, reading about the real-life adventures of World War II fighter pilots or the development of specialized aircraft like the Lockheed SR-71 Blackbird. Michael's library opened up a whole new world to me. For the first time in my life, I began to wonder what it would be like to fly aboard a real airplane. Maybe, I thought, one of these days . . .

Paul's father, Dan Brazell, was the Mr. Goodwrench of the neighborhood, and he had the same effect on me as Mr. Marsh. At first Mr. Brazell was wary of me, but eventually he grew to tolerate my standing over his shoulder, quizzing his every movement. Sometimes Paul, Dave and I would peek into Mr. Brazell's garage and stare in awe at whatever projects he was building from scratch. Whenever he left the garage for a few minutes, Paul would strut in, while Dave and I followed in Paul's footsteps for fear of disturbing a piece of metal or a placed tool. However, as soon as the door opened, the three of us would scurry out of the garage before Dan caught us. We knew that the garage was a special domain where Dan, Michael and a host of other men from the neighborhood gathered for their daily meetings.

Sometimes during the daily gatherings, a few of the men from the neighborhood frowned at me, as they complained about the fear of "plummeting real estate values in the local area." Mr. Marsh always came to my rescue. "Back off, boys," Michael once warned. "I have plans for my young ward. I predict that Mr. Pelzer here will become the next Chuck Yeager or Charles Manson. As you can see, I'm still working on the details."

I smiled at the compliment. "Yeah," I nodded in defiance, "Charles Manson!" I did feel a little foolish that I did not recall Charles Manson as an Ace fighter pilot.

My times at Duinsmoore were the best in my teenage life. At night, after reading one of Mr. Marsh's "borrowed books," I'd fall asleep to the scent of flowers from a soft outside breeze. Every day after school carried a new adventure, waiting for *my* two friends and me to discover.

My stay at the Walshes was not so good. Raging arguments were a daily occurrence, and at times both of them would storm out of the house, leaving me to watch their children. Sometimes I'd try to time the fights, so that before John and Linda began to hit each other, I could grab the youngest child and order the other two children to follow me outside until things calmed down.

As much as I loved Duinsmoore, I knew I couldn't keep living like I did. I felt that *I had to do something.* Finally, after an explosive argument I called Mrs. O'Ryan, my probation officer, and begged her to move me, even if it meant returning to The Hill. Mrs. O'Ryan seemed pleased with my decision and thought she could convince the Turnboughs to take me back.

Leaving Duinsmoore was one of the hardest decisions I had to make. In a matter of months, in the tiniest fraction of my life, Duinsmoore had given me so much.

I made it a point not to say good-bye. Paul, Dave and I seemed choked up, but we hid our feelings behind our age. At the last moment Dave gave me a hug. Mr. Brazell saluted me while holding a wrench, while Mr. Marsh presented me with a book on airplanes—the same book I had sneaked out of his house dozens of times. "This way you won't have to break in my house . . . you hooligan." He also gave me an autographed Delta Airline postcard. On it he scrawled his address and phone number. "Stay in touch, Slim," Michael said, as I felt myself beginning to get emotional. "Day or night, Sandra and I are here for you. Hang tough, Airborne! Get some!"

Before climbing into Harold Turnbough's ancient, blue-and-white

Chevy pickup, I cleared my throat, then announced in my Michael Marsh-like voice, "Shed no tears. Have no fear . . . for . . . I shall return!" As Mr. Turnbough and I motored away from Duinsmoore Drive, I saw *The Brady Bunch* woman, who stood on her immaculate front porch with her arms tightly across her chest. She gave me a sneering smile. I smiled back before shouting, "Love you, too!"

Almost an hour later I burst through Alice Turnbough's screen door. After a quick hug she pushed me away. "This is the last time," she warned. "Speak now or forever hold your peace."

I nodded before replying, "I know where I belong: 555-2647!"

CHAPTER
10

Break Away

*D*uring the middle of my sophomore year in high school, I grew frustrated and bored. Because I had moved so much and never stayed in one school for more than a few months at a time, I was placed in a class for slow learners. I fought the idea at first, until I discovered that very little was expected of me. By then I abandoned all of my academic studies, for *I* knew my future lay outside the school walls. I was putting in over 48 hours of work a week through a string of jobs, and I believed that nothing I learned from high school could be used in the real world.

My hunger for work was fueled by the fact that I was 17 and had less than a year to go in foster care. During sixth period, I'd race from school to Alice's home, change clothes, then speed off again to one of my jobs at a fast-food restaurant or the plastic factory, where I worked until one or two in the morning. I knew that the odd hours and lack of sleep were taking their toll on me. In school, teachers had to prod me awake as I snored in their classes. I resented the kids who laughed at me. Some of these same kids acted high and mighty whenever they saw me labor at the restaurants, strutting in to show off their dates or flashy clothes, knowing they would never have to work like I did in order to survive.

Sometimes during my free period, I'd stroll over to visit my English teacher, Mr. Tapley. Since he didn't have class that period, Mr. Tapley used his time to correct papers. I'd plant my elbows on his desk and bug him with an endless stream of questions about my future. He knew how hard I struggled, but I was too embarrassed to tell him why

I would always fall asleep. Mr. Tapley would look up from his pile of work, run a hand through his thinning hair and feed me just enough advice to get me through the weekend—to bury myself in my homework assignments.

As much as I labored through the week, I tried to schedule every other weekend off, on the off chance of visiting Father in San Francisco. Over the years, I had left hundreds of messages to all the fire stations throughout the city. Father never called back. One afternoon I lost it when a hesitant fireman tried to put me off. "Is this the right station?" I pleaded. "Just tell me, what shift does he work?" I begged, raising my voice.

"Uhh . . . Stephen works at different stations at different times. We'll get the message to him," the fireman said before the line went dead.

I knew something was horribly wrong. Alice tried to stop me from fleeing her home. "My dad's in trouble," I shouted, my chest heaving.

"David, you don't know that!" Alice blasted back.

"That's exactly what I mean," I said, pointing a finger at her. "I'm tired of living in the dark . . . of hiding secrets . . . of living a lie. What can be so bad? If my dad's in trouble . . ." I stopped for a moment as my imagination began to take hold. "I just have to know," I said, kissing Alice on the forehead.

I hopped on my motorcycle and sped off to the heart of San Francisco. On the freeway I dodged and swerved through the traffic, and I didn't slow down until my motorcycle rumbled into the alley next to 1067 Post Street—the same fire station Father had been assigned to since I was a baby.

I parked my motorcycle by the back entrance of the station. As I walked up the steep incline, I noticed an old familiar face. At first I thought the face belonged to Father, but I knew it wasn't him when the face smiled. Father never smiled. "My Lord, son! How long has it been? I haven't seen you boys in . . . I don't know how long."

I shook hands with Uncle Lee, my father's longtime partner and best friend. "Where's Dad?" I asked in a stern voice.

Uncle Lee turned away. "Well . . . he just left. He just went off shift."

"No, sir!" I demanded. I knew Uncle Lee was lying—firemen changed shifts in the morning, not in the middle of the afternoon. I lowered my defenses. "Uncle Lee, I haven't seen Dad in years. I have to know."

Lee seemed choked up. He rubbed a tear from the corner of his eye. "Your father and I started out together, ya know. I got to tell ya, your old man was one hell of a fireman. . . . There were times when I thought we wouldn't make it. . . ."

I could feel it coming. My insides became unglued. My eyes searched for something to grab onto, to keep me from falling. I bit my lip. I nodded my head as if telling Uncle Lee to just let it out and tell me.

Lee's eyes blinked, showing that he understood. "Your father . . . doesn't work for the department anymore. Stephen—your father— was . . . asked to retire early."

I let out a sigh of relief as I fought to control my feelings. "So he's alive! He's okay! Where is he?" I shrieked.

Uncle Lee laid it all down, telling me that Father had not had work for over a year. So when his money ran out, he moved from place to place, and at times Lee feared that Father slept on the street. "David, it's the booze. It's killing him," he said in a soft but firm tone.

"So where is he now?" I begged.

"I don't know, son. I only see him when he needs a few bucks." Uncle Lee stopped for a moment to clear his throat. He looked at me in a way he never had before. "David, don't be too hard on your old man. He never really had a family. He was a young man when he first came here to the city. He loved you kids, but the marriage destroyed him. His job wasn't easy on him, either. It's all that kept him going. He lived for the station. But his drinking . . . it's all that he knows."

"Thanks, Uncle Lee," I said, as I shook his hand. "Thanks for not putting me off. At least now I know."

Uncle Lee walked me down to my motorcycle. "I should see your dad in a few days. Hell, maybe you can help him out of this mess."

"Yeah," I replied, "maybe."

Two weekends later, I rode on a Greyhound bus to the Mission district of San Francisco. At the bus station I waited for Father for over an hour. From outside I spotted a rundown bar. I took a chance, walked across the street and found Father slumped over on top of a table. My head swiveled around, searching for help. I couldn't believe how people strolled by Father's table without the slightest concern, or sat by the bar nursing their drinks as if my father were invisible.

I gently shook my childhood superhero from his slumber. Father's coughing seemed to awaken him. His stench was so bad that I held my breath until I could help him stumble from the bar. The outside air seemed to clear his head. In the sunlight Father looked worse than I ever imagined. I deliberately did not look at his face. I wanted to remember my father for the man he once was—the tall, rugged, strong firefighter with gleaming white teeth, who placed himself in danger to help a fellow fireman or rescue a child from a burning building.

Father and I walked for several blocks without saying a word. I knew better than to question him on his drinking or his lifestyle. But Uncle Lee's warning about doing something, anything, to help Father echoed in my mind. Without thinking, I closed my eyes, spun around and held out my hand, stopping him. "What happened, Dad?"

Father stopped and let out a hacking cough. His hands trembled as he struggled to light a cigarette. "You'd be better off forgetting all about it, the whole thing—your mother, the house, everything. It never happened." Father took a deep drag. I tried to look into his eyes, but he kept dodging my glance. "It's your mother. She's crazy. . . . You'd be better off forgetting the whole thing," he ordered with a wave of his hand, as if sweeping the *family secret* under the carpet for the final time.

"No, Dad, it's you! I'm worried about you!" A chill blew across my face. My body shuddered, and I clamped my eyes shut. I wanted to cry out to Father, and yet I didn't have the guts to tell him how much I was scared for him. My brain struggled with what was right and what was proper. I knew by Father's look that his life was his business and that no one ever questioned a father's authority, but he was a walking death. His hands rattled every few seconds and his eyelids were dropped so low that he could barely see. I felt so awkward. I didn't want to make Father mad, but I soon found myself becoming upset. *Why weren't you there for me? Couldn't you have at least called me? Can't you be like a regular dad, with a job and a family, so I could be with you and play catch or go fishing? Why can't you be normal?* my brain screamed.

I sucked in a deep breath before I opened my eyes. "I'm sorry. It's just that you're my dad . . . and I love you."

Father wheezed as he turned away. I knew he had heard me but he couldn't bring himself to reply. The river of alcohol and the destroyed family life had stripped him of his innermost feelings. I realized that inside, my father was truly dead. Moments later he and I continued our journey to nowhere, with our heads bent down, looking at no one—especially not ourselves.

Hours later, before Father loaded me onto the bus, he pulled me aside. "I want to show you something," he said with pride, as he reached behind him and plucked out a black leather covering with the emblem of the fireman's shield on it. Father smiled as he opened the casing, revealing a bright, shiny silver fireman's badge. "Here, hold it," he said, as he gently placed the badge in my open palms.

"R-1522," I read aloud, knowing that the R signified that Father was indeed retired and not fired as I had feared, while the numbers were those assigned to Father when he first joined.

"That's all I have now. That's one of the only things in my life that I didn't screw up too badly. No one can ever take that away from me," he stated with conviction, pointing to his prize. "Someday you'll understand."

I nodded my head. I understood. I always had. In the past I had imagined Father dressed in his crisp, dark blue fireman's uniform, as he strolled to a podium to receive his badge of honor in front of a frenzied crowd shouting his name, with his beautiful wife and family standing by his side. As a child, I had dreamed of Father's big day.

I now looked into his eyes as I gave him his lifetime achievement. "I'm really proud of you, Dad," I said, gazing down at the badge. "I truly am." For a split second Father's eyes gleamed. And for a moment in time his pain disappeared.

A few minutes later Father stopped me on the steps of the bus. He hesitated. His eyes looked down. "Get out of here," he mumbled. "David, get as far away from here as you can. Your brother Ronald joined the service, and you're almost at that age. Get out," Father said as he patted my shoulder. As he turned away, his final words were, "Do what you have to. Don't end up like me."

I pressed my face to the window of the bus and strained my eyes as I watched Father disappear into the crowd. I wanted to jump off and hug him, to hold his hand or sit by his side the way I did as a child whenever he read his evening paper—like the dad I knew so many years ago. I wanted him to be a part of my life. I wanted a dad. As the bus lumbered out of San Francisco, I lost control of my emotions and cried inside. I clenched my fist, as the tremendous pressure I had stored for years burst inside my soul. I realized the horribly lonely life that Father lived. I prayed with all my heart that God would watch over him and keep him warm at night and free from any harm. A mountain of guilt weighed on my shoulders. I felt so bad for everything in my father's life.

After visiting Uncle Lee, I had fantasized that maybe I could buy a home in Guerneville and have Father move in. Only then could I help ease his pain or could we spend some time together as father and son. But I knew, as always, that fantasies were dreams and reality was life. I cried throughout the bus ride to Alice's home. I knew that Father was dying, and I became terrified that I would never see him again.

Months afterward, during the summer of 1978, after dozens of interviews, I landed a job selling cars. Selling cars was mentally exhausting. The upper managers would threaten the sales staff one day, then bait us with money incentives the next. The competition was fierce, but I somehow managed to keep my head above water. If I had a weekend off, I'd race off to Duinsmoore and forget about having to be an adult, as Paul, Dave and I searched for new adventure on four wheels—loaned to me by the car dealer. Once, after seeing a movie on Hollywood stuntmen, the three of us sat facing forward as I drove backward in a perfectly straight line, without looking behind my back. Our stunt caused a few wrecks with confused drivers, and the three of us had a few minor scrapes with the law. But I knew my adventurous times would be coming to an end when Paul and Dave matured and began to look for jobs, too.

More than ever, I sought guidance from Duinsmoore Drive. One time Dan drove to Alice's home so he could talk me out of my pipe dream of becoming a Hollywood stuntman. With his son Paul by his side, Mr. Brazell spent hours of his time telling me how foolish I was. I had always been fond of Dan, and as I walked him and Paul outside after abandoning my lame idea, I realized that I was closer to Dan than to my own father.

The Marshes were just as caring. Many times I'd help Sandra with her housework, as I learned other ways to become self-sufficient. Mr. Marsh recommended that I join the service. Immediately I'd think of the Air Force, but as a freshman in high school I had taken the aptitude test and failed miserably. I had convinced myself that I could make it in the outside world without any schooling.

Summer passed, and I decided—because I was almost 18 and had to make money in order to survive—to drop out of high school. Alice was livid, but my career as a salesman was on the rise. Out of a sales staff of over 40, I was consistently one of the top five salesmen. But months after my 18th birthday, the recession hit, gas prices shot up, my savings withered and the reality of going nowhere fast hit me in the face.

To escape my troubles, one Sunday I rode off in my beat-up, orange

'65 Mustang and headed north to find the Russian River. I didn't know exactly how to get there, but I drove by instinct, relying on my memories as a child. When I sensed the correct exit, I turned off. I knew I was close when the towering redwood trees filled my windshield. My heart seemed to skip a beat when I parked my car at the old Safeway supermarket. My eyes gaped at the same aisles I had strolled through as a child. At the checkout counter, I dug through my pant pockets and spent the last of my splurge money on a stick of salami and a loaf of French bread. I sat on a deserted sandbar of Johnson's Beach and slowly gnawed on my lunch, listening to the rippling sounds of the Russian River and the scraping metal of an oversized motor home that rumbled its way across the narrow evergreen bridge. I found myself at peace.

In order to fulfill my vow of living at the Russian River, I knew I had to first find myself. I couldn't do it living so close to my past. I had to break away. As I collected my trash and walked away from the beach, the sun shone on my shoulders. I felt warm inside. I had made *my* decision. Turning to face the river one last time, I felt like crying. If I wanted to, I could move to the river, but I knew it wouldn't be right. I took in a deep breath and spoke in a slow voice, renewing my lifelong promise. *I will be back.*

Months later, after obtaining my high school G.E.D. and completing a series of tests and background checks, I proudly enlisted into the United States Air Force. Somehow word got to Mother, and she called me a day before I reported for basic training. Her voice wasn't that of the *evil mother*, but *my mommy* from years ago. I could almost see Mommy's face on the other end of the phone as she cried. She claimed that she thought of me all the time and that she had always wanted nothing but the best for me. We talked for over an hour, and I strained my ear in hopes of hearing the three most important words I had wanted Mom to say all my life.

Alice stood beside me as I cried into the telephone. I wanted to be with my mom. I wanted to see her face in hopes of hearing those three words. I realized that I was being foolish, but I felt I should at least try. It took all of Alice's persuasive powers to keep me from visiting Mom. But in my heart I knew that *Mother* was just toying with my emotions. For over 18 years, I wanted something I knew I would never receive—Mom's love. Without a word, Alice opened her arms. And as she held me, I suddenly realized that my lifelong search for love and acceptance had finally ended in the arms of a foster parent.

The next day I stood tall as I looked into Harold's blue eyes. "Be good now, son," he said.

"I will, sir. You watch. I'll make you proud."

Alice stood beside her husband. "You know who you are. You've always known," she said, as she held out her hand and gave me a shiny yellow key. "This is your home. It always has been and always will be your home."

I pocketed the key to my home. After kissing Alice, *my mother*, and shaking Harold's, *my father's*, hand, I opened my mouth to say something appropriate. But this moment in time needed no words, for we knew what we all felt—the love of a family.

Hours later, as the Boeing 727 banked its way from California, I closed my eyes for a final time as *a lost boy*. I pictured "The Sarge," Michael Marsh, in all his glory, with his eyes pierced toward the sky when he had said, "Well, Airman Pelzer, any thoughts?"

"Well," I had replied, "I'm a little scared, but I could use that to my advantage. I have a master plan. I'm focused, and I know I'm going to make it."

Then my mentor had glanced down on me and smiled. "Good on you, Pelz-man. Get some."

Aboard my first plane ride, I opened my eyes for the first time *as a man named Dave*. I chuckled to myself. *"Now the adventure begins!"*

Epilogue

December 1993, Sonoma County, California—*I'm alone. On the outside I'm so cold that my entire body shivers. The tips of my fingers have been numb for some time. As I exhale, a frosty mist escapes through my nose. In the distance I can hear the rumbling sounds of dark gray clouds colliding against each other. A few seconds later, thunder echoes from the nearby hills. I can see a cloudburst approaching.*

I don't mind. I'm sitting on top of an old rotted log in front of a long stretch of empty beach. I love gazing at the splendor of the powerful dark green waves that form into a curl before pounding the beach. A coat of salty spray covers my glasses.

On the inside I'm warm. I'm no longer afraid of being alone. I love spending time by myself.

From above, a flock of seagulls squawks at each other as the birds comb the beach in search of any morsel of food. Moments later a single gull struggles to maintain flight. As much as the bird pounds its wings, it cannot keep up with the flock, let alone maintain altitude. Without warning, the gull crashes beak first into the sand. The bird flops up and hobbles on a single, webbed orange leg. After a short search, the seagull finds a fragment of food. Suddenly, out of nowhere, the flock of seagulls returns, hovers above the beach, then dives to pick on the weaker gull for its meal. The gull seems to know it cannot flee, so it stands its ground and pecks at the other birds with furious intensity. Within a blink of an eye the struggle is over, and the flock of birds flies off in search of an easier victim.

The seagull screeches at the flock as if telling them that it was victorious, then turns toward me and squawks a warning. As I study the gull's movements, I recall how its battle mirrored my own challenges while in foster care. Back then nothing was more important than wanting to be accepted and finding the answers to my past. But the more I matured on the inside, the more I realized I had to carve my own path. I also learned to be content in not finding all the answers of my quest. But like most things in my life, my answers seemed to come without effort after I joined the United States Air Force, where I achieved my lifelong dream of flying. As an adult I came full circle. One of the things I accomplished was visiting my mother and asking her the most important question of my life: Why?

Mother's own secret made me cherish the life that I lead even more.

The screeching sound of the seagull breaks my trance. In front of me my hands quiver, but it's not from the cold. I wipe a stream of tears from my cheeks. I don't cry for myself as much as I do for my mother. I begin to cry so hard that my body shakes. I can't stop. I cry for the mother and father I never had and the shame of the family secret. I become unglued because at times I have doubts about making a difference in the lives of others, and I feel unworthy for the recognition I've received.

I cry to let everything out.

I close my eyes and say a quick prayer. I pray for the wisdom to become a better, stronger person. As I stand up, facing the dark green ocean, I feel cleansed inside. It's time to move on.

After a relaxing drive with the windows rolled down and listening to Pat Metheny's Secret Story, *I park my 4-Runner in front of my second home—the Rio Villa in Monte Rio. The owners, Ric and Don, wave as they scurry about to prepare for incoming guests. The serene beauty of the Rio Villa still takes my breath away. For years now Ric and Don have gone out of their way to make my son, Stephen, and me feel a part of their family. To be welcome means so much to me.*

After I wrestle him to the floor, Stephen wraps his arms around my neck. "You okay?" he asks. Even though he is only a child, in so many ways Stephen's sensitivity is beyond his years. I'm amazed that at times he can feel my innermost feelings. As much as he is my son, Stephen is also one of my closest friends.

The two of us spend the remainder of the day designing multicolored Creepy Crawlers plastic toys, and playing Sorry and Monopoly over and over and over again. I quickly discover that my years of training in military strategy are no match for the mind of a ruthless seven-year-old, who acquires both Park Place and Boardwalk, with hotels. (I still owe Stephen back rent.)

After several annihilating lessons of Sorry, Stephen and I make our way down to the deck by the Russian River. A thick odor of burning wood mixes in with the sweet aroma of redwood trees. The shallow green river becomes transparent, with only a soft trickling sound that makes the water real. As the sun disappears behind a hill, the reflection of a Christmas tree shimmers from across the river. A blanket of fog seeps down from the hills. Without a word, Stephen and I join hands. I can feel a lump creep up my throat as we tighten our grip.

Stephen clamps onto my leg. "Love you, Dad. Happy birthday."

Years ago, I truly doubted whether I'd make it out alive. In my former life I had very little. Today, as I stand in my utopia, I have what any person could wish for—a life and the love of my son. Stephen and I are a family.

*P*erspectives on Foster Care

David Pelzer
Foster Child

There is not a doubt in my mind that had I stayed with my biological mother much longer, I would have definitely been killed. Foster care was not only an escape, but literally a whole new world. At times it was extremely difficult to adjust, for I never quite knew what to expect.

As an adult survivor, I am forever grateful to "The System" that so many in society ridicule without mercy. It would have been easy for me to exploit the weakness of social services and foster care and all that they entail. That was *never* the premise of the story, but rather to take the reader into a world rarely seen by the general public— through the eyes of a tortured, programmed-to-fail child who is "placed" into the care of others.

My social worker, Ms. Gold, stays etched in my mind simply because of her genuine concern for *my* safety and security. Though I thought retracting my statements within days of my disposition was unique to my case, this is an everyday occurrence for most of those who work in her field. Very few people truly know what Child Protective Service workers go through.

There are many who believe that social workers are nothing more than homewreckers who barge into a private residence and pluck a child from the arms of a loving parent. Or that they *never* respond to a *real* case involving child abuse. The reality of the situation is far more horrifying. In 1973, in California, I was among several thousand cases reported. Twenty years later the same state reported more than 616,000 cases.

There are too few social workers available to respond to the never-ending siege of "youth at risk." For them, it is a matter of triage—a minor who is in harm's way the most receives immediate attention first. Then, once a report is under investigation, *no* information can be given to the general public on the status of the case, which causes stress to those who dared to file the report in the first place and who in turn may surmise that social services never follows through. Again, the operating principle of social services is to preserve the privacy, safety and security of the *minor*. Needless to say, burnout plays a major role for these angels—whose *sole* purpose is that of saving the life of a child.

As for my foster parents, *they* made me the person I am today. *They* took in a heap of hideous mass and transformed a terrified child into a functional, responsible human being. I owe each of them so much. Unfortunately for them, I put my foster parents through absolute hell—especially the Catanzes, during my critical "adjustment phase." They saved me from almost certain doom. The Turnboughs were a godsend, with something so simple as teaching me how to walk, talk and act like a *normal* child, while assuring me that I was worthy and could overcome any challenge that life had to offer.

This is the work that *foster parents* do!

As an adult I will never understand why *these* people put up with so much. One can barely fathom what it is like to deal with a child who came from a past like mine, let alone the half a dozen other foster children residing in the average foster home.

And yet the general public rarely, if ever, hears of the love and compassion for what some folks dub *F-parents*—as if the words *foster parent* belonged to a deadly epidemic. These same individuals may assume that foster parents "are only doing it for the money," that foster parents are nothing more than parental mercenaries, making a profit off of society's ills. If this is true, then why is it that over 65 percent of the foster parents in Iowa end up adopting their foster children, thus making the foster parents ineligible for financial assistance? Like most foster parents, they fall victim to the emotion of love. To be adopted is the highest honor bestowed on a child who longs to become a member of a family.

But society is never made aware of those stories. It appears that foster parents only receive attention when a child is hurt while under the guardianship of foster care. The press clamors to "inform" the public of a child victim becoming victimized again. Investigations are made, and it is most likely that the foster parents in question may not have been suited as foster parents. An obvious answer! Because of such publicity, the question brought up by many is, has "The System" failed the child again? Hardly!

Don't get me wrong; harming a child is absolutely wrong and should never be tolerated! However, those cases are rare, and they undermine the incredible work that foster care performs. The *real* question is, how did those adults receive a license as foster parents in the first place? The answer may be for the simple reason that so many children need to be placed into homes—yesterday. Again, society's ills tax "The System" to overwhelming proportions. There are literally millions of children in need and only several thousand homes available. Alleviating the situation may lie with a thorough screening process for those who apply for foster licenses, including background checks— much like those used for any county or government job. Perhaps training programs on how to deal with the endless and various needs of the foster children could help as well.

On the other hand, the press was kind enough to pay homage to Charlotte Lopez, a foster child for 15 of her 17 years, who won the title of Miss Teen USA in 1993. I was extremely intrigued by Charlotte's confidence and inner beauty. I wonder where Miss Lopez received her esteem and poise from? Could it have been from her foster parent, Janet Henry? One can only imagine the endless hours that Janet and Charlotte spent together. I can only assume that Charlotte's main concern was not so much for her smile or her technique for strolling down the runway, as it was for her inner fear, which most foster children possess—seeking answers to their condition, while struggling to fit into an ordinary world.

There are other dedicated foster parents, like Debbe Magnusen, who takes in babies, in the middle of the night, that were born addicted to crack cocaine. Like so many others, Debbe, too, has adopted her former foster children. Legends in the field of foster care include Nina Coake, Judy Fields and Lennie Hart, who have each been in service to children at risk for over 35 years, fighting for the care and rights of foster children. Another is Pamela Eby, who literally dedicated her life to saving children until losing her final battle to cancer.

I cannot begin to state how much I cringe when I hear the term "cop" or "pig." Again, one can only imagine what type of world we would live in if it were not for our police officers, who rescue children from abusive situations and wear bulletproof vests for fear of being killed in a domestic dispute. When folks gripe about our educational system, they may fail to realize that the teachers and staff see victims of child abuse firsthand and are the ones who are overburdened. If this statement sounds doubtful, step into a classroom holding 75 students. I don't call that teaching as much as I do crowd control. Besides parents and legal guardians, who has the most influence over our children's lives but teachers? As for those who work in social services—from counselors at juvenile halls, Child Protective Service members, juvenile probation officers and Court Appointed Special Advocate (CASA) volunteers to foster parents—I can never admire and respect *their* efforts enough.

There are organizations that play a priceless role for "youth at risk" in our communities, such as the members of the United States Junior Chamber of Commerce, better known as the Jaycees. The main purpose of the Jaycees, who are volunteers, is the service of humanity. For instance, every year the state of Nebraska raises several thousand dollars for its Aid to Foster Children program. During the Christmas season, Jaycee chapters from across the nation donate Christmas trees to children who have never seen, let alone smelled, a Douglas fir. Their dedication doesn't stop there. Jaycees invade stores with hundreds of children in tow—children who have never shopped for toys for themselves. These children never crave such niceties as Game Boy or Nike Air Jordan shoes. Instead, these children wish for clothes that are a size too big—so as to get more wear out of them.

Another organization is The Arrow Project, a nonprofit organization that addresses the needs of children and families in several states by providing foster care, diagnostic and educational services and other interventions.

In March 1994 I was in Ohio presenting a keynote address to local law enforcement officers, teachers and social service workers. The lady who preceded me made a statement that made everything crystal clear: "It takes a community to save a child!"

All too often, as a result of dissolving families and values, a lack of concern for minors and a lack of proper guidance, children grow up to become "killing machines." By investing in our "youth at risk" today, does society not stand a better chance of a "higher yield" tomorrow—an adult serving our community rather than rotting away in some jail?

While "The System" is not perfect, it does in fact work. In my estimation "The System" will never be perfected—the demands from society are just too much. Many of us look toward "The System" and demand that "they" solve our problems, to our satisfaction, right now.

Like the Jaycees and The Arrow Project, maybe society can ease some of the frustrations of those in their chosen field. Maybe *we* can mail a card to a teacher for no special reason and just say thanks, or give a small bunch of flowers to a social worker. Perhaps the next time *we* see a police officer, *we* can smile and wave hello; or present a foster family with a pizza. If *we* can treat those in entertainment and sports like gifts from the gods, why can't *we* show a little bit of gratitude to those who play such a priceless role in *our* community?

As much as this book takes the reader behind the scenes, its main theme is always that of the child who seemingly comes from another planet. Some people may believe that once a child is removed from a threatening environment, the minor's problems instantly disappear. The actuality is, that is when the troubles begin. Like so many other children who enter "The System," I was brought up in a violent, controlled environment. My problem was twofold: first, the need to deprogram my hideous past; and second, the need to be guided into mainstream society.

In so many ways I was so lucky. I was able to use my dark past to propel me to a brighter future. But like so many other lost children, in the beginning I failed to realize that I could take the same techniques I had used to survive my abusive past and apply them to the real world. In general, foster children are far more mature, resilient and focused on their futures than mainstream children because foster children have had to adapt at an earlier age. (The key word is adapt, not give up!) Foster children, for the most part, do not sit around waiting for the silver spoon—they rely on themselves. I could have fallen through the cracks and then blamed my failed future on my past, had it not been for proper guidance and a little bit of love. However, the single biggest mistake I've ever made was dropping out of high school.

But like most foster children, I simply had to adapt and overcome. After being exposed to a different world, in order to make it, I knew *I had to want it more.*

While at times foster care was frustrating, it did give me the chance to see how other families lived. Like a great deal of those in foster care, I didn't know how good I had it until I moved out on my own. Foster children *never* forget their foster parents. I am the same. Like others, I have many regrets. One of them is that Harold Turnbough passed away before I had my son, Stephen. Another regret was not being able to present Harold with my first book, which was nominated for a Pulitzer Prize. However, today Alice Turnbough lives hours from my home. The highest compliment I can pay to my foster mother is this: Alice is my son's grandmother. That's how much foster care means to me.

In January 1994 I had the privilege of presenting a training program in Ottumwa, Iowa, for a group of foster parents who had traveled from throughout the region during the middle of a snowstorm that closed down that part of the state. I presented a program on working with children who come from abusive backgrounds and how to better deal with them. During the course, I gave an illustration of how I used to escape my pain by dreaming of a hero. On the outside my hero did not fit into mainstream society, yet on the inside my hero knew who he was and wanted to do good for others in need. In my dreams I saw myself as my hero. I flew through the air, I wore a cape of red and I had an "S" on my chest. I *was* Superman. When I stated this, the foster parents erupted with applause. As tears rolled down some of their faces, they held up a bumper sticker that read, *SUPERMAN HAD FOSTER PARENTS.*

To all of you who work with *The Lost Boys and Girls*, God bless *YOU!*

Alice Turnbough
Foster Mother

Dave came to us when he was 13 years old. I guess I'm still his foster mom. At first I think he was a combination of scared and defensive. He was a little wild and extremely frustrated, but for the most part did what he was told.

At the time Dave came to us we had all teenage girls. He drove them a little crazy, following them and tattling on them all the time. Plus, Dave was a neat freak, and the girls weren't. He didn't have much, but what he did have he treated like gold. And everything needed to be in the right place. A lot of foster children are like that.

Dave never acted his age, period. He always tried to act older, staying busy and finding work. He was 13 going on 20 and was always thinking ahead.

I have been a foster parent for 30 years, fostering approximately 75 children. It all started when a gentleman introduced me to two children who needed help.

We never got into morals. These children were just like other children—except for the treatment they received from others. For the most part, foster children need someone to talk to. As a foster parent, I would like to see improved screening processes in order to better place children in the right homes, rather than dropping them off and hoping for the best.

One of the rewards of being a foster parent is seeing the kids turn out the way you had always hoped they would.

I always knew that David would make it. One of the most memorable moments was when David joined the Air Force. He had a devil of a time enlisting. I had to get used to him always flying away. Harold and I were very surprised and proud that he took it upon himself to carve out his future. Many foster children don't have the motivation.

Although I always knew that Dave would do all right, I never thought he'd go as far as he has. The day I found out that he had received the Ten Outstanding Young Americans (TOYA) award was one of my proudest days as a foster parent. Foster children hardly ever achieve that kind of status because they allow the prejudices of our society to hold them back.

Dave was the last foster child to leave my home. I'm proud to be Dave's mother.

Dennis Tapley
Teacher

I have been teaching for more than 20 years. When I was a freshman teacher in San Bruno, "special education," as we now know it, had just received major support from the federal government. The special education program recognized that some children with minor learning disabilities had not been receiving an appropriate education. Children who had difficulty in learning basic skills were to be given special instruction to remedy those weak or unlearned skills.

There was talk about teachers being aware of some negative emotional concerns among these students. Some families produced schoolchildren who brought their family confusion with them to school. The confusion was evidenced in schoolyard social difficulties or classroom learning problems.

Teachers were as aware as we could be in working with the parents of these children. But this was two decades before Dave Pelzer published his book, *A Child Called "It"* (and Jane Smiley her *1000 Acres*, and Susan Griffin her *Chorus of Stones*). We did not know—and were cautioned not to know—too much, for fear of being accused of interference.

From the 1970s point of view, foster care was not accepted. For a child to go to foster care meant there was something wrong—a complete failure in parenting. This was a failure that society did not want to face, even when given details of some drastic home situations. Because of this, foster care was twisted into something very negative. Individuals involved in foster care—both parents and children—were seen as second-class. The viewpoint even went so far as to believe that foster children had done something bad—unlike an orphan who was an innocent victim, for example. It has taken, and still takes, a long time to come to grips with what foster care, and the parents involved, can accomplish.

Today, child-rearing dynamics, awareness of the dysfunctional family, and direct evidence of the product of loveless or abusive parenting are matters of public record and psychological and educational research. Teachers and counselors are being trained to manage, test, evaluate and intervene.

I have been teaching special education now for 12 years. I have seen learning disabilities and delays in learning in specific areas. But family dysfunction and abuse cause emotional disturbances and learning delays that can be horrendous. I have seen students steal to gain attention, or carve the life out of shop and cooking equipment for the complex pleasure of artistic revenge. Such students are incapable of social self-restraint, and press their peers and teachers to react.

The disability of poor parenting is more likely to cause disruption in a child's intellectual and social growth than a physical disability. A child who has supportive parents and a reading disability may be delayed in reading, but in my mind has a better chance of general life success than an abused child without a disability.

David Pelzer is an exception. Although all I knew about him was that his home life had been incredibly bad, I was very aware that he was an extreme individual. In class he wasn't as "shifty" as the others, but very restricted in movement. I knew him because he was a demanding student who pressed his questions and pressed for answers. No other high school kid would stay after class, actually sitting on my desk to gain attention. He made sure he was noticed. Students would often visit their teachers with the simple intent of being friendly, but David was more purposeful and demanded consideration through his attitude and posture.

David is—even now, after 20 years—a rare student in his forcefulness and his directness. He is to be congratulated for his success.

Carl Miguel
Chief Probation Officer

Dave Pelzer, a seriously abused child, was booked into the San Mateo County Juvenile Hall in 1974. As a result of Dave's background, his case was immediately reviewed by a team of juvenile hall staff that included a doctor, psychologist and detention supervisor. It was decided to house Dave on C-Wing—a living unit for children that were suffering from physical, psychological or sexual abuse. This was a special unit with an excellent staff-to-child ratio and a program designed to have a high degree of one-to-one, staff-to-child counseling.

Dave's case was reviewed by C-Wing staff, and he was assigned to me during his stay at juvenile hall. Dave thrived on the individual attention and the behavior modification program. He established a bond with all the staff and demonstrated phenomenal growth both socially and emotionally. Dave entered the juvenile justice system at a time when resources were available to focus on the individual.

Dave left San Mateo Juvenile Hall in a much healthier state than when he arrived. In 1989, 15 years later, Dave and I met again in the most unusual manner. I was the superintendent of the Yuba/Sutter Juvenile Hall, and Dave was stationed at Beale Air Force Base in Yuba County. Dave came to the juvenile hall to volunteer his services to the youths detained there. Dave worked as a very effective volunteer and was eventually hired as a part-time staff person until being transferred by the Air Force.

It is with great pleasure and deep personal and emotional satisfaction that I have had the opportunity to see Dave rise above his excruciating childhood. He is a living example and a model to others who have suffered under similar circumstances. As Dave walked out of juvenile hall in 1974, as a child, I bade him good luck. And as he walked back into juvenile hall in 1989, as a counselor, I felt a tear in my eye and simply said, "Bravo."

Michael Marsh
Mentor

One day in 1976, in the quiet, blue-collar California neighborhood of Menlo Park, I walked out of my garage and was disheartened to view the driveway scene next door. For almost a year now, houses in the neighborhood that came on the market were being snapped up by opportunistic Realtors and turned into rental properties. The house next door was such a house, and its tenants were scruffy-looking people who derived a significant amount of their income from the state of California by being foster parents.

What I was viewing on this day was their latest "acquisition"—a tall string bean of a kid in a filthy, sleeveless, ribbed T-shirt. He was working on a miniscooter engine, had a sort of leering grin—as a natural part of his facial features—and had intense eyes that darted about from behind a thick pair of glasses.

Initially I resented him, feeling that my hard work and that of my wife toward purchasing our first home in a decent neighborhood was being defeated by real estate speculators who were making a buck off importing families into *my* neighborhood. But David Pelzer wasn't shy—in fact, he was persistent in his friendliness. As I got to know David a little, I began to see he was bright and had a keen sense of humor, in spite of the fact that he had been kicked around in a dismal childhood and what was looking to be an even drearier adolescence.

At first it was somewhat like housebreaking a pet. As we got more familiar, he was at our house more and more, asking about my Vietnam experiences, pursuing my aviation library and wanting to talk about almost anything. My wife and I began to require things from him—small, essential things like courtesy and consideration. He was to knock before entering the house. Some of his conversational manners were horrid, and his telephone and table manners were nonexistent.

The day came when David left the neighborhood. His "foster parents" simply weren't acceptable to him, and I still don't blame him one iota for having the courage to pull up stakes and seek something better. But he stayed in touch and started showing up on weekends, wanting to be with friends he had made in the neighborhood and wanting to stay at our house. We finally told him that he would be welcome under most circumstances on most weekends but that he must call in advance, ask and make "reservations." This he began to do, and some time passed before there was trouble. Trouble in a nearby park. Trouble with a pellet pistol. Trouble with neighbors who felt David was a bad influence on their children. These things were discussed, and I made it very clear to David that any more trouble, and it was bye-bye to the neighborhood that he loved to come and visit.

When pressed about his past or his school, he was always purposefully vague, so we never really knew what was going on in his life. A couple of years went by with intermittent trouble and calls from the Menlo Park police. David was never an angry, rebellious individual—he was just thickheaded and had a penchant for finding trouble or letting it find him. Maybe it was from some sort of misguided sense of adventure; I don't know. But there came the day when I asked him how his school was doing, and he said, "Oh, I quit." I hit the ceiling and chewed his butt out for an hour. When I asked him what he was going to do, he mentioned he was going to sell cars. I went ballistic again. A skinny, wimpy, pimply-faced kid was selling cars in the Bay Area? Get real, kid. A week or so later he called to say he had the job and was looking forward to being the "Salesman of the Month," which bore the distinctive honor of driving a Corvette for a 30-day period. Right, Dave . . . something to shoot for, all right.

A couple of months later I received a telephone call from David, who said he wanted to visit. I said, "No, I have to go up to San Francisco International to pick up my paycheck." "Great," he says, "I'll drive you up there. I want to show you something." What he wanted to show me was, of course, a black Corvette that he was the owner/operator of for the next month. A few months later David arrives in an El Camino—his company car—with a motorcycle strapped to the back. Dave mentioned that he might try a new job. I asked what he was planning, and he replied, "Well, I'm going to Hollywood to become a stuntman." There was what a writer would describe as a pregnant pause, as the impact of his words crashed into my unbelieving psyche. I chastised him, focusing on his lack of athletics and experience, his clumsiness and, of course, the absence of contacts in L.A. I then ripped into him for another half hour with heavy emphasis on the importance of a high school diploma.

Months later, although wounded, David was considering another plan. He wanted to go into the military. So we went to the recruiters and began watching videos of paratroopers and rangers. They, of course, looked good. To the United States Army, however, David didn't. No diploma? Sorry. Perhaps it took that letdown for the importance of a high school diploma to sink into David's concrete-thick head. He called me a few weeks after and said, "I'm in! The Air Force will take me and get me a G.E.D." He had pursued it *on his own* and was finally going out into the world. I was gratified, hopeful and proud of him for getting down to personal pragmatics, so to speak.

Shortly after David joined the Air Force, we moved to Denver, Colorado. David had stayed in touch and ended up training at Lowry Air Force Base in Denver. He was there to visit the first week we were in our new home. He subsequently went to Florida and was unhappy with his assignment—which was cooking. I counseled patience, and he ultimately made the best of an unhappy assignment by finessing his way into cooking for the Ranger School candidates stationed in the jungle/swamp phase of the Army Ranger program in Florida. *Then* he finagled a slot in the Army Parachute School, known as the Airborne Course, and on receiving his silver jump wings, became a member of an extraordinarily proud fraternity.

Then once again David persisted and ultimately found a niche: boom operator on an aerial tanker! He landed an assignment "booming" on the supersecret Mach 3 spy plane—the SR-71 Blackbird. He was hooked for years. During this period he became involved in the community around him, on and off base. His awareness of what he had and who he was brought to the surface a drive within him to diminish other people's hurts, to wade in and solve problems, and to contribute some positive payback.

In January 1993 I sat in the Center for the Performing Arts in Tulsa, Oklahoma, as David received an honor. He was out of the Air Force and had not just moved on, but moved forward. On this evening, which was actually the culmination of a week's festivities, David was being honored as one of the Ten Outstanding Young Americans in the United States by the National Junior Chamber of Commerce organization. The list of previous recipients reads like a *Who's Who* of American industry, politics and society. And there he was, David, the wannabe stuntman, who had pulled off the Big One, and had done it with determination, guts and resolve, and maybe a little luck. I'm proud of who you were, David—that hurt person who refused to "die." And I'm more proud of who you've become—a caring, giving, fixing person, the guy with the same sense of humor and that deft, sensitive touch. Good on you, David. I love you.

*R*esources for Help

The **National Association of Social Workers** constitutes 50 percent of the nation's social workers. With various degrees in social work, social workers in general work directly with individuals and families, at times in dire circumstances, resolving issues such as health problems, substance abuse, disabilities, poverty and violence. *Child protective social workers tread a fine line of saving children while maintaining the fabric of society.** For more information, please write 750 First St. NE, Suite 700, Washington, D.C. 20002 or call 800-638-8799.

The **National Court Appointed Special Advocate Association** (CASA) is composed of specially trained volunteers who are appointed by a judge to speak on behalf of abused and neglected children in court. By reviewing records, collecting information from parents, teachers, family members and the child, CASA's unique services enable judges to make informed decisions regarding the best interests of the child. For more information, please write 100 West St., North Tower, Suite 500, Seattle, WA 98119 or call 800-628-3233.

---

* Author's perspective.

The National Foster Parent Association is the national voice for foster parents. NFPA strengthens foster families through nationally focused legislative advocacy, training and education, publications, and linkages among foster parents, state and local foster parent associations, and child welfare organizations. Help save a life by loving a child. For more information, call the NFPA Information and Services Office at 800-557-5238.

Parents Anonymous, Inc., is the nation's oldest and largest child abuse prevention program dedicated to strengthening families through innovative strategies that promote mutual support and parent leadership. As the nation's premier family strengthening program, Parents Anonymous encourages parents to ask for help early—whatever their circumstances—to effectively break the cycle of abuse to protect today's children and strengthen tomorrow's generation of parents. Annually, more than 100,000 parents and their children come together in more than 2,300 Parents Anonymous groups throughout the United States to learn new skills, transform their attitudes and behaviors, and create long-term positive changes in their lives. Parents Anonymous builds on the strengths of parents to ensure that children live and grow in safe, nurturing homes by offering families help today and hope for the future. For more information or to locate a Parents Anonymous group in your community, please contact Parents Anonymous, Inc., at 909-621-6184.

The Arrow Project (TAP) is a Christian, nonprofit agency that serves communities by promoting and enhancing the well-being of children and families through preventive, supportive and therapeutic services. Through various programs including therapeutic foster care, diagnostic assessments and alternative education, the agency supports over 1,000 children annually in more than 300 foster homes and other facilities in Texas and Maryland. TAP solicits the support of individuals and corporations nationally to assist them in "fighting the battle for our kids." TAP believes in Psalm 127, that "children are a gift of the Lord, like arrows in the hand of a warrior." For more information, please write 350 N. Sam Houston Parkway, Suite 101, Houston, Texas 77069, or call toll free 877-92ARROW.

*A*bout the Author

A retired Air Force air crew member, Dave played a major role in Operations Just Cause, Desert Shield and Desert Storm. Dave was selected for the unique task of midair refueling of the then highly secretive SR-71 Blackbird and F-117 Stealth Fighter. While serving in the Air Force, Dave worked in juvenile hall and other programs involving "youth at risk" throughout California.

Dave's exceptional accomplishments include personal commendations from former Presidents Ronald Reagan and George Bush. While maintaining a rigorous, active-duty flight schedule, Dave was the recipient of the 1990 J.C. Penney Golden Rule Award, making him the California Volunteer of the Year. In 1993 Dave was honored as one of the Ten Outstanding Young Americans (TOYA), joining a distinguished group of alumni that includes Chuck Yeager, Christopher Reeve, Anne Bancroft, John F. Kennedy, Orson Welles and Walt Disney. In 1994 Dave was the *only* American to be selected as one of The Outstanding Young Persons of the World (TOYP), for his efforts involving child abuse awareness and prevention, as well as for instilling resilience in others. During the Centennial Olympic Games, Dave was a torchbearer, carrying the coveted flame.

Dave is currently working on a book based on overcoming obstacles and achieving one's innermost best, as well as on the third part of his trilogy, entitled *A Man Named Dave*.

When not on the road or with his son, Stephen, Dave lives a quiet life at the Russian River, in Guerneville, California, with his box turtle named Chuck.

*K*eynotes, Workshops, and School Assemblies

Dave is recognized as one of the country's most effective and respected communicators addressing corporate America. Dave is often dubbed "the Robin Williams with glasses," and his unique presentations and delivery target overcoming obstacles, positive self-esteem and goal achievement. Additionally, he provides specific workshops for those in the human services, educational and law enforcement fields. Dave also spends time working with "youth at risk," and junior high and high school assemblies, as well as presenting programs on child abuse prevention, drug and alcohol awareness, and personal responsibility.

For additional information on Dave's programs, write or call:

D-Esprit
P.O. Box 1385
Guerneville, CA 95446
phone: 707-869-2877
fax: 707-869-4424